S0-BXY-903

Women, Violence and Social Control

Women, Violence and Social Control

edited by
Jalna Hanmer
Lecturer in Sociology and
Co-ordinator of Women's Studies
University of Bradford
and
Mary Maynard
Lecturer in Sociology and
Co-ordinator of Women's Studies
University of York

HUMANITIES PRESS INTERNATIONAL, INC.
Atlantic Highlands, NJ

First published in 1987 in the United States of America by
HUMANITIES PRESS INTERNATIONAL, INC., Atlantic Highlands, NJ 07716

© British Sociological Association, 1987

Library of Congress Cataloging-in-Publication Data
Women, violence, and social control.
Bibliography: p.
Includes index.
1. Violence. 2. Women—Crimes against. 3. Social
control. I. Hanmer, Jalna. II. Maynard, Mary,
1950–
HM291.W5395 1987   303.6'2   86-27294
ISBN 0–391–03514–2
ISBN 0–391–03515–0 (pbk.)

All rights reserved. No part of this publication may be reproduced or
transmitted, in any form or by any means, without permission.

PRINTED IN GREAT BRITAIN

Contents

List of Tables

List of Abbreviations

AllER   All England Law Review
BSA   British Sociological Association
ESRC   Economic and Social Research Council
NCADV   National Coalition Against Domestic Violence
NWAF   National Women's Aid Federation
USCCR   United States Commission on Civil Rights

Notes on the Contributors

R. Emerson Dobash and Russell P. Dobash are members of the Department of Sociology at the University of Stirling. Since 1973 they have been working with Scotish Women's Aid, conducted research on violence against wives and have published extensively on the problem. Their major work is *Violence Against Wives*. They are currently completing a book comparing the British and North American response to violence against women.

Anne Edwards is Senior Lecturer in Sociology at Monash University, Melbourne, Australia. Before going to Australia in 1968, she held teaching and research positions in Newcastle and Durham. She is a feminist sociologist whose main areas of teaching, research and writing are women and gender, social theory and deviance/social control. Her publications include *Social Deviance in Australia*, which she edited with P. Wilson.

Susan S. M. Edwards is currently a Research Fellow at the Polytechnic of Central London, where she is engaged in a study of domestic violence and spousal homicide focusing on, amongst other things, the response of the police and the courts. She also lectures on criminology, medical sociology and women's issues courses. She contributes regularly to law, sociological and medical journals, and is the author of *Female Sexuality and the Law* (1981) and *Women on Trial* (1984), and the editor of *Gender, Sex and the Law* (1985).

Eileen Green is Senior Lecturer in Sociology at Sheffield City Polytechnic where she teaches joint courses with Diana Woodward in women's studies and sociological perspectives in the field of medicine. Her past research includes a qualitative study of the working lives of mothers employed on a part-time basis in various local industries in Sheffield. She is currently researching women's leisure on a project funded jointly by the Sports Council and the ESRC.

Jalna Hanmer is co-ordinator of the Dip/MA Women's Studies (Applied) at the University of Bradford. She taught at the London School of Economics from 1974 until moving north in 1977. Her main areas of research and writing are on violence against women and the effects of the new reproductive technologies on the lives of women. She is author (with Sheila Saunders) of *Well-Founded Fear: A Community Study of Violence to Women* and is currently researching into the policing response to the physical and sexual abuse of women. Her interest in violence against women began ten years ago with the development of refuges for battered women and she remains active in Women's Aid.

Sandra Hebron is a Research Associate at Sheffield City Polytechnic working in the area of women's leisure on a project funded jointly by the Sports Council and the ESRC.

Diane Hudson lives and works in Leeds, and is at present in charge of a rehabilitation hostel for the mentally ill. She is interested in all aspects of women and mental health, but has published articles particularly on women and psychosurgery.

Liz Kelly has recently completed her doctorate on sexual violence. She has been involved since 1973 in a number of local groups and national campaigns around violence against women and is still a member of her local Women's Aid Refuge Collective. She teaches Adult Education Women's Studies courses in Norwich and hopes to do further research on child sexual abuse and prevention programmes.

Sandra McNeill has been an active member of the Women's Liberation Movement for ten years, mainly in campaigns around male violence and in women's employment and training initiatives. She is editor with dusty rhodes of the book *Women Against Violence Against Women*. She has given lectures on feminist theories at the Adult Education Department of Leeds University and is currently working for ICOM Women's Link-up and researching her next book.

Mary Maynard is a Lecturer in Sociology at the University of York, where she is also involved in running and teaching the MA in Women's Studies. She has written about domestic violence and housework and is author (with Arthur Brittan) of *Sexism, Racism and Oppression*. Her current work is the preparation of a book on feminist thought.

David H. J. Morgan is Senior Lecturer in sociology at the University of Manchester. He is particularly interested in the sociologies of the family and of gender, the latter with particular reference to masculinities. His most recent publication is *The Family, Politics and Social Theory* (1985).

Jill Radford is a feminist who has been active in feminist campaigns against men's violence. She has taught part-time for various institutions, including the Open University and the Polytechnic of the South Bank. Since 1983 she has been a worker at the Wandsworth Policing Campaign, with responsibility for the *Violence Against Women – Women Speak Out Survey*, a study of violence against women in the London Borough of Wandsworth which has been funded jointly by the Greater London Council's Women's and Police Committees.

Lorraine Radford studied sociology and economics in London and sociology and law at Brunel University. She is presently engaged at Bradford University in full-time research on law and violence against women.

Caroline Ramazanoglu is a lecturer in sociology at Goldsmiths' College, University of London. She has worked in a number of institutions of higher education in England, Uganda and Turkey, specialising in development studies and analysis of labour migration. She is currently working on the inter-relations of class, ethnicity and gender in the subordination of women.

Elizabeth A. Stanko is an Associate Professor of Sociology at Clark University, Worcester, Massachusetts. She is concerned primarily with issues of male violence to women. Her two books, *Judge, Lawyer, Victim, Thief* (edited with Nicole Rafter) and *Intimate Intrusions*, focus on women and their treatment in and by the criminal justice system. Dr Stanko was a founding member of a battered women's refuge in Worcester, Massachusetts, and has participated in police training, both in the US and UK, around issues of policing male violence to women.

Diana Woodward is Senior Lecturer in Sociology at Sheffield City Polytechnic, where she teaches courses with Eileen Green in women's studies and sociological perspectives in the field of medicine. Her past research includes the career patterns and experiences of women graduates. She is particularly interested in developing a feminist methodology and is currently researching women's leisure in a project funded jointly by the Sports Council and the ESRC.

1 Introduction: Violence and Gender Stratification

Jalna Hanmer and Mary Maynard

The papers in this volume (together with its companion, *The Sociology of War and Peace*), are a selection of those presented at the 1985 Annual Conference of the British Sociological Association, which had as its theme, 'War, Violence and Social Change'. Despite the violent nature of the society and world in which we live, sociology has had little to say about the social causes, effects and, more importantly, the prevention or elimination of violence. The conference aimed to remedy this deficiency by including research on different forms and kinds of violence, ranging from that involving war and the militarisation of the State to work which focuses on the interpersonal and everyday experiences of violence. Some of the dominant themes to emerge from the conference concerned gender and violence, with a significant number of papers concentrating on men's violence towards women.

Although violence towards women, particularly rape and the sexual abuse of girls, is being given an increasingly high profile in the media, mainstream sociology has yet to address it as a central issue. The reason for this is due partly to the ways in which conventional sociological practices have tended to marginalise women and render them invisible in all but the most obvious areas of study, such as the family. However, whereas questions of gender are now being raised in many areas of sociological research on topics as diverse as paid employment, education, popular culture and health, women's experience of violence is rarely submitted to scrutiny or analysis either as a topic in its own right or as a constituent feature of any of the sub-areas of the discipline. We hear little, for example, of sexual harassment as it may be experienced at work, school or college, nor is much attention paid to the ways in which women are forced to modify their behaviour and activities through fear of attack.

Although a few sociological analyses of rape and domestic violence have appeared during recent years, these are not regarded as part of mainstream concerns. Furthermore, as Anne Edwards notes in this volume, the authors of this work have tended to ignore the significance of gender relations as a central factor in understanding violence towards women. They have avoided introducing the concept of male power either as a feature of all interpersonal male–female encounters or as a structural dimension of society. As a result, many studies have emphasized only victim precipitation and individual psychopathology as causative factors in male–female violence. It has been left to feminists to challenge such stereotypes and widen the context within which violence to women must be discussed.

The chapters in this volume together constitute examples of some of the most recent feminist work in the area. They are particularly indicative of the ways in which both the theoretical discussion and the empirical base of our understanding of violence and gender is being extended. However, such work has not developed in a vacuum. Feminists have been grappling with the phenomenon of violence for many years, both in their writing and in their political activity, so that there is now a considerable amount of feminist literature devoted to the subject. In Chapter 1 Anne Edwards uses this literature to document the changes and developments in feminist views of male violence since the early 1970s. Her overview of work in the field provides an important backdrop against which the subsequent chapters in the book may be understood.

Edwards' thesis is that a significant shift has occurred in feminist thinking on violence. In the 1970s it was usual for analysis and activities to be organised around specific types of violence, which tended to be treated in a discrete fashion. Thus it was commonplace for studies and campaigns to focus on a particular form of violence – sometimes rape, sometimes domestic violence, sometimes incest, etc. Today male violence is more often treated as a 'unitary phenomenon' which is regarded by feminists as important, along with other forms of male power, in the reproduction and maintenance of male dominance and female subordination. Edwards supports her claim for this shift in emphasis by looking at material from the 'early' and 'later' stages of second-wave feminism. Early classic texts saw force and violence as residual categories in man's domination of woman which was regarded as being maintained through mainly ideological devices. The active involvement of feminists in the 1970s with women who had been physically or sexually abused led to an increasing emphasis on the significance of male violence and to the development of concepts and a vocabulary through which it could be described and analysed. Subsequently, this analysis has moved to a concern with heterosexuality as a system of social control of women. Edwards provides us with a perfect example of how theory develops as a response to material conditions. She highlights how the present focus of the feminist approach to the study of violence towards women has developed.

Although the substantive context of each chapter ranges widely, including studies of psychiatry, the courts and judicial judgements, leisure and indecent exposure, there are many ways in which the chapters are interrelated and together contribute generally to the analysis of violence and gender. Six main themes highlight their significance and interconnections.

1. Several of the contributions are concerned with new and important fields of empirical study, confirming the findings of other works in the area, that violence and its threat, in various forms, are common and inhibiting features of most women's lives. Jill Radford's piece, based on research conducted in the London borough of Wandsworth, is significant both for including non-white women in its respondents (a serious omission in so much of the literature) and for the coverage given to women's experiences of and feelings about the police response to violence against women. Although the women involved in the Wandsworth survey reported a high incidence of male violence, they were very reticent of going to the police and critical of the latter's response when an incident was reported to them. Similarly, although the women in Liz Kelly's research were aware of the threat of violence and most had experienced forms of sexual harassment, they had learnt to 'cope' with this rather than feeling it could be dealt with directly.

The work of Jill Radford and Liz Kelly demonstrates some of the ways in which feminists have developed alternative research strategies for the study of violence against women. Both are concerned with what women themselves define as violence, rather than some objective measure of it; both are concerned to let women speak for themselves; both are concerned to extend the range of women included in gender and violence studies. The sample of women which is the focus of the Wandsworth survey was collected through door-to-door interviewing, but Kelly publicised her research through the local media and by giving talks in the local community, and invited women to participate in her study. Both contributors have gone beyond the confines of existing work, most of which has concentrated on those women who can be contacted through official or voluntary agencies. They demonstrate that a healthy scepticism about conventional ways of drawing samples and measuring social phenomena such as violence, can have a significant impact on and be of value to sociological research.

Other chapters in the book are also devoted to new empirical concerns. Sandra McNeill extends the common-sense notion of the kinds of events to be included in the category of violence, by focusing on indecent exposure. 'Flashing' is often culturally trivialised as a topic of farce and treated as pathetic or funny. By concentrating on what the *victims* experience, McNeill shows that the women involved often feel frightened, humiliated and degraded. Furthermore, the uncertainty as to what a man who exposes himself may do next means that women frequently think of and fear death during harassment of this kind. McNeill is highly critical of the existing literature on indecent exposure, which tends to view it as an individualised mental problem. Her work challenges this kind of formulation and provides the first sociological account of flashing and how women are affected by it.

Similarly, Diane Hudson also extends our ideas on what may properly be labelled as violence. Her study of psychosurgery, which focuses on leucotomy, is concerned with an area of physical intervention which is normally characterised as medical treatment. Yet Hudson argues that many operations on the brain are more properly regarded as violence towards women. Her research shows that it is women who are the prime targets for such 'treatment' and that the surgery is performed with the expressed aim of modifying women's behaviour, particularly when they are defined as not being able to cope with the traditional aspects of their gender role. Furthermore, the operations do not appear to be 'successful', largely, Hudson argues, because many of the causative factors in a woman's life, for example, the violence of a man, are ignored by the psychiatric profession. This is an extremely disturbing chapter and one which raises many new questions about psychiatry's attitude to and behaviour towards women.

2. The second link between several of the chapters in this book lies in their concern with the question: what is violence and how should it be conceptualised? Until now those researching violence towards women have been mainly preoccupied with the task of describing the most obvious forms. However, as the above discussion suggests, feminists are extending both their empirical range and their conceptual framework to embrace activities and personnel not previously included in the literature of the subject. We have already commented on McNeill's research: flashing as a form of visual violence. Similarly,

Hudson in her chapter extends both her definition of what constitutes violence and our understanding of where and by whom it can be committed by focusing on psychiatric treatment and professional psychiatrists.

Other contributors also raise conceptual questions about definition and usage of terms. Caroline Ramazanoglu's sensitive chapter uses personal experiences and observations to study the sexual politics of academic life. Following the Quaker Pinthus, she argues that: 'Violence should be understood as any action or structure that diminishes another human being' and that institutions can be as violent and intimidating as individuals. Ramazanoglu is dealing with phenomena that do not involve physical attack. Instead she concentrates on the 'insults, leers, sneers, jokes, patronage, bullying, vocal violence and sexual harassment' which are the common experiences of working women. Although universities exude a veneer of liberalism, the reality is that women are kept subordinate through these various strategies, which are not simply the perogative of particular men, but rather institutionalised through the male-dominated hierarchy. The insults and leers which Ramazanoglu describes are regarded as forms of violence by her because they are specific mechanisms for keeping women in their place. Moreover, the woman who resists is marginalised and labelled as deviant by the academic community, for such resistance undermines their deference system and exposes the mechanisms of social control. Ramazanoglu's work, by extending the notion of what we mean by violence, elucidates the process whereby the patriarchal order is reproduced within the higher education environment.

A further elaboration of the concept of violence is supplied by Liz Kelly. Kelly focuses on the idea of a continuum of sexual violence, which is beginning to be used by researchers in the area. She is critical of the ways in which it has been employed as a vehicle for understanding women's experience of violence. Kelly moves the discussion from the perception of a continuum as a way of describing the severity of attacks to an emphasis on the incidence of various forms of violence and the range of possible experiences of and responses to this. Her point is that all forms of violence towards women are serious and have consequences for them. She challenges the linear and dichotomous thinking adopted by most of those who talk in terms of a continuum. Since, as her research shows, all women experience sexual violence, the division of women into those who are victims and those who are not is exposed as false. For Kelly, the concept of a continuum is only useful when conceived as a series of planes in which experiences intermesh and merge. Further, she emphasizes that women's own evaluations of the seriousness of the violence towards them does not necessarily correspond to the definitions and categorisations used by agencies such as the media or the criminal justice system.

3. Ramazanoglu and Kelly provide detailed conceptual justifications for broadening the connotations of violence in the ways previously described. Other writers are specifically concerned with including threat or fear of violence as constituting violence towards women. This, then, is the third general theme of the chapters in the book.

In 1978, Hanmer argued for the first time that not only should a definition of violence be based on the perspective of the victim, but that women's definitions covered a wide spectrum of abuses:

> A sociological definition of violence needs to include both the use of force and its threat to both compel or constrain women to behave or not to behave in given ways.

Although feminists implicitly took this on board in the range of harassments they began to investigate, it is only recently that the significance and consequences of being threatened with or fearing violence have been explored. As Kelly, Hudson, McNeill and Jill Radford show in this book, the fear of violence limits women's freedom of movement. It constrains what they can do, where they can go and with whom they can go. In other words, both the reality and the threat of violence act as a form of social control. The chapters by Stanko and by Green *et al.* develop this position further.

Elizabeth Stanko, in her chapter on precautionary strategies, focuses on the role played by gender in understanding criminal victimisation and men's and women's fears of such victimisation. She points out that while official victimisation surveys indicate that women seem to suffer violence less frequently than men, their fear of attack is shown to be significantly higher. She argues that contemporary discussions about fear of crime in fact omit many women's experiences of violence by concentrating only on 'outside' crime and fear of attack by strangers. However, it is well known that certain sorts of violence against women are under-reported, particularly those of a sexual nature involving someone known to the victim and occurring 'inside'. Thus, although women's *fear* of violence has formed the focus of analysis, their *experience* of it has been ignored – at least by governmental and official bodies. Stanko suggests that part of the reason for this is that most non-feminist research has adopted a gender–neutral approach towards the problem, but women fear attack by virtue of being women in a male-dominated society. Stanko goes on to elaborate on the nature and extent of women's fear by discussing the precautions they take to avoid attack. She leaves us in no doubt that feelings of fright, vulnerability and lack of protection are common features of women's lives and contributory factors in the way these are circumscribed.

This issue of social control is taken up again by Eileen Green, Sandra Hebron and Diana Woodward. The theme of their discussion is women's leisure activities – an area which, at first glance, appears to be governed by few constraints. However, based on several sources of empirical data including their own research, Green *et al.* argue that leisure is one of the areas in which women's behaviour is most regulated, in both private and public spheres. Although much of the control of women's free time rests on conventionally-accepted notions of how women should behave and is thus control via 'consent' rather than 'coercion', they emphasise that when this form of constraint breaks down men have other regulatory methods at their command. Among these are both the exercise and the threat of physical and other forms of violence.

4. A fourth focus of the book is on how violence against women is processed within the civil and criminal justice systems. Over the years various kinds of data have been collected detailing the reactions of state agencies, such as the police and social services, to incidents such as rape and domestic violence, and the outcome of cases that have come to court and the operation of relevant legislation have been monitored. It has been less usual, however, for researchers to consider the grounds and the procedures upon which decisions have been reached in courts of law. The chapters by Susan Edwards and Lorraine Radford contribute to the development of work in this area.

Edwards demonstrates that violent assaults against wives or cohabitees are frequently marginalised and trivialised within the legal system. With the use of case data, she shows that one of the ways this is achieved is by suggesting that women precipitate the behaviour against them – what Edwards calls 'provoking their own demise'. She outlines some of the ideological constructs concerning the appropriate behaviour and conduct of women which are regularly used by the police and courts in dealing with cases of domestic violence. It appears that, even in cases of spousal murder, the concept of provocation can be taken into consideration by the court, although the female victim is, of course, no longer able to speak for herself on this matter. However, when the wife is an offender in a murder trial, the plea of provocation is less likely to be accepted. Edwards suggests that this is because what is regarded as provocation contains a clear gender bias. Women are expected to put up with a far greater degree of provocation than men, which means that their actions are more likely to be defined as premeditated than seen as committed in self-defence or retaliation. The result is that women who are battered are the 'victims' not only of the unequal power relationship which exists within the family, but also of a legal system which, according to Edwards, provides them with little real protection from assault.

Lorraine Radford uses the decisions reported from higher courts, which form the basis of 'case law', to focus on what the law defines as acceptable or unacceptable behaviour for the two sexes and how this affects judgements about violence between men and women in the family. Like Edwards, therefore, she is concerned with the ideological aspects of law. Focusing on the language used in reported decisions, she concentrates on four discursive strategies which may be used to render domestic violence as less serious or less dangerous than other forms of attack. Radford concurs with Edwards that domestic violence is often trivialised by the law and treated as merely a welfare issue. She also shares her conclusion that although the law has the power of intervention in domestic violence cases, this is frequently kept to a minimum.

5. In this introduction so far the impression may have been given that this book conceives women's response to male violence as one which is simply passive and submissive. This is by no means entirely the case and the fifth theme explores how violence from men is challenged and resisted. Jill Radford, for example, details some of the suggestions made by women in the Wandsworth survey as to how public transport and housing estates could be made safer for women. The victims of flashing, interviewed by McNeill, speak of anger as well as resignation. Caroline Ramazanoglu refers to campaigns against sexual harassment and the ways in which feminism forces women to see abuse and assault as a general, rather than an individual problem and one which can be challenged. It is rare, however, that the history of women's responses to the violence committed against them is recorded. Rebecca and Russell Dobash have attempted to do this for the movement which has been concerned with domestic violence. Their chapter records the struggles, setbacks and successes which are a feature of the women's

aid movements on both sides of the Atlantic. They chart the 'discovery' of the problem, its emergence as a social issue and the variety of responses which came from the women's liberation movement and the state in each country. Their discussion covers the development of networks of refuges and shelters, legislative reform and the formation of national organisations to campaign on behalf of battered women. Although Dobash and Dobash highlight many of the similarities between the movements in Britain and America, they also stress some of the differences, emphasising that their diversity is as significant as their 'sheer volume of accomplishments'. Their chapter is testimony to the collective campaigning of feminists and what it is possible to achieve.

6. The sixth theme focuses on men and masculinity. It has been argued elsewhere that many studies concerned with gender concentrate solely on the oppressed, that is, women, and neglect the mentality, culture and practices of the oppressors, that is men *qua men* (Brittan and Maynard, 1984). The social construction of maleness and masculinity has yet to be properly analysed in sociology, which means that when reference is made to 'gender', it is assumed that only women will be the subject of study. This is particularly true of the study of violence where, until now, attention has primarily been only on women as gendered subjects. The fact that it is, in the main, *men* who systematically abuse women, *men* who fight wars, *men* who revel in the sub-cultures of the gang and the hooligan, has been concealed, except in feminist work. It is, therefore, important that we have in this book one of the few attempts to explore the links between masculinity and violence: the final chapter by David Morgan.

Morgan argues that the relationship between masculinity and violence is more complex than has previously been acknowledged, partly because both notions are themselves more variable and diffuse than is usually recognised. Thus, he claims, is it more useful to pluralise the terms and to talk about masculinities and violences. Morgan explores the relationship between the social construction of masculinities and the ways in which violence is legitimated and explained. He also examines the links between different levels of violence, ranging from the interpersonal to militarism and warfare. Morgan's point is that to present too uniform a model of male violence can make it appear innate. Not only may this result in the power of patriarchy being understated, it also precludes the possibility of being able to alter violent practices or eliminate them from society and thus denies any chance of social change.

Morgan leaves us with an important question – when do differences between masculinities merge into similarities when examined in relation to violence against women? On the one hand, it may not matter which masculinity is projected, as men with different masculinities may assault women; but on the other, men whose masculinities do not allow this type of expression may still receive deference from women as a result of their more generalised fear of violence and its consequences.

Taken together, the contents of this book comprise a concerted attempt to develop a sociology of violence with particular reference to the violence of men against women. One focus for this is on the relationship between the social construction of heterosexuality, and the ways in which men's abuse of women supports their power and control over them. Another is the interdependence of forms of control at various social levels. If self-regulation by individual women through fear of or actual violence from men is not effective, then other social processes may be activated. For example, women who resist sexual harassment may be labelled deviant by the larger social grouping within the workplace and controlled through exclusion. Other forms of shifting control by the State may be through treating women more harshly than men; for example, psychosurgery for sex-role deviance, or longer prison sentences for killing men, or refusal by the courts or police to meet women's requests for protection. However, the importance of the volume goes even further than this: it also contributes to the developing critique of the almost obsessive concern in sociology with the concept 'social class' in describing and analysing issues such as inequality, power and oppression. For our purposes two particular aspects of such criticism are significant.

Firstly, it has been pointed out that there are gender as well as class differences in the social fabric of our society and these, as was stated at the beginning of this introduction, increasingly feature in empirical sociological studies. Secondly, questions concerning how gender issues should be conceptualised and how this relates to class measurement and theory are beginning to feature in the literature of the subject. The outcome of these developments is not, in our view, entirely satisfactory. The tendency in empirical work is either to focus on gender issues separately from those of class (this is a feature, for example, of the sociology of education) or to subsume them within an overall class analysis (characteristic of research on employment). The major conceptual issue, as evidenced in recent volumes of the BSA journal *Sociology*, is on whether women can be incorporated within the framework of 'social class' and how this is to be achieved. Although differing in what they mean by, and how they use, the term 'class', the protagonists seem to agree that the problem is one of 'fit': what alterations need to be made to conventional practices or arguments to ensure that women may be included? As Delphy remarks: 'The concept of a class system as a stratification system is exhaustive in the sense that it is supposed to cover all the possibilities in a given society. This aim is never challenged even by those who criticise specific features of the concept or criteria used' (Delphy, 1981). Such a conception of class raises difficulties for those working in certain areas of gender- or woman-orientated studies, particularly those studying violence.

In all this recent debate, in both the empirical and the conceptual literature, the attempt has been to revise 'class' to encompass gender 'problems', thus maintaining 'class' as pre-eminent. But there is increasing evidence from feminist research on women that gender cannot be subordinated in this way. Studies of education and ageing, for example, suggest that many social processes which effect women occur *across* different social groupings, even though there may be different material circumstances among women as a group. More importantly, work on 'violence' is testimony to the fact that many issues of central importance to women's lives, and of paramount importance to the power inequalities of male and female, are common to all women. In understanding violence against women the concept 'class' is simply not a significant factor in identifying either victim or offender. Nor is it relevant in explaining why this violence occurs. To ignore these issues is to obscure the central power dimension of gender stratification. To put it bluntly, the realities of male violence and the sociological language of class seem entirely divergent.

Instead, the chapters on gender and violence included here display, in stark relief, the hierarchical nature of a society where gender stratification is fundamental and violence plays a major role in the social control of women. This is both from individual men and via the institutionalisation of violence in a social structure dominated by men as a group (or class). The term 'gender stratification' underlines the unequal power relationship between men and women in both the public and private spheres. The analysis of violence, including the threat and fear of violence, demonstrates some of the mechanisms through which that domination and subordination is maintained and reproduced. Current feminist research reveals, therefore, the existence of a complex social structure where power, inequality and oppression operate along socially-constructed gender lines. Only if sociology is able to distance itself from the legacy of nineteenth-century class analysis, which did, after all, ignore gender issues almost entirely, can we begin to understand the complexities of power relationships and of stratification. The use of the concept of gender stratification is, we hope, a move in the right direction.

2 Male Violence in Feminist Theory: an Analysis of the Changing Conceptions of Sex/Gender Violence and Male Dominance

Anne Edwards

. . . the victim is the one who is acting out, initiating the interaction between her and the offender, and by her behaviour she generates the potentiality for criminal behaviour of the offender or triggers this potentiality, if it existed before in him.   (Amir, 1971, p. 259)

That the basic elements of rape are involved in all heterosexual relationships may explain why men often identify with the offender in this crime. But to regard the rapist as the victim, a man driven by his inherent sexual needs to take what will not be given to him, reveals a basic ignorance of sexual politics. For in our culture heterosexual love finds an erotic expression through male dominance and female submission. A man who derives pleasure from raping a woman clearly must enjoy force and dominance as much or more than the simple pleasures of the flesh.   (Griffin, 1971, p. 29)

Through the process of consciousness-raising, women moved on from the discovery that sexual assault was not just an individual and unique experience to the realization that rape, as an issue, was a means of analyzing the psychological and political structures of oppression in our society.   (New York Radical Feminists, 1974, p. 3, written about their Rape Conference in 1971)

We are not accustomed to associate patriarchy with force. So perfect is its system of socialization, so complete the general assent to its values, so long and so universally has it prevailed in human society, that it scarcely seems to require violent implementation. Customarily, we view its brutalities in the past as exotic or 'primitive' custom. Those of the present are regarded as the product of individual deviance, confined to pathological or exceptional behaviour, and without general import. And yet, just as under other total ideologies . . . control in patriarchal

13

society would be imperfect, even inoperable, unless it had the rule of force to rely upon, both in emergencies and as an ever-present instrument of intimidation. (Millett, 1972, p. 43, first published 1969)

. . . investigations reveal rape, incest, sexual harassment, pornography, and prostitution as not primarily abuses of physical force, violence, authority, or economics. They are abuses of sex . . . They are sexual because they express the relations, values, feelings, norms and behaviours of the culture's sexuality, in which considering things like rape, pornography, incest or lesbianism deviant, perverse or blasphemous is part of their excitement potential. Sexuality, then, is a form of power. Gender, as socially constructed, embodies it, not the reverse. (MacKinnon, 1982, p. 533)

Of these statements, all made by Americans on the subject of male violence against women, the first four appeared around 1970. The 1970s was a critical decade in the modern history of women, since it marked the period of development of the second-wave feminist movement. Modern Western feminism involved both the construction of a distinctive body of social theory and socio-political activity on a broad range of issues to publicise and work towards changing the conditions of women's oppression. Around 1970 academic sociology began to come under attack for gender blindness and sexism with respect to its inadequate treatment of women and of sexual divisions and inequalities in society.[1]

There is no area where androcentric bias is more visible and systematic than that of male violence against women. Sociological analyses of male violence started to appear in the early 1970s, in particular Amir's (1971) theory of victim-precipitation in rape and work by family sociologists[2] on domestic violence, and these have continued to be influential. Though at last giving social factors more weight than individual psychopathology, these male authors still failed to perceive the central importance of sex and gender in all male–female interactions, and their relevance wherever violence is involved, nor did they place much emphasis on power or on the broader structural dimensions of gender relations and sexual politics.[3] This chapter will explore the contribution of modern feminists to our understanding of sex/gender and violence,[4] and the main source of material is the published writings of modern English and American feminist theorists[5] over the last fifteen years or so.

The choice of particular theorists is ultimately a personal one though in this case there are a number of well-known and obviously significant writers who must be included. The focus on published works, however, is more problematic given feminism's equal commitment to the pursuit of knowledge and to personal/political action, and the close interrelationship between theory and practice, ideas and experience. It must therefore be acknowledged that relying on published feminism may not do full justice to the experiential and activist side of the movement, to the importance of the efforts and insights of numerous nameless women, and to the direct influence these have had on feminist theorising.

Since the main purpose of the chapter is to trace some patterns of change and development in feminist theory from 1970 to the present day, particularly in the conceptualisation and treatment of male violence, we will first consider feminist writing in the early 1970s and then turn to more recent work. From the earlier period there are two relevant sources of theoretical ideas: one is the classic texts of modern feminism (Millett, Firestone, Mitchell and Rowbotham, for example) and the other is feminist analyses of male violence that emerged from the movement's active involvement with and on behalf of women who were victims of male physical and sexual abuse. Work on rape is of particular importance (Griffin and Brownmiller being key examples). From the later period (and no precise dates can be set on what is necessarily a continuously developing, diverse yet interconnected body of knowledge) we examine more recent theories of male violence and the control of women (by such writers as Barry, Dworkin, Rich and MacKinnon). These are viewed against the background of the changing nature and concerns of contemporary feminist theory as a whole. Some feminists, of whom Daly is the prime example, span the two periods and contribute both to feminist understanding of physical and sexual abuse of women cross-culturally and to general theories of male dominance and female oppression. A deliberate decision was taken to present feminist theory through the writings of individually-identified women. The alternative, to use general categories such as 'Marxist' or 'radical' feminist to refer to different schools or 'brands' of feminist thought, leads to oversimplification and distortion, as similiarities within and contrasts between the various perspectives are necessarily overemphasised.[6]

It appears that a significant shift has occurred within feminist thought over the decade. This is evident in the conceptualisation of male violence against women, which moved from separate accounts of specific types of violence to an appreciation of male violence overall as being at some level a unitary phenomenon, and in the theoretical importance attached to violence – as well as other forms of male power – in the analysis of what different writers describe as patriarchal, male-dominated or male-supremacist society.[7]

EARLY MODERN FEMINIST THEORISING ON MALE DOMINANCE AND THE SOURCES OF WOMEN'S OPPRESSION

At around the same time, the early 1970s, as both academic 'malestream' sociology and the emerging women's movement were giving attention, though of very different kinds, to the issues of rape and domestic violence, the early classic texts of second-wave feminism were being published. As we shall discover, Firestone, Millett, Mitchell and Rowbotham – and de Beauvoir before them – did not give male violence a central place in their theories of male dominance. Rather, they all adopted the position that in the modern Western world force is no longer a major technique for patriarchal control over women. Male dominance is seen to rest on a variety of social, economic, political and ideological institutions and practices, all of which are regarded as more or less 'normal' and 'natural' by both male and female members of society. Indeed, from de Beauvoir (1949) on, women's oppression is attributed to society, not biology; to male-dominated institutions, not individual men; to the social structures of production and reproduction, not to the physiological differences between men and women; to the cultural construction of masculinity and femininity as a polarity or dichotomy. The male is seen as subject and agent, the female as object or other. Gender differences are traced back not to any innate physical or psychological qualities such as aggression or timidity, though as de Beauvoir and many others have pointed out, one of the most insidious elements of patriarchal ideology is that it (mis)represents the female nature as biologically, not culturally, determined. It therefore appeared logical to these modern feminist thinkers to look for the sources of male power not in men's greater physical strength or their alleged aggressive instinct, but rather in the major institutions of contemporary capitalism:

> . . . the military, industry, technology, universities, science, political office, and finance – in short, every avenue of power within society, including the coercive force of the police, is entirely in male hands. (Millett, 1972, p. 25)

Indeed, given the male monopoly on all formal and legitimate sources of power and authority, why would men need to resort to physical means of coercion?

This general perception is one shared by all four feminist writers and all, except Firestone, make specific reference to the relatively minor role of physical force or the use of violence in modern patriarchies. Mitchell, for example, building her analysis around the four major social structures of production, reproduction, socialisatation and sexuality, recognises the importance of 'social coercion', but argues that 'force may not be actualized as direct aggression . . . Coercion has been ameliorated to an ideology shared by both sexes' (1971, pp. 103 and 105). Rowbotham too is far more concerned with social structural features of capitalism, such as the sexual division of labour and the 'cultural colonisation' of women's consciousness by male ideology (1973, p. 37), than with direct methods of male coercion. She does suggest, however, that the pressures and contradictions of capitalism ensure that violence in male–female and adult–child relationships remains, even if most of the time it is submerged or repressed in the modern family (1973, pp. 59 and 77). Firestone gives more weight to biology, specifically women's reproductive capacity, but still argues that the basis of the social order and male power is psychosexual and cultural. She is often interpreted as a biological determinist but most of her chapters are devoted to accounts of the social aspects of patriarchy. As she says (1971, pp. 20–1), her book is an attempt to extend historical materialism beyond the analysis of class divisions and modes of production to sex divisions and reproduction.

Millett's (1972) position is somewhat less straightforward on the question of force and violence. The bulk of the chapter called 'Theory of Sexual Politics' in her book originally published in 1969 is devoted to an examination of the ways in which the conventional institutions of society, such as the family, the state, ideology and culture, are responsible socially and psychologically for producing and reproducing patriarchy. She explicitly rejects biological reductionist arguments. However, not only does she have a section in the chapter entitled 'Force' (pp. 43–6), but in it she explicitly acknowledges that all control ultimately rests on force. She then goes on to discuss in a few pages rape and pornography, the link between 'cruelty and sexuality' and the 'variety of cruelties and brutalities' to women that have occurred in the 'history of patriarchy'. She mentions specifically suttee, footbinding, clitoridectomy, child marriage and other practices, pointing out that all of these have cultural 'rationales' to justify the injury and injustice incurred. Interestingly, she alone of these four authors perceives the continued existence of male violence and sexual aggression even in what is apparently a highly 'civilised', rationalistic (in the Weberian sense), well-established system of male domination, and its problematic status. With her insights into the nature and role of men's use of force against women in modern society and the linking together of a number of culturally sanctioned abuses of women's bodies found throughout human history, she anticipates, and no doubt influenced, both the work of Griffin on rape and Daly's conceptualisation of five major 'barbarous rituals' as comprising the 'sado-ritual syndrome' (to be discussed later).

Other ideas to be found in these four early classics of modern feminism which became major themes in later feminist theories are the psychology of femininity and sexual repression, pursued by Firestone and Mitchell, and the changing character and increasing commercialisation and objectification of sexuality, taken up by Mitchell and Rowbotham.

At the same time, other feminists were giving male violence a prominent place in their analysis of male dominance. Within the women's movement, at least in America, rape in the early 1970s was *the* feminist issue. It symbolised women's unique vulnerability to attack from men at any time and an attack involving a fundamental violation of their physical and sexual being. Unlike other issues at the time, such as prostitution or abortion, rape had the advantage of uniting all women, whatever their status, values or beliefs. Indeed, it has been wrily observed that on rape, and on rape alone, women on the radical right and on the radical left find themselves in agreement. Susan Griffin's classic article entitled 'Rape: the All-American Crime' appeared in 1971. Here are contained most of the ideas which have come to characterise American feminist treatments of rape. Issues were raised which were later developed in more detail by Brownmiller (1975), Clark and Lewis (1977), Medea and Thompson (1974) and Russell (1975), as part of radical feminism's analysis of male sexual violence and its contribution to the maintenance of patriarchy throughout history and under capitalism. These issues are: the close interconnection between sexuality, aggression and violence as the primary component of masculinity in many societies; a difference in degree only, not quality, between rape and 'normal' heterosexual intercourse; the contradiction between men as predators on and guardians or protectors of women; the paradox that femininity, socially constructed as the complement of masculinity, not only undermines women's capacity for sexual (and social) self-determination but actually increases their physical and psychological vulnerability to male attack; the perception of rape as more a political than a sexual act, one which represents the collective domination of men over women and thus is an act akin to terrorism; and the failure of the legal and judicial systems to extend to women the support, protection and redress their injuries deserve.

Brownmiller's (1975) book is the most famous of the radical feminist works that deal with rape. For her, rape is a mechanism of male social control over women that relies as much on generalised threat and fear as on the actual use of force. Rape is not an act of sexual gratification but an exercise in power and intimidation made possible by the anatomical differences between men and women (p. 14). She argues that 'the ideology of rape is fueled by cultural values that are perpetuated at every level of our society' and encapsulated in what she terms 'machismo' or 'the theory of aggressive male domination over women as a natural right' (p. 389). She makes a connection between rape, prostitution and pornography as part of this general cultural 'perception of sexual access as an adjunct of male power and privilege' (p. 392). She apparently sees, however, a distinction between 'deviant' and 'normal' heterosexuality, placing the former in the category of violence, and the latter in that of sexuality (MacKinnon, 1979, p. 219). Brownmiller also exposes the sexist biases in the modern legal and judicial systems' attitude to rape and the extensive opportunities for, and legitimisations of, rape provided for men in every type of society by virtue of their occupancy of positions in particular institutions, settings and authority structures which license such conduct.

The problems with this type of feminist analysis arise from its generality. The case for rape having a common function across all situations and societies must ultimately rely on biological essentialist arguments and ignore cultural and historical variations in definitions and conditions related to sex/gender, sexuality and sexual behaviour. Differences between societies in the form and frequency of male violence in general and sexual violence in particular, and in the patterns of relationship between interpersonal violence, male dominance and other social variables have to be denied or overlooked (Sanday, 1981b).

As the 1970s progressed, feminists and feminist-inspired social scientists turned their attention to other, less dramatic or less obvious, forms of female abuse, intimidation and exploitation by men – both individually and collectively – abuse which did not necessarily rely on the use of direct physical force or violence. It was during this time that feminist theoretical analysis was progressively uncovering the complex, pervasive and devious workings of patriarchy, and the feminist movement was campaigning for the extension of the principle of self-determination to more and more areas of women's lives. This included their physical and psychological health, their sexuality, their fertility and reproductivity, their mothering, their intellectual and educational development, their participation in the paid work-force, and so on. For example, in the health field, as early as 1973 Barbara Ehrenreich and Deirdre English exposed the sexist assumptions and practices of modern Western medicine (such as the nineteenth-century advocacy of surgery on women's genital and reproductive organs for reasons other than disease or physical malfunction – surely a form of legitimated violence).[8] Later in the 1970s, sexual harassment emerged as another such issue (McKinnon, 1979).

In each of these cases, certain key social institutions and core values traditionally regarded as highly desirable and necessary features of society are subjected to the feminist perspective and revealed as having important, if covert, functions for the maintenance of the gender order and for the legitimation of male power and the use of violence. One could begin to see parallels between the treatment of women workers at the hands of their employers, supervisors and male colleagues, the treatment of wives by their husbands, and the treatment of female patients at the hands of their doctors. All these involve institutional settings with a number of common structural and ideological features where men are dominant and women dependent and subordinate.

Particularly significant later in the 1970s is Mary Daly's book 'Gyn/Ecology' which was published in America in 1978. Daly (1978) shares some characteristics with each of the groups of feminist theorists identified here and in some ways her book provides a bridge between earlier and later feminist thought. Male violence in the form of what she calls the 'sado-ritual syndrome' (pp. 131–3) is presented as a major aspect of male power. She and Brownmiller have a number of ideas in common: both share the basic assumption that men and women are fundamentally very different types of beings; both believe that men fear and despise women while at the same time desiring and using them to meet their own various needs; and both describe how male aggressive sexuality and propensity to violence dictates the pattern of relationships between men and women. Daly's use of language to describe male power is similar to that of both Griffin (1971) and Brownmiller (1975). All three use terms like 'terrorism' to characterise the social and psychological effects of male violence on women and liken the battle of the sexes to war generally. In this respect there are also similarities between Daly and Dworkin, one of the more recent feminists who will be discussed later. Like Brownmiller and some of the earlier radical feminists, Daly is also vulnerable to criticism for her reliance on essentialist notions of male and female human nature (albeit not in her case simple physiological ones[9]) and a lack of any sense of historical or contextual specificity and variability in the conditions and forms of women's oppression. At the same time, Daly (1978) emphasises that in the modern world the 'possession of women's minds' (p. 2) is more important than physical intimidation. 'Mind-rape' (p. 110) is far more powerful than body-rape. In this respect she has more in common with Millett and the other early modern theorists. She also anticipates some of the later feminist writing in looking beyond the particularities of any one form of abuse to common underlying elements, like her five 'sado-rituals' (1978 ch 3–7)[10] and eight 'male-functions' (pp. 30–1), in a diverse range of cultural and social practices that oppress women.

No comparable body of feminist work on male violence was being produced in England at this time, though there was the much pub-licised book by Pizzey (1974) on wife-beating and the accompanying refuge movement (Women's Aid). On the whole, neither this nor other forms of male violence against women generated the same levels of theoretical interest among feminists (this was the period of the 'domestic labour debate'). Later in the 1970s, however, there were two important contributions made by feminists in England to the issue of male violence. Smart (1976), pointed to ways in which the double standard of morality and gender stereotypes are reflected in the criminal law and justice system (and in academic criminology), resulting in discrimination against women both as offenders and as victims, comparing particularly prostitution and rape. Hanmer (1978) in a theoretical paper which anticipates some later American feminist analysis, argues that 'force and its threat is never . . . residual or secondary . . . rather it is the structural underpinning of hierarchical relations' (p. 229) and she identifies the state as a significant agent of male dominance and female dependency.

There are limitations in both the two major types of feminist analysis. A number of American radical feminists following Griffin linked male sexuality and violence. However, they paid more attention to the manifestations of men's sexual aggressiveness than to its sources (indeed, it was often assumed to be biological) and largely ignored the processes by which male sexuality, and even more importantly female sexuality, are socially constructed (Shulman, 1980). At the same time, those American and British feminist theorists who were engaged in exploring the social and structural bases of sexual divisions and inequality attributed only a minor role to the use of force and coercion. When considering the institutions and ideologies believed to be responsible for women's oppression they dealt mainly with gender and neglected both sex and sexuality (English *et al.*, 1982, p. 42).

LATER FEMINIST THEORY AND MALE VIOLENCE: SEXUALITY, HETEROSEXUALITY AND SOCIAL CONTROL

Three issues are relevant to our analysis of more recent feminist writers and to comparisons between feminist theory in the earlier and later phases of the modern period. The first is whether or not force and violence are considered major factors in the maintenance of male domination. The second is whether those who do recognise its role look at the various manifestations of male violence as separate phenomena or as part of a general pattern or process. The third concerns the recognition of the social construction of sexuality and heterosexuality (in particular, heterosexism) and their relationship to violence, power and male control over women.

While still attempting to further our understanding of the material conditions of women's oppression and of the nature of the relationship between capitalism and patriarchy (Delphy, 1977, 1984; Hartmann, 1981; Sargent (ed.), 1981), contemporary feminist theory has turned its attention to social and cultural mechanisms for defining, shaping and constraining female (and male) sexuality as fundamental elements in male power over women and as of critical importance to patriarchy. Many, including Marxist-feminists, emphasise the contribution of ideology in particular to the social construction of gender and sexuality (Barrett, 1980; Chodorow, 1978; Rich, 1980; Women's Studies Group, Birmingham, 1978). Such writers identify various ideological forms, specifically romantic love, monogamy, motherhood and the cultural identification of femininity with the emotional, 'private' sphere and masculinity with achievement and the 'public' sphere, thus reinforcing men's economic and political power position and female dependency. In the view of modern feminists, heterosexism or 'compulsory heterosexuality' (Rich, 1980), essential as the normative underpinning of modern marriage and the family and as the cornerstone of patriarchal ideology, 'was dismissed' in the earlier period as a 'political problematic by radical feminism's dismissal of men' (Campbell, 1980, p. 3). Campbell shows how feminist analyses of normative heterosexuality and male definitions of sexuality for both males and females help us understand why 'sexual permissiveness' in the 1960s and 1970s did not result in sexual liberation for most women.

In general, these ideological notions are seen to support, and be supported by, social practices in the major institutions of capitalist patriarchal society: that is, marriage and the family, the sexual division of labour, the economic system, law and the state. One of the major concerns of feminist theorists in the 1980s is the exploration of the ways in which dominant ideologies, particularly those of heterosexuality, monogamy, motherhood and the public/private dichotomy contribute to the maintenance of male dominance and capitalist patriarchy. For example, Smart's (1984) recent work on the theory and practice of the law with respect to divorce reveals its ideological function in upholding the notion of the traditional family and reinforcing female dependency. Elsewhere (1982) she has exposed the fact that while the law and the state now intervene more directly in marital and family life, the main result is a further legitimation of 'the very structure of the family' (p. 744) which oppresses women (Edwards, 1981; Loseke and Cahill, 1984; Stanko, 1985; Stark *et al.*, 1979). Dobash and Dobash in a series of publications from the late 1970s and Klein (1979) explore various aspects of the institutional regulation of marriage. They focus on the legal system and the state in particular. They and others discuss the way in which official judicial and professional responses to wife battering and rape deny, excuse or justify male violence and allocate blame instead to the female victims, even in some cases to the feminist movement. Analysis of the state is an increasingly significant part of feminist work, however, as MacKinnon (1983, pp. 635–45) argues, feminism lacks as yet its own theory of the state and is thus forced to work within the existing Marxist and liberal individualist alternatives provided by malestream social science.

A significant development in feminist work, however, is the attempt to formulate a perspective which can encompass several or all of the various forms of male violence, abuse and exploitation of women and to link them all to the underlying struggle by men to retain and reinforce their dominant position as a group over women in society. Patriarchy or the sex/gender order as a social system concerned with the control of women has at its disposal a whole range of technique and mechanisms of control. Among these are force and physical violence. Patriarchal social relations rely on different modes of exerting power and control over women under different socio-historical conditions (Collier and Rosaldo, 1981; Rosaldo, 1980; Young and Harris, 1978).

The central argument of Rich and Barry is that heterosexuality should be 'recognized and studied as a political institution' (Rich, 1980, p. 637) and that it manifests itself directly or indirectly in a whole variety of forms of male power over women's bodies, sexuality, labour, fertility, children, creativeness and access to knowledge. Feminists talk of 'female sexual slavery (Barry) and 'sexual colonization' (Dworkin) to capture the central significance of the essential components of power and sexuality in male domination of women and to expose the real nature of 'normal' heterosexual relations. Rich, Barry, and the other writers discussed here who share their view, basically contend that the sexualisation of the relationship between males and females is a major form of social control over women. Klein and Tong, for example, examine the types of male violence that are subject to legal regulation and observe that the fact common to all crimes of violence against women is that women are 'injured *as women*: as childbearers, sexual objects for men, and nurturers' (Klein, 1981, p. 64). Like other devalued and minority groups, women are particularly vulnerable to stereotyping, objectification, exploitation and scapegoating by members of dominant groups (Tong, 1984; Hirsch, 1981). Parallels can also be found between the sexual exploitation and abuse of women in the marital and personal relationship context and sexual harassment in the workplace (MacKinnon, 1979). In both situations men are able to use their superior power position to treat women as objects, and primarily as sex objects, rather than as human beings. These feminists argue that in sexual harassment, like wife battering, the problem is not 'offensive behaviour' as much as 'abusive power' (Tong, 1984, p. 77). 'Male domination is the expectation that men will be gratified by women and that they will get their own way' (Schechter, 1982, p. 221).

In the modern Western world, pornography has come to be seen by feminists as another area where links between male power, male-defined and imposed sexuality, violence and the physical and sexual abuse of women can be demonstrated.[11] Rich (1980), Dworkin (1981),

Kittay (1984) and Lederer (ed.) (1980) all contribute to our understanding of the way images of sexuality, heterosexuality and the interconnection between sex and violence reflect and reinforce masculinity, male power, and the depersonalisation, objectification and degradation of women. In this process aggressive male sexuality and the dominance of men is legitimated and women are portrayed as creatures for whom 'sex is essentially masochistic, humiliation pleasurable, physical abuse erotic' (Rich, 1980, p. 641). Their critique is not so much in terms of direct connections between media representations and behaviour but at the level of the frightening implications of the preoccupation with sado-masochism and the celebration in much modern pornography of the 'male erotic trinity' of sex, violence and death (Dworkin, 1981, p. 30). Dworkin links her analysis to a broad conceptualisation of 'male sexual domination' as a multidimensional phenomenon operating both as a material system and an ideology (p. 203). She lists what she sees as the seven main forms of male power: 'metaphysical assertion of self', 'physical strength', 'capacity to terrorize', the powers of 'naming', 'owning', 'money', and 'sex' (pp. 13–24). Dworkin and MacKinnon are currently involved in proposals for legislative control of pornography, which has become a major area of feminist politics.[12] The notion that violence is interwoven with sexuality and that both are fundamental to male power, also that violence is an essential component of relations between men and women are highlighted in recent work on women's perceptions and experience of male violence as a general and pervasive phenomenon and on the kinds of official and media responses to male violence, such as the case of the so-called Yorkshire Ripper (Bland, 1984; Hanmer and Saunders, 1984; rhodes and McNeill (eds), 1985; Stanko, 1985).

Another important contemporary feminist theorist who develops a general theory about the role of physical and sexual violence and coercion in male dominance, which she sees as applicable to all kinds of male abuse of women (rape, incest, sexual harassment, pornography, prostitution, domestic battery, and so on), is MacKinnon (1982 and 1983). In the first of two complex and challenging articles on feminism, Marxism, gender, power and the state, she expands on the feminist conception of sexuality as 'the primary social sphere of male power' (1982, p. 529). Not only sexual violence but heterosexuality itself should be interpreted as examples of what she calls the 'eroticization of dominance' (1983, p. 650). Sexuality cannot be separated from power, but the power dimension must be seen as the fundamental one (1982, p. 533). In the second article she formulates her conception of the state as the institutionalised agency of 'male control over women', that is, over women's sexuality (1983, p. 645). She then illustrates how this operates with respect to rape, which she takes as paradigmatic of male power and the eroticisation of dominance. Part of her argument rests on her analysis of the role of the law in upholding male rights and male interests while at the same time claiming to be objective, abstract and neutral in its adjudication of cases.

Over the period 1971 to 1984, then, certain changes in the conceptions of male violence have occurred and there has been a trend towards convergence of views between those contributing to the main body of feminist theory and those feminists whose special interest is in rape, wife battering, pornography or one of the other manifestations of male violence and abuse of women. Violence has come to be seen as a socially-produced and often socially-legitimated cultural phenomenon, rather than the 'natural' expression of biological drives or an innate male characteristic. Masculinity and femininity, 'man' and 'woman', male and female sexuality are all socially constructed. Therefore cultural practices involving sexual aggression, violence, abuse and exploitation of women by men must be the result of social and historical conditions, not primarily of human (male) biology. This kind of analysis is applied not only to violence against women, but to sport (Graydon, 1983) and war (Roberts, 1984).

At the same time, sexuality as socially created has itself become a central issue for feminists. To the extent that sex/gender, sexuality and heterosexuality determine the lives of women (and men) and, in so far as society is based on divisions and inequalities between men and women, power, gender and definitions of sexuality become the closely interrelated bases of women's oppression. Blatant examples of male brutality towards women can be located in a continuum of male power over women, along with a variety of economic, psychological and social mechanisms of control. Whether or not there seems to be a conscious or overt sexual element in particular instances of male violence or coercion, there is an emerging consensus among feminists that sexual politics and sexuality as socially constructed are inseparable. Though there is some disagreement among feminist writers over the relative importance of power and sex, most of the writers considered here would regard sexuality and heterosexism specifically as the central site of gender struggle and the key area for male control and female liberation.

We will conclude by identifying briefly a few issues raised by feminist analyses of sexuality, heterosexuality and male power. The basic proposition is that violence and sexuality are socially constructed in ways that serve the interests of male dominance. Non-violent forms of heterosexuality also become problematic since they help maintain patriarchal structures and ideologies. The alternative strategies of lesbian separatism or the negotiation of 'new' types of relationships between men and women both assume that, if conscious of it, one may escape or modify one's cultural and sexual conditioning. However, as MacKinnon (1982, p. 533–4) points out, how can women (and presumably men) know or act on anything other than the sexual nature they have acquired from the patriarchal societies within which they all live? The question of a biological link between something in male (and perhaps also female) human nature and aggression and aggressive sexuality is also left open. This problem is central to the current controversy amongst feminists over sado-masochism both in reality and in media representations, and over the question as to whether obtaining pleasure from the violent acts of oneself or others is ever acceptable. These sorts of questions clearly point to the need for further feminist theory and research. However, feminists are also committed to personal and political change and on the basis of existing knowledge, alternative and sometimes competing strategies present themselves. Issues include: Where are alliances to be formed? Are these to be with women generally, with gay men, with blacks and other oppressed minority groups, and/or with 'the working class'? Should the struggle be focused in certain key areas or in as many places as possible? On what level should the struggle take place – at the level of personal life, the community of women and/or the major centres of power in society? The feminist analysis of the legal and judicial systems and of the state in general, and their roles in relation to male violence and the oppression of women, for example, can be read either as a warning against any strategies that assume 'the system' will ever do anything against men as a group and for women, or as useful information which helps us locate the places and ways in which structural contradictions can be exploited to women's advantage. However, past efforts show us that it is only through a combination of theoretical work, political action and attempts at social change that women's oppression can be understood and, hopefully, be overcome.

REFERENCES

1. Early examples of the feminist critique of sociology include Bart (1971), Bernard (1973), Millman and Moss Kanter (eds) (1975), Oakley (1974b, ch. 1) and Smith (1974).
2. The first article on this subject was by Goode (1971) but the major writer in the field has been Strauss; his first book was published in 1974 (co-edited by Steinmetz), later works include Strauss, Gelles and Steinmetz (1980), and Strauss and Hotaling (eds) (1980).
3. Major critics of Amir include Clark and Lewis (1977), Smart (1976) and Weis and Borges (1973), and of Strauss – Breines and Gordon (1983), Dobash and Dobash (1977 and 1978), Stark and Flitcraft (1983), Wardell *et al.* (1983)
4. Though earlier feminists favoured making an analytical distinction between 'sex' (biological) and 'gender' (socio-cultural), some feminists (for example, Eichler, 1980; Jaggar, 1983, pp. 106–13; MacKinnon; 1983, p. 635, note 1) have expressed doubts as to the validity and utility of this distinction. One solution, which is adopted here, is to use the two terms in conjunction.
5. For much of my understanding of feminist theory I am greatly indebted to Feminism in Social Theory, a Melbourne discussion group, which for more than three years has been a significant intellectual and social force in the lives of its members.
6. For a recent discussion and critique of classifications of feminist theory, see McFadden (1984).
7. Not only does the terminology vary but there are differences between feminist writers in what they perceive as the basis of male power, what mechanisms and processes are seen as responsible for men's dominant and women's subordinate positions and whether these are regarded as universal or historically variable. Writers who discuss these differences include Barrett (1980, ch. 1), Beechey (1979), Edholm *et al.* (1977), Rosaldo and Lamphere (eds) (1974), Rubin (1975), Sargent (ed.) (1981).
8. Others (Chesler, 1974; Smith and David (eds), 1976) produced a feminist critique of the role of the mental health system in turning women with 'problems in living' into psychiatric patients.
9. Neither Daly nor O'Brien (1981), another more recent feminist theorist, see biology or sexuality as the basis of the fundamental division and antagonism between men and women. While Daly (1978) talks of male terror and envy of female creativity and life-producing capacity, she interprets this very broadly to cover spiritual and mental creative energy and not only biological reproductive powers (pp. 58–64). O'Brien (1981) does link male–female differences to differences in the reproductive process, but it is the social relations and practices of reproduction she has in mind, not the facts of 'mute, brute biology' (p. 44). She goes on to argue that the cultural elevation of sexuality over reproduction is part of the male attempt to overcome the effects of female's superior role and consciousness in the reproductive process. It is this difference, she claims,

that is responsible for male–female differences in attitude to and capacity for violence (pp. 110 and 206–7).
10. To Millett's list, Daly added European witch-hunting and modern western gynaecology.
11. However, this view is not shared by all feminists and, unlike the other manifestations of male violence and sexual power, pornography has become a highly controversial issue for modern Western feminism, particularly in America: see *Feminist Review*, issue 11, 1982; *Signs* 10(1), 1984, pp. 102–35; Barry (1982); Bart (1983); Wilson (1983b).
12. See Blakely (1985) for an account of the current situation; Kittay (1984), Lederer (ed.) (1980) and Tong (1984) discuss the specific issues that legal modes of control over pornography raise.

3 Policing Male Violence – Policing Women

Jill Radford

This chapter, based on existing literature concerning women and violence and the Wandsworth *Violence Against Women – Women Speak Out Survey*, examines the nature and extent of men's violence to women and the police response. Its starting point is the recognition that men's violence to women is a political issue, expressing the basic power relations of patriarchy by maintaining and reproducing men's dominance and women's subordination. It argues that by formulating the problem of men's violence in the context of the social control of women by men, we are able to see its contribution to the general policing of women and to understand why, with certain crucial exceptions, women have *not* been the object of formal policing by the State. This mode of analysis also provides insights as to why the State's concern with containing violence has not included the day-to-day forms of violence which women routinely experience from men. Locating the problem in a theoretical context is crucial in terms of exploring effective interventions, for example in unpacking some of the contradictions around calling for State support (such as reforms of police practices and the legal system generally) in relation to combating men's violence.

THE WANDSWORTH VIOLENCE AGAINST WOMEN SURVEY[1]

This survey of women's experiences of violence was centred on the London borough of Wandsworth. Three hundred and fourteen women, ranging in age from 16–88 years were interviewed. Of these forty-six (15 per cent) were black, thirty-nine (12 per cent) were Asian and included women from Vietnam as well as India, Bangladesh and Pakistan, and 229 (73 per cent) were white and included Jewish, Irish, Italian, Greek, Spanish and Polish women. One hundred and twenty-one were in full or part-time employment, ten were students, three were school students and thirty-five defined themselves as unemployed.

Our approach to the survey was informed by an awareness of the ways in which women's experiences are discredited, particularly when men see them as threatening. The methodology was constructed to be consistent with our practice of feminism but in a way which could not be dismissed as 'atypical' or 'non-representative'. Therefore it was decided to conduct door-to-door interviewing and draw on the concept of randomness, rather than ask for volunteers or approach local networks of women, because any self-defining group could be labelled as non-representative. The women interviewed reflected a wide variety of backgrounds and living situations, although it is never possible to claim that a group selected for interview is ever completely representative of any wider group. More important is the fact that the women interviewed were a group of very real women who were prepared to share personal and often very painful experiences. In some cases, we were the first women they had spoken to about their experiences of male violence.

The questionnaire used was based on that initially constructed by Hanmer and Saunders in Leeds (Hanmer and Saunders, 1984), and adapted for a London context after a pilot study. The final questionnaire was made up of four sections: the first was concerned with how safe women found their neighbourhood, buses, underground and other trains; the types of precautions they took when going out; and their attitudes towards and experiences of self defence. The section concluded with questions asking how women had in the past dealt effectively with male harassment. It was considered vital in a study of this nature to include 'strong stories' of women's day-to-day survival. The second section was the most sensitive, asking women about their experiences of men's violence within the past year. It included specific questions on sexual and racist harassment, violence in the home and harassment at work as well as more public violence. The third section was concerned with what women thought could be done about men's violence, and included questions about policing. The final section was about the women themselves.

Before interviewing, we engaged in various forms of publicity using the local press and radio, discussions with local women's and community groups and leafleting in all the streets selected, since we thought it right to give advance notice of the survey. Additionally, we prepared a list of useful addresses consisting of contacts and brief descriptions of support groups like Women's Aid, the Rape Crisis

Centre, Incest Survivors Group, self defence classes and women's centres. These were given to all women interviewed as part of our attempt to avoid the 'hit and run' type of interviewing. This commitment also involved calling meetings after we had interviewed in an area, for women who wanted to follow the progress of the survey, set up local support groups and arrange self defence classes. Also, because we met women who needed personal support around the issue of men's violence, we visited some women regularly during this stage of the survey and sometimes put women in touch with Women's Aid and Rape Crisis Centres ourselves. Two methods of analysing the interview material were adopted: the quantitative material was put through a computer and the qualitative material was examined by content analysis.

Throughout the survey, during interviewing, analysis and writing-up we have made no attempt to define the terms 'violence', 'harassment' or 'threat'. Rather than engage with competing malestream experts' views on the subject, we considered it important for the women interviewed to interpret these terms according to their own experiences.

WOMEN'S EXPERIENCE OF MEN'S VIOLENCE IN WANDSWORTH

The experiences of these Wandsworth women demonstrate the ways in which the threat and reality of men's violence to women severely limits women's lives. They confirm the 'circular spiral of violence' outlined by Hanmer and Saunders, which depicts the way women learn fear as a result of their own and other women's experiences and from the media, the press and police warnings (Hanmer and Saunders, 1984). The fear of public violence results in the belief that home is the safest place. This discourages women from getting involved in social, political or even work activities. They become more dependent on individual men for protection from men generally. This dependence on individual men, together with women's resultant isolation, make it easier for those men to assault or abuse the women in the privacy of their own homes. They can do this in the knowledge that it is difficult for women to retaliate or get redress, since such behaviour is supported in the dominant male culture.[2] Legal statements, reproduced in the press, complete the circle by making it clear that men's violence against women is not a concern of the state.[3]

This process is illustrated in our findings. Of women interviewed, 88 per cent said that their neighbourhood was not safe for women during the night, and 25 per cent found it unsafe during the day. The effect of the threat and reality of men's violence is to limit freedom of movement. Without this freedom, women's lives are fundamentally controlled. Other freedoms, such as equal pay, equal opportunities and child-care facilities loose their impact when freedom of movement is denied. This was shown in the large numbers of women who said they 'never', 'hardly ever', or 'only when necessary' went out. Other women said that they were in a state of constant anxiety when they did go out. Others, again, reported that they were totally dependent on men – their husbands, boyfriends, fathers or sons – for lifts or protective company. For this last group, freedom of movement was contingent on men's goodwill – a goodwill which can be withdrawn at a moment's notice and as such is itself a form of male control. The threat or reality of men's violence pushes women into dependent and controlled relationships with men from whom, according to official sources, they are at most risk.

Aware of the threat of men's violence, 87 per cent of the women reported that they took precautions when they went out. Becoming 'street wise' was the most common expression of this. As described to us, this involved being aware of who else is in the street, walking close to other women, avoiding men, keeping to well-lighted areas, going the long way round if necessary and being 'psychologically' aware by checking whether they were being followed and wearing shoes and clothes they could run or fight back in. Some women, in addition, carried articles they thought could be used in self defence, but took care that they had a legitimate reason for carrying them, in case they were stopped by the police. Others put their own safety before legal concerns and carried such things as bricks, milk bottles, sprays and pepper, which they knew could be classified as 'offensive weapons'. A few women carried alarms, but the consensus was that these were not reliable, or that other people would not respond to them. This account makes it very clear that for many women, using public space was perceived as using alien or occupied space.

It was not just the streets that were seen as being colonised by men. Public transport was viewed in the same way: eighty-two per cent of women interviewed stated that the Underground was unsafe for women at night, 68 per cent thought the buses were unsafe at night and over a third of women experienced the buses and the Underground as unsafe during the day. Suggestions were put forward as to how public transport could be made safer for women. Schemes like the 'late night lift service' operating in Lambeth and the Lewisham 'safe women's transport service' were thought useful. (Both these schemes are lift services run by and for women). Sixty-five per cent of women thought that women-only carriages should be reintroduced into the trains and Underground, but other women disagreed, arguing that these could actually target women travelling alone. The new 'one person operated' buses were criticised as being unsafe and many women who used to sit near the conductor in the old buses did not use buses now. Another demand was for frequent and properly timetabled services which would give women the power to plan their journeys, without long waits at badly-lighted bus stops or stations. All these demands are contrary to current philosophies of cutting the cost of public transport.

Women also had suggestions for improving lighting in the area, and for improvements in estate design. These included the 'bars and bolts' approach favoured by Wandsworth Council, plus things like proper lift maintenance, and the scrapping of underground car parking in high rise estates. As well as specific suggestions, many women expressed the view that much could be done if women were included in the design process. It was pointed out that currently most planners and architects are men who can have little understanding of what it is like for women to live in their man-made environment. Other demands were for more safe women-only spaces, such as women's centres and girls' nights at youth clubs, where women could meet socially or take their children. In these discussions women made it clear that it was not dark streets, unlighted commons or underground tunnels that attacked women, but the men who (mis)used them. This underpinned demands made by some women for a curfew on men.

There was strong support, too, for women's self defence classes run by and for women: thirty-nine (12 per cent) of the women interviewed had been to such classes, a figure which included two self defence teachers. Self defence instruction was thought to be a good idea by 91 per cent and 56 per cent said they would go to classes if they were organised locally at convenient times and with a crèche. Some women thought they were too old to participate but were please to hear of specific classes being run for older women. Seven disabled women interviewed pointed out how additionally vulnerable they felt and thought more classes should be run for disabled women. Other women, however, resented the fact that the onus was being put on women to defend themselves and felt that this might reach the stage where not having attended self defence classes would be seen as complicity in or even inviting attack.

In response to the second section of the questionnaire the 314 women interviewed reported 1046 incidents of men's violence which had happened to them, to women they knew well or which they themselves had seen within the past year. Breaking these figures down: 280 women reported being racially and/or sexually assaulted or harassed; 137 women reported being the target of a violent attack; forty-one reported having been threatened in a public place; thirty-two had been threatened or attacked by a stranger in their home; thirty-five had received obscene telephone calls; 121 reported sexual harassment at work; and thirty-nine reported being threatened and/or attacked by men they were living with. Sixty-four of the women had seen another woman being threatened or attacked and 206 women knew (well) other women who had been attacked. It should be emphasised again that all these instances occurred during the previous year.[4]

These findings cast real doubt on the figures cited in the British Crime Survey which reported a very low rate of offences against women and which is discussed elsewhere in this book (Hough and Mayhew, 1983).[5] Perhaps one way of accounting for this discrepancy is that whereas they are investigating 'crime', we are exploring 'violence against women'. One of the problems with the legal definition of crime is that it is often difficult to apply it to women's experience of men's violence. For example, in theory at least, rape is acknowledged as a 'serious crime', although the experiences of women reporting rape belie this. However, routine harassment and assault, such as being followed, flashed at or verbally abused are such regular experiences for women and so readily dismissed as 'trivial' or discounted on the grounds that 'nothing actually happened' that few women even consider them as worth reporting to the police. Yet, it is clear from the accounts we heard that these attacks are as much a form of terrorism as those acknowledged by the patriarchy as 'criminal'. As one woman put it:

> A man got threatening. It was the usual sort of thing. He was accosting me with remarks, racist abuse and sexual threats. I ignored him. He became very angry and came running after me shouting that I was a filthy, snobbish, black bitch. It made me angry and scared. Men must know how their abuse terrorises women. They may think they are harmless, but we never know, not till afterwards . . . I didn't report it to

the police. They would say 'nothing happened'. They are not interested in things like that.

As this woman said, while threats or harassment are actually occurring, women do not know, and have no control over where they will end. It is only afterwards that it can be said that 'nothing happened', meaning 'you've not been raped or murdered'. Yet in that phrase, 'nothing happened' women's experience of terror is negated.

POLICING MALE VIOLENCE

Another issue of concern in this survey was women's experience of the response to violence against women. Our findings suggest that, in Wandsworth, women are very unimpressed by the response of the police. Excluding incidents which happened to other women known to her, where a woman herself may not have been in a position to go to the police, reports were made to the police in respect of less than 25 per cent of the incidents mentioned in the survey. The most common reasons for not reporting were: that women did not think the police were concerned about routine sexual and racist harassment; they did not think the police could or would do anything about the incident; they knew the police were unpleasant to women reporting sexual attacks and unsympathetic to women generally; it was the police themselves who were responsible for the harassment; or the women just wanted to put the incident out of their minds and get on with life. The following accounts are illustrative:

> I was raped on the Common about 6 months ago. It upset me badly. I was off work for ages and didn't think I could tell anyone. I don't really want to go into details. I've still not told anyone much. I didn't go to the police. It was on TV about how awful the police are to women who've been raped.

> I was hassled in the street about 4 months ago. I was 7 months pregnant at the time. I was very angry. I told these women near by, that this man was hassling me. They were very good about it. There's no point telling the police, they don't even catch rapists unless they're put under a lot of pressure.

> I got off the train at Waterloo one evening last week and was making for the Underground, when these two men passed me. When they'd passed, one grabbed my arm and said 'got you'. I was really scared and tried to

scream, but nothing came out. It was early evening and there were lots of people on the station, but no one seemed to notice, somehow. . . . Eventually they let me go and I went on my way, shaken and wobbly. There were two policemen further down the station. I didn't go to them. I didn't see what they could do and I just wanted to get home from work. I have to do this journey every day, so I've tried to put the fear out of my mind. If I'd gone to the police, it would have been a lot of hassle and after all, from their point of view, nothing had happened, had it?

So, few women reported incidents to the police. Further, the majority of the few who did were dissatisfied with the police response. Their main complaints were that the police were not interested, were slow to respond, did not follow up the initial report or tell them what had happened, or that they expressed attitudes that were racist and/or hostile to women. The following accounts are illustrative:

My daughter was chased by a man with a knife, at school. He was an intruder and the police were called to the school. They never came to see me or her Dad, or warned the other Mums waiting at the gate. We never heard if he was caught. I was really annoyed with the police about that.

The man next door came round to my side window with a meat cleaver and a hammer. The man's crazy and I live alone . . . I was very frightened and rang the police. They didn't want to come out. They said it was 'domestic'.

I was flashed at by a man who was following me. I just carried on, pretended I'd not seen, but it was disturbing. I met a policeman and told him and even pointed to the man. The policeman just looked at me. They give you too many of those looks.

A man attacked me in the park in the day time. He couldn't get my zip undone as I'd fastened it on the inside with a safety pin. He knocked me down and I tried to talk to him to calm him down. A police car stopped on the road outside. I shouted and the man made off. The policeman asked who he was and made out I knew him. They kept asking me what I was doing there and were really unpleasant. I said 'just forget it' and walked home.

My husband and I have been divorced for some time now. I had to go to Women's Aid because of his violence and he'd started to batter the baby who was a few weeks old. One evening last month, I came out of my front door with the baby . . . He suddenly materialised from behind the hedge and snatched the child and threw a carton of orange juice on my hair and tried to make off. I snatched the child back and got kicked a lot. I managed to get past him and rushed down the street to the phone box. I rang the police. They told me to stay in the phone box till they came – that was 45 minutes later. I got into the police car, one said, 'Don't be sick in my car'. They took me to a friend's house and dumped me there without checking she was in. They wouldn't take me to my sister's, they said it was too far. As it happened my husband was there, upstairs in my friend's house, looking out of the window. So I just had to walk back home feeling terrible. I've had lots of problems with him on other occasions too, with him prowling round the house and posting letters saying he'll kill the children. The police don't usually come, they say it's 'domestic'. I'll try one of those injunctions, I don't suppose it can make things worse, it might help, you never know.

The minority of women who were satisfied with the police response were those reporting theft or damage to property, combined with threats or violent attacks. Most of these were older women and with two exceptions, white.

I was attacked and hit around, you know, badly bruised. They took £250. I told the police. They sent an Asian woman to take details. After that I received threatening letters from their friends. I reported that to the police too. The police were very helpful and told me I could get Criminal Injuries Compensation, but I've heard nothing since. They didn't take action on the letters.

I was attacked and robbed. I had to go to hospital for 2 weeks. The police were very good.

ATTITUDE TO THE POLICING OF MALE VIOLENCE

Included in our questions concerning 'what can be done about men's violence' was a section on policing. Only three, that is 1 per cent of women interviewed, made a straight call for more policing. This very small number should go some way to challenging the stereotype that women are reactionary with respect to 'law and order' politics. Forty-five women (11 per cent) called for more foot patrols. In their comments, however, it was made very clear that they were not just asking for more of the same:

More police on the streets but not those bumptious smart alecs who are rude and harass women and black people.

Its dodgy, we do need protection and police on the streets could help, but I do believe they stir up trouble where none exists.

Community Policing?

Several women touched on notions of community policing, which is not surprising given the amount of police energy which has gone into advocating it as a panacea for all inner-city problems. Their comments reflect the varying interpretations of 'community policing' which characterise the wider debate. Thirteen women adopted an approach close to the 'multi agency' strategy currently advocated by Sir Kenneth Newman, Commander of the Metropolitan Police:

> They should liaise with community groups including women's groups. They should listen to what Women's Aid has to say about violence against women.

> More community police, specifically for this purpose, not to harass black youth. They need to change their attitude towards women who are attacked and not make us feel guilty.

Fifteen women took a view of community policing which included an element of local accountability, a view favoured by the Greater London Council:

> The police are out of touch with the public because they are not controlled by the public. they are not sympathetic to women who are attacked. They should have regular meetings with the people of the areas they work in. We have a 'community' cop but we never see him. He knows the shopkeepers and that's it.

> More community police, but they need to change their attitudes to black women and black people generally. They need anti-racist and anti-sexist awareness programmes. They should work for the local community, not harass us.

> They could try community policing, but the police must be controlled by the community. They should stiffen up their selection to exclude those with racist and women-hating ideas and they must do a thorough weeding out of racist police and those who attack women.

These responses show that twenty-eight women (9 per cent) looked to community policing as a strategy that might help to deal with violence against women. They show that, while there are different understandings of 'community policing', something more than merely administrative change in police strategy is being called for.

Changes in Police Attitudes and Practice?

One hundred and eighteen women (38 per cent) demanded changes in police practices and attitudes towards women. These included:
  (i)   An increased sensitivity in the police response to violence against women.
 (ii)   A greater readiness to respond positively when faced with violence against women, and for it to be treated seriously.
(iii)   Improved and more sensitive treatment to women who have been raped.
(iv)   Improved, swifter and more sensitive response to 'domestic' violence calls.
 (v)   That the police receive anti-racist and anti-sexist awareness training programmes.
On the other hand, fifty-four women (17 per cent) said that they thought it pointless for women to either look to the police for protection from men's violence or to change their attitudes:

> The police do more harassing than anyone, that's the problem.

> I don't think the police are sympathetic to women. Look at the palaver when a woman is raped. The police say you encouraged it. They would, being men. The police is a male-dominated institution, there's no point in relying on them.

> It's a difficult one. In one way I'd like more police, like when I'm harassed by men in the street, but I don't like the idea of police everywhere. I worry about their abuse of power and the amount of power they have already. They are racist and anti-women. I don't think its possible to look to the police.

> No the police will never help women. Its against the interests of the status quo. Their job is to keep the status quo, a status quo that is white, male and middle-class.

Women Police Officers?

Women expressed mixed views about the value of having women officers in the police force: 138 (44 per cent) thought women officers might be more helpful and understanding in relation to violence against women, 100 women (32 per cent) thought not. Those who thought women officers might serve women's interests argued that they were more sympathetic to raped women and that raped women would be more at ease if they only had to talk to women police. Similarly, it was argued that they would be better in dealing with domestic violence. Many said that, in such situations, they would prefer to speak to women police officers. Others made the point that women officers are valuable in favourably influencing their male colleagues. A second group argued, however, that women police were no better than the men, pointing out that their only strategy for success in a male-dominated institution was being 'harder' than men:

> They are too hard. Its the macho cult of the police. Women need to be hard to survive it. They should be more sensitive, but there's no room in the police for sensitivity. We have to get rid of their macho culture.

> They don't behave like women, they can't, not in the police. They are usually more sarcastic than policemen. They don't give any impression of sympathy.

> I don't like them. They are aggressive. They are trained like men, but become worse than men. I like the idea of women police. They could be helpful to women, but a lot would have to change before that would be possible.

CONTRADICTIONS IN THE POLICING OF MEN'S VIOLENCE

These divided views reflect a major contradiction faced by women seeking strategies for the combating of men's violence to women. On the one hand, the police are a paid full-time, professional agency, theoretically concerned with protecting citizens from violence and crime. Many women do turn to the police after being attacked and it is right that they should be treated with respect and sensitivity. Withholding protection from women adds to their humiliation, pain and insecurity. Further, the failure to condemn men's violence legitimates violence as an acceptable means of controlling women. On the other hand, the role of the police is to protect the status quo which, as one of the women interviewed pointed out, is 'white, male and middle-class'. The police failure to provide an adequate response to men's violence is perfectly consistent with this role.

History may throw some light on this contradiction. Fitzgerald, *et al*. (1981) identify the police role as 'maintaining the social order and the legitimation of particular class relations in that order'. Policing in the nineteenth century, they argue, was about controlling the working or dangerous classes, political radicals and the unemployed who had to be watched, supervised, segregated and their behaviour changed:

> when the word 'police' is used in early 19th century Britain, it means a system of protection partly involving police office men, partly the law, but partly matters of habit, training – in short particular social relations between groups.   (Corrigan, 1977)

This analysis is valuable to our understanding of the modern as well as the nineteenth-century inner city, but here concern is primarily with the class basis of nineteenth-century policing. A similar analysis can be adopted to throw considerable insight into the policing of women in contemporary society.

POLICING WOMEN

If, as is argued here, the control of women by men is a primary form of control, then it is important to explore the ways in which women are watched, supervised, segregated and have their behaviour changed.

In the history of policing there have been far fewer confrontations between women and the police than, for example, between the police and strikers, the unemployed and in public order confrontations. Women have featured in these struggles, but usually in support of men, and they have rarely been considered 'dangerous' by the state. The exceptions are interesting: the Greenham women, like the suffragettes, have been heavily and violently policed. It is, apparently, when women have acted autonomously *as women*, that they have been the targets of heavy policing. A similar point can be made with respect to the policing of prostitution in the nineteenth and twentieth centuries. It seems that it is only when women have broken away from being responsible to, and controlled by, individual men that they have been deemed 'worthy' of state policing. This argument could be extended to explain, for example, the heavy policing of lesbians on recent marches and demonstrations in Britain. The role of the police can be theorised as providing a last defence of the status quo, when routine control of women by men is cracking.

Thus, routine policing such as watching, supervising, segregating and changing the behaviour of women is left to others, either individual men or men collectively in groups. One important agency for this is the institution of heterosexual monogamy, the family. Inside the family husbands exact unwaged sexual, emotional and physical servicing from women in exchange for protecting them from other men. Sanctioned by the ideology of privacy, this almost feudal relationship has only recently been theorised in terms of power relationships. When the power relationships between men and women in the family are examined, woman or wife abuse and the sexual abuse of girl children take on new meaning. Their role in the maintenance and reproduction of monogamous heterosexuality becomes clearer. It is the family which is the first line of defence of patriarchal power, the state is the last. In between is the whole range of watching, supervising and controlling of the behaviour of women through the various forms of sexual harassment, abuse and violence described by women in this survey. Through jokes and innuendo, as well as in legal responses which define women as guilty or innocent in respect of violence committed against them, women are subjected to segregation and supervision by men (Hanmer, 1978). Through sexual harassment and official warnings by the police (such as those issued in West Yorkshire concerning the danger of being out at night while the Yorkshire Ripper was at large), women are continually reminded of the ways men control and attempt to alter their behaviour, whether at work or in public places. In this context, it is not surprising that men's use of threat or violence is rarely condemned by the state.

The role of the state, whether in the interrogation of raped women, the conduct of rape trials or in the police and courts' handling of what they insist on calling 'domestic' violence, is to define the limits of violence appropriate for the control of women. The purpose is to discriminate between the violence which is 'acceptable' and that which is 'excessive' and the legitimacy or otherwise of the targets. Legitimate targets are those women an individual man has the right to control, that is, who belong to *him* and not another man's wife, girl friend, lover or daughter except when they step out of line and 'ask for it' – by being out late at night, for example. Women, especially lesbians and prostitutes, who refuse to be directed and restrained by specific, individual men can be controlled by any men. Furthermore, by stepping outside the normal parameters of male control, they are frequently denied the kind of protection against violence that may be afforded by the legal system to 'innocent' or 'decent' women. Thus it becomes clear that men's violence is used to control women, not just in their own individual interests, but also in the interests of men as a sex class in the reproduction of heterosexuality and male supremacy.

The divisions within patriarchy around race, class and the

distribution of privilege for men and for women intervene and are themselves mirrored in the state's treatment of violence against women. Men, high in the privilege hierarchy, are accorded more rights. Initially the institution of privacy ensures their violence is less visible and when visible it is treated with greater leniency. Less privileged men are accorded less leniency. Paralleling this are the different levels of protection accorded to women under patriarchy. Women with wealth, living in better-protected neighbourhoods, with access to their own transport, may be less vulnerable to certain forms of men's violence. However, this protection for the vast majority of women remains contingent on male goodwill. Women most vulnerable to public violence are poorer women who spend more time on foot or on public transport. Factors such as racism result in black women or women of colour being additionally the targets of racist violence. Lesbian women and others who live separately from men may be less likely to be victims of violence in the home, but at work or in public they are readily pinpointed for anti-lesbian attacks or abuse. Similarly, older and disabled women are easy victims of men's violence, although their age or disability may later allow them to qualify for state protection and concern.

An analysis which locates men's violence as the fundamental form of social control of women in patriarchal society demonstrates that, in the absence of any fundamental change in the power relations between men and women, the problem addressed will not be resolved by minor reforms in policing or law reform. So long as the state remains committed to enforcing existing power relations only marginal reforms – such as the curbing of the excesses of misogyny – are winnable, and then only with a struggle. Given the energy required and the uncertainty that any gains can be secured through reform, it is perhaps more useful to look to alternative strategies.

The best way forward may be to continue to concentrate on drawing positively on women's energy and support, as evidenced in the activities of Women's Aid, Rape Crisis Centres, Incest Survivors and Women Against Sexual Harassment groups.

REFERENCES

I would like to thank the following women for their time, help, advice and support as interviewers and/or members of the survey support group: Anne, Annie Robinson, Adalia, Betsy Stanko, Cabby Laffy, Dorretta, Dorothy Kelly, Em, Erika, Gloria, Jackie Trimmer, Lee Pollak, Katia Duncan, Margie

Wood, Sue Sanders, Sui Jackson, Rachel, Ros, Veronica Perrin. Thanks to my co-workers at the Wandsworth Policing campaign for their support, and to the WPC management committee for their help and advice and for coping with the chaos in the office that the survey produced. Thanks also to the many women who offered advice and support at many stages in the survey including women from Central London Women Against Violence Against Women, women from the Departments of Law and Social Sciences at the Polytechnic of the South Bank, the South West London Women Studies Group, and women from many community groups in Wandsworth and the BSA study group on violence against women. I also acknowledge, with gratitude, the debt owed to the women in Wandsworth who agreed to be interviewed for the survey: without their time and willingness to share painful and personal details, the survey would not have been possible. Because of our guarantee of anonymity, these women cannot be named here. This work is a tribute to the strength of these women and to all those in this country and throughout the world who are survivors of men's violence. It is also in memory of those, including my friend Mary, who were less fortunate.

1. The *Violence Against Women – Women Speak Out Survey* was sponsored by Wandsworth Policing Campaign, and funded by the Greater London Council's Police and Women's Support Committees from September 1983 until August 1984.
2. See, for example, Pahl (ed.), 1985.
3. See, for example, Stanko, 1985.
4. At the time of writing the 'other' category relating to additional forms of violence contains ninety-one items which are still to be analysed.
5. See Elizabeth Stanko, 'Typical Violence, Normal Precaution: Men, Women and Interpersonal Violence in England, Wales, Scotland and the USA' – Chapter 9 in this volume.

4 The Continuum of Sexual Violence
Liz Kelly

This chapter discusses the application of the concept of the continuum of sexual violence to research on, and discussion of, the issue of sexual violence. Two of the original aims of the research were to explore the links between the different forms of sexual violence and to investigate the idea, which arose whilst working in a refuge for battered women, that most women have experience of sexual violence in their lifetime.[1] Whilst analysing the in-depth interviews carried out with women, the concept of a continuum of sexual violence was used to describe the findings in the two areas.

METHODOLOGY

The research data consists of in-depth interviews with sixty women and follow-up interviews with forty-eight after they read a transcript of their original interview. The first interview covered childhood, adolescence and adulthood, in order that experiences of sexual violence were discussed within the context of each woman's life. Every woman was asked if she had experienced any of a number of forms of sexual violence, and each self-defined experience of rape, incest or domestic violence and its effects was discussed in depth. The follow-up interview was included to assess the effect of the first interview on the women. It also functioned as an internal validity test, enabling further discussion of areas that were unclear in the original interview. It also resulted in the recording of incidents of sexual violence which the women forgot to mention initially, or decided to divulge as a result of the first interview.

Women volunteered to take part in the project. It was considered crucial that the women chose to discuss, in depth, what might well have been distressing memories. Moreover, one of the research aims was to interview a wider spectrum of women than merely those who could be contacted through official agencies (the police, courts, social services, therapists), or voluntary agencies (refuges for battered women, rape crisis centres, self-help groups). Much of the available research to date has drawn samples only from such sources. Given the suggestion that the incidence of sexual violence is underestimated in official statistics and in victimisation studies (the recent British Crime Survey documented only one case of attempted rape from interviews in 11 000 households), it is important to reach women who do not officially report their experiences. A number of methods were used to contact women including letters and articles in newspapers and magazines and a local radio appearance. The most successful method of contact was through talks given to a wide range of local community women's groups and students.

Given the research aims it was essential that the various forms of sexual violence were adequately covered within the interviews. The sample was, therefore, split into two groups of thirty. Initially, women were asked to volunteer only if they had experienced rape, incest or domestic violence (samples of ten were selected for each type of assault). When these samples were nearly complete, women were asked to volunteer irrespective of any particular experience (this produced a further group of thirty).

The sample consisted predominantly of white women, with only two non-white women, both of mixed race. The sample was varied in other respects, however. It included women from different socio-economic backgrounds with varied experiences of employment and who had made different decisions regarding marriage, motherhood and sexuality. The proportion of women in the sample who had been or were at that time still in further education was higher than within the population generally, although a number of these women came from working-class backgrounds and/or went into further education as mature students. Whilst not representative, the sample drew on the experience of a group of predominantly white women seldom recorded in other research: those who do not report their experiences to welfare agencies, women from middle-class backgrounds, and women holding professional jobs.

THE CONCEPT OF A CONTINUUM

As the interviews were transcribed and analysed it became clear that most women had experienced sexual violence in their lives. It was also clear that there was a range of possible experiences within each form of sexual violence discussed in the interviews. It was in response to these findings that I began to use the term 'continuum' to describe the extent and range of sexual violence in women's lives. The concept was used in a number of talks given to a variety of women's groups (some were feminist groups involved in work around male violence, some were local community groups). Many of the women present found it helpful in understanding their own experiences and sexual violence generally.

Women in these groups found the common-sense meaning of the word 'continuum' useful, and it is this meaning which is intended here. The Oxford English Dictionary provides two meanings which were used: 'a basic common character that underlies many different events' and 'a continuous series of elements or events that pass into one another and cannot readily be distinguished'. The first meaning enables discussion of sexual violence in a general sense: the basic common character underlying the many different events is that men use a variety of forms of abuse, coercion and force in order to control women. The second meaning enables documenting and naming the range of abuse, coercion and force that women experience. At the talks given, women used this second meaning to locate their own particular experiences within the category of sexual violence. This meaning also allows for the fact that there are no clearly defined and discrete analytic categories into which women's experiences can be placed. The experiences women have and how they are subjectively defined shade into and out of a given category such as sexual harassment, which includes looks, gestures and remarks as well as acts which may be defined as assault or rape.

In both senses, the concept is intended to highlight the fact that sexual violence exists in most women's lives, whilst the form it takes, how women define events (Kelly, 1984a) and its impact on them at the time and over time (Kelly, 1984b) varies. The meaning of continuum, as used in this chapter, does not refer to the meaning common in social science which involves the application of statistical measurement to clearly defined, discrete categories. The concept should not be seen, therefore, as a linear straight line connecting the different events or experiences. There are a number of dimensions which affect the meaning for, and impact on, women of experiences of sexual violence at the time they happened and later in time. Amongst these are the particular nature of the assault, the relationship between the man and the woman or girl, whether the assault was a single incident or part of ongoing abuse, the extent of threat perceived by the woman at the time and the context of the assault for the woman, including how she defined the man's behaviour and whether it connected to previous experiences.

Nor should the term continuum be interpreted as a statement about seriousness either at the time or over time. Marie Leidig (1981), the only other writer to suggest using the concept of a continuum in relation to sexual violence, uses seriousness as the basis of her analysis. She argues that those forms of violence which she places at the extreme end of her continuum – domestic violence and incest – are necessarily more serious and, therefore, have greater negative effects. But the impact of sexual violence on women is a complex matter. With the important exception of incidents of sexual violence which result in death, the effects on women cannot be read off simplistically from the form of sexual violence women experience. How women react to and define their experiences at the time and how they cope with them over time differs and a complex range of factors affect the impact of particular experiences. The testimony of previously-battered women (Dobash and Dobash, 1979; Pagelow, 1981; Schecter, 1982) about the effects of mental/emotional violence, and the finding by McNeill (see Chapter 7) that what women fear most when they are flashed at is death, suggest that creating a hierachy of abuse based on seriousness is inappropriate.

Such a perspective necessarily requires making judgements about what is more serious and what are greater negative effects. It would be equally possible to argue (although this argument is not used here), that forms of sexual violence, such as the threat of rape and street harassment, which most women experience and which have the effect of limiting women's access to and freedom within public space, are more serious than, say, domestic violence, which fewer women experience.

The perspective of this chapter is that all forms of sexual violence are serious and have effects: the 'more or less' aspect of the continuum refers only to incidence. It will be argued that there are forms of sexual violence experienced by most women in their lives, which are also more likely to be experienced on multiple occasions. These more common forms are also more likely to be defined by men as acceptable behaviour, for example seeing sexual harassment as 'a bit of fun' or 'only a joke', and they are less likely to be defined as crimes within the law.

HOW THE CONCEPT CAN BE USED

Several researchers investigating rape have used the idea, if not the actual concept, of a continuum linking rape to heterosexual sex (Russell, 1975; Vogelman, 1979; Williams and Holmes, 1981; Wilson, 1978). Gilbert and Webster (1982) are representative of this approach:

> Many rapes merely extend traditional heterosexual exchanges, in which masculine pursuit and feminine reticence are familiar and formalized. Although rape is a gross exaggeration of gender power, it contains the rules and rituals of heterosexual encounter, seduction and conquest. (p. 114)

Clark and Lewis (1977), and Marolla and Scully (1979) explicitly use the term in discussing rapists:

> At one end of the continuum is the man who makes no attempt to disguise his behaviour . . . At the other end of the continuum is the rapist who will try to avoid seeing his actions as rape. (Clark and Lewis, p. 101)

> It is equally relevant to ask if, rather than a distortion, rapists may not represent one end of a quasi-social sanctioned continuum of male sexual aggression. (Marolla and Scully, p. 316)

Herman (1981) also explicitly uses the word, defining incest as:

> only the farthest point on a continuum – an exaggeration of patriarchal family norms, not a departure from them. (p. 110)

In each case, these writers are linking specific forms of sexual violence to more common, everyday aspects of male behaviour. However, whilst several researchers have used the term 'continuum', it appears as a descriptive word rather than a developed concept. The underlying analysis is often implicit and the importance of developing the idea in relation to all forms of sexual violence is not drawn out.

Feminist theory is increasingly linking a critique of heterosexuality, as currently constructed, with discussion of male violence (see, for example, Rich, 1980). Many discussions of rape suggest that force and coercion are often present in heterosexual encounters (Clark and Lewis, 1977; MacKinnon, 1982). Other writers illustrate how aspects of domestic violence (Schecter, 1982), incest (Herman, 1981; Ward, 1984) and sexual harassment (Farley, 1978) link to more commonplace interactions between men and women/girls. The concept of a continuum of sexual violence enables this theoretical analysis to be applied to empirical data and to women's own experiences.

Most previous research concentrated on particular forms of sexual violence, such as rape or domestic violence. The samples often include only women who had defined their experience in terms of the particular form of sexual violence in question. Koss and Oros (1982), discussing research on rape, suggest that this has resulted in a concentration within research on the extremes of sexual violence. They note the need for research which explores the range of sexual violence, including verbal coercion and the threat of violence, alongside the use of physical force. The concept of the continuum of sexual violence draws attention to this wider range of forms of abuse and assault which women experience, illustrating further the link between more common, everyday male behaviour and what Koss and Oros term the 'extremes'. Several questions in this research project were designed to investigate everyday forms of abuse and the following quote from a follow-up interview shows how invisible this may be to women themselves:

> You asked me if I knew women who had these experiences. Talking about it afterwards there were a surprising number who had been sexually harassed – none who had been raped. I do feel that's really invisible. We don't say someone flashed at me last night or – so it seemed that it's happened to so many women but it's not recognized.

Stanko (1985) offers a possible explanation for this non-recognition:

> Women's experiences of male violence are filtered through an understanding of men's behaviour which is characterised as either typical or aberrant . . . In abstract we easily draw lines between those aberrant (thus harmful), and those typical (thus unharmful) types of male behaviour. We even label the aberrant behaviour as potentially criminal behaviour . . . Women who feel violated or intimidated by typical male behaviour have no way of specifying how or why typical male behaviour feels like aberrant male behaviour.   (p. 10)

The concept of the continuum of sexual violence enables women to specify the links between 'typical' and 'aberrant' behaviour and therefore enables women to locate and name their own experiences.

The following two sections use data from the research interviews to illustrate how the continuum of sexual violence can be used in relation to incidence and experience. It is important to note that these two aspects interconnect. When analysing the range of experience within each particular form of sexual violence the incidents of experiences which are closer to everyday male behaviour is more common. The continuum of incidence applies within the continuum of experience.

THE CONTINUUM OF INCIDENCE

In viewing sexual violence as a continuum and widening the range of possible forms of abuse women may experience, research on incidence becomes both a wider and a more complex area of investigation. Additional questions must be asked which add to the range of possible experiences and yet do not presume a shared definition of forms of sexual violence. The existence of a continuum of events which are not easily distinguishable implies that women may not share the same definition of a particular incident. In this project, a number of questions were included in order to explore the more hidden aspects of women's experience. For example, women were asked if they ever felt pressured to have sex, if they picked up sexual messages in the family, and if they remembered any negative sexual experiences as a child. In response to these questions many women recalled experiences of abuse that they would not have considered relevant if questions had been limited to rape or incest (see also Russell, 1985, for a detailed discussion in relation to her incidence study).

In order to analyse the interviews, it was necessary to apply analytic concepts to the women's experiences. The definitions used by the women have been reflected as accurately as possible, however.[2] Table 4.1 presents the incidence of experiences of sexual violence in the lives of the sixty women interviewed.

The continuum of incidence is shown in this table, which moves from experiences which were most common in women's lives to those which were least common. The particular placing of forms of sexual violence in this table is intended only to reflect the experiences of the sixty women interviewed and it is not suggested that this pattern is generally applicable. It is suspected, however, that the most common forms in this table would be similarly placed if this analysis were to be applied in other research projects. It is also important to note that aspects of sexual violence which most women experience are not reflected in this

Table 4.1 Women's experiences of sexual violence

Form of violence	Number of women	Percentage of sample
Sexual harassment	56	93
Sexual assault	54	90
Pressure to have sex	50	83
Sexual abuse	43	72
Obscene phone call (37 asked)	25	68
Coercive sex	38	63
Domestic violence*	32	53
Flashing	30	50
Rape*	30	50
Incest*	13	22

* These three categories include those women who initially volunteered to take part in the research specifically because of their experiences of these types of violence.

table, particularly the threat of violence and emotional/psychological abuse.

Every woman interviewed was aware of the threat of violence and most had experienced sexual harassment, sexual assault and pressure to have sex during their lives. These forms of sexual violence are also more common in the sense that they were more likely to occur on multiple occasions. Women were far more likely to comment on the commonness for them of sexual harassment and pressure to have sex. Many referred to sexual harassment as something they were coping with on a daily basis:

> It's something that happens so much – you just experience it in the street all the time, its almost a background of what going out of doors seems to mean.

Hanmer and Saunders (1984) interviewed 129 women in Leeds. They found that within the previous year 59 per cent had experienced 'threatening, violent or sexually harassing behaviour'.

Women coped with the common forms of sexual violence in a variety of ways including ignoring them, not defining them as abusive at the time and, very commonly, forgetting them. This process was confirmed by the fact that, whilst typing up the transcripts, two women on the research team remembered or redefined a number of experiences from their own lives which they had either forgotten or minimised. Incidence, as recorded in the interviews, is therefore likely to be an underestimate. Further research is needed to investigate the extent of sexual violence at the more common end of the continuum and its impact on women's lives.

The continuum of incidence also applied within specific forms of sexual violence. Only ten women had never experienced violence within a heterosexual relationship. Thirty-two women defined their experiences as domestic violence. The major factor influencing this definition was whether the violence was repeated and occurred over time. It was also clear that many men used the forms of control common within domestic violence (emotional outbursts which included violence to objects, emotional withdrawal, absence, controlling women's social contacts, questioning women's performance of household tasks) but did not use physical violence. This pattern was also clear in relation to incest: more women picked up sexual messages from fathers than actually experienced father/daughter incest. On reflection, most women recalled being disturbed by this behaviour, but it was difficult both at the time and over time to explain why. Again, the patterns of control recalled by women who were sexually abused by their fathers were experienced by other women who were not sexually abused. These patterns clearly illustrate that more common patterns of male control are linked to behaviours that are defined as criminal by the legal system.

THE CONTINUUM OF EXPERIENCE – HETEROSEXUAL SEX TO RAPE

This section illustrates that women's experiences of heterosexual sex are not either consenting or rape, but exist on a continuum moving from choice to pressure to coercion to force. The illustrations from the interviews clearly show how the categories I have used to record women's experiences, pressure to have sex, coercive sex and rape, shade into one another. This point is relevant to recent discussions of pleasure and danger as two opposing frameworks within which women's experiences of sex are conceptualised by feminists (see, for example, DuBois and Gordon, 1983). The concept of a continuum suggests that pleasure and danger are not mutually exclusive opposites but the desirable and undesirable ends, respectively, of a continuum of experience.

Dworkin (1983) and MacKinnon (1982) have argued that one of the key problems in 'proving' rape in a court of law is that forced or coerced sex are common experiences for women. Both challenge the assumption that all sexual intercourse that is not defined as rape is, therefore, consensual. Responding to Dworkin's argument, Bart (1983) suggests conceiving of heterosexual sex as a continuum which moves from consensual sex (equally desired by woman and man), to altruistic sex (women do it because they feel sorry for the man or guilty about saying no), to compliant sex (the consequences of not doing it are worse than the consequences of doing it), to rape. This is similar to the continuum of heterosexual sex developed in this project in order to reflect the ways women define their own experiences. Bart's 'altruistic' and 'compliant' sex would be equivalent to the category 'pressure to have sex'. 'Coercive sex' is the term used in this research to cover experiences women interviewed described as being 'like rape'.

Evidence from the interviews demonstrates the validity of this approach. Data is drawn from answers to a number of interview questions – in particular, whether women found it easy or difficult to say no to sex, whether they had ever felt pressured to have sex, and whether they had ever been raped.[3]

One group of women recalled that saying 'no' to sex had been a problem in the past, but described how they developed a belief in their right to say no and a commitment to themselves only to have sex when they desired it. This was not an easy process for any of these women. In this group, women currently involved in a heterosexual relationship were more likely to feel sex was consensual:

> I think this is probably the first sexual experience where I've felt equal and I haven't felt used because I've definitely said no if I haven't wanted to.

A larger group of women felt that saying no, particularly in an ongoing relationship, was not something they found easy to do. Many of these women referred to occasions when they had sex when it was not what they wanted. They clearly felt that they 'owed' sex to their partners regardless of their own feelings. Aspects of this group's current heterosexual relationships fit Bart's 'altruistic sex'. This quote, whilst retrospective, refered to a relationship that had just ended:

> When I was living with Mark I'd come home from work and I'd be shattered and I'd just want to go to bed and sleep, and he'd start cuddling up and touching me and I'd think 'oh here we go again'. It was like a *duty*, that was sort of paying the rent – I had a roof over my head and that was what I was expected to pay.

A number of women discussed altruistic sex within long-term relationships. They felt guilty refusing sex on a long-term basis, even where sex gave them little pleasure and made them feel used:

> I think he preferred to be satisfied rather than satisfy me. It did have an effect on me for a long time afterwards.

Most women's initial response to the question 'Have you ever felt pressured to have sex when you didn't want to?' was to say that this had happened but that physical force was not used. The presence of physical coercion clearly made it easier for women to define their experience as abusive. Bart's 'compliant' category applied to experiences woman discussed where sex was the price for improving the situation or preventing men becoming unpleasant:

> Generally in relationships I've felt that I've had to do it to save myself the trouble of persuading him not to want it. I mean I would do it because it was easier than spending a whole day with him sulking about it.

The above quote, and the one which follows, are examples of the responses many women made to this question. They felt pressure to have sex in many, if not all, of their sexual relationships with men:

> I felt pressured to have sex by nearly *everybody* I met at university – apart from one who did actually ask – I felt pressured by the bloke I was engaged to, I just felt *obliged* to have sex with him.

Pressurised sex seemed to cover situations in which women chose not to say no, but in which they were not freely consenting.

The term coercive sex covers experiences of forced sex which women discussed either in response to the question about pressure to have sex or the question about rape. The responses were more likely to refer to particular experiences in which there was explicit pressure from the man, often including the threat of or some physical force. Women's consent was overtly coerced. At the time of the interviews, women did not define these experiences as rape:

> I couldn't call that rape . . . I mean there was that one *bad* case of it, he's forced sex on me a number of times, that's what I would call a woman being taken for granted.

> We'd had a row and I'd gone to sleep in the other room and he came in and got me by the arm and he *dragged* me into the bedroom and said 'you will remember this when you're old – meaning I will remember this wonderful sexy scene where this guy is showing me his wonderful masculine strength and desire and passion – I wasn't turned on by it at all.

Women also gave examples of feeling coerced in relation to specific sexual practices:

> I'm not a women's libber but I thought it was time I started to go out as he was out every night. He objected strongly, to put it mildly, put my clothes in the sink, put a dirty poker over my face so I couldn't go out. The only way I could get out in the end was to have some kind of sex, usually oral, before I went out.

One of the ways in which the concept of the continuum is useful is that it can allow for definitions of experiences to change over time. The following quotes illustrate how, in retrospect, women made explicit links between pressurised or coerced sex and rape:

> I didn't say to him that I didn't want to, I didn't dare to [pauses] you know you don't want to, but you are still doing it. That's why in my eyes now it's rape with consent. It's rape because it's pressurized but you do it because you feel you can't say no, for whatever reason.

> Where do you define rape? The pressure to have sex was overwhelming . . . I was made to feel guilty. It isn't rape but *incredible* emotional pressure was put on and I wanted that man out of my room as soon as possible.

> No not rape not in the [sighs] . . . not actually physically forced to have sex, only . . . coerced I think yes.

She added later in the interview:

> I remember an occasion where he wouldn't let me get up, and he was very strong. He pulled my arms above my head, I didn't put up much of a

struggle. I mean I wouldn't have seen that as rape because I associated rape with strangers, dark, night and struggle. I didn't put up much of a struggle, but *I didn't want to*, so in a sense that was rape, yes.

Many of the experiences women defined as rape are similar to those included in the 'coercive sex' category. How women subjectively define experiences of sexual violence at the time and over time is too complex a topic to discuss adequately in this chapter (see Kelly, 1984a, for a more detailed discussion). The factors which made defining an incident as rape more likely included that the rapist was a stranger, that the assault happened outside and at night, that physical force was used, and that women resisted. Many of the experiences women defined as rape were not defined as such by them until some time after the assault. As the above quotes illustrate several women did not define assaults as rape until they were interviewed.

The examples demonstrate that many women experience non-consensual sex which neither they nor the law and, even more unlikely, the man, define as rape. Women do, however, feel abused by such experiences and a number of women recalled short-term and long-term effects that were similar to those experienced by women who defined their experience as rape at the time. There is no clear distinction, therefore, between consensual sex and rape, but a continuum of pressure, threat, coercion and force. The concept of a continuum validates the sense of abuse women feel when they do not freely consent to sex and takes account of the fact that women may not define their experience at the time or over time as rape. It also allows us to explore how and why women's definitions might change over time.

CONCLUSIONS

This chapter explored the usefulness of using the concept of a continuum when researching and discussing sexual violence. Continuum was defined as a basic common character underlying many different events and as a continuous series of elements or events that pass into one another. The common underlying factor is that men use a variety of methods of abuse, coercion and force to control women. The concept of a continuum was applied to the incidence of forms of sexual violence and the range of possible experiences within each form of sexual violence. The continuum should not be seen as a linear connection, nor can inferences be made from it concerning seriousness or the impact on women.

Using the concept of a continuum highlights the fact that all women experience sexual violence at some point in their lives. It enables the linking of the more common, everyday abuses women experience with the less common experiences labelled as crimes. It is through this connection that women are able to locate their own particular experiences as being examples of sexual violence.

An important implication of this way of viewing sexual violence is that a clear distinction cannot be made between 'victims' and other women. The fact that some women only experience violence at the more common, everyday end of the continuum is a difference in degree and not in kind. The use of the term 'victim' in order to separate one group of women from other women's lives and experiences must be questioned. The same logic applies to the definition of 'offenders'.

REFERENCES

1. The term 'sexual violence' is used as a general term to cover all forms of abuse, coercion and force that women experience from men. There are both empirical and theoretical reasons for using this term. When the interviews were analysed it became clear that it is not possible to make neat distinctions between physical and sexual violence. Many battered women are raped or coerced into having sex; many raped or incestuously abused women and girls also experience physical violence. On a theoretical level the term draws attention to the fact that it is violence committed by one sex, men, directed at the other sex, women. It also links to MacKinnon's (1982) analysis of sexuality as a system of power through which men attempt to control women.
2. The categories used in this table emerged out of women's own definitions and data analysis. Sexual harassment covers experiences at work, in the street, in public places. Pressure to have sex covers experiences where women felt pressured by the man's behaviour or expectations, but they chose not to say no. Coercive sex covers experiences women described as being 'like rape', where their consent was coerced or participation forced. Sexual abuse covered all forms of sexual violence women experienced before the age of sixteen which were not already counted in the incest category. Sexual assault contains experiences of sexual violence after the age of sixteen not already counted in other categories; a number of attempted rapes are included in this figure. Rape, domestic violence and incest, flashing and obscene phone calls contain experiences women defined as such.

3. A number of women were lesbians and/or celibate at the time of the interview. However, they all had had heterosexual relationships in the past and were asked to discuss these in response to the question about saying 'no' to sex.

5 Sex and Violence in Academic Life or You Can Keep a Good Woman Down

Caroline Ramazanoglu

Thirteen years of teaching in universities has at last disclosed to me the secret that there is no second sex in academe. There is only one sex: male.   (Adams, 1983, p. 135)

AUTHOR'S INTRODUCTION

British universities, and institutions of higher education in general, are still male institutions with very limited and rigid career patterns. Characteristically, they are run according to hierarchical systems of organisation which are not consistent with the democratic and liberal ethic adopted by these institutions. Although women comprise important elements of the student body and various workforces, they are plentiful in traditional female and service roles, notably cleaning, catering and clerical, and rare in the higher reaches of administration, research and teaching. The contradiction between the liberal ideology and scholarly aims of higher education, and the realities of competitive academic careers in male-dominated hierarchies, leads to widespread defence of male privilege and to institutionalised forms of violence.

I do not set out to *prove* these points with any positivist intention but, working from the precept that the personal is political, to argue from personal observation and experience that there are general structural mechanisms in higher education which reproduce a patriarchal order, which construct academic women as actual or potential threats to this order, and which act to subordinate female academics.[1] These specific mechanisms for keeping women in their place need to be understood as forms of violence.

The chapter is based on the insults, leers, sneers, jokes, patronage, bullying, vocal violence and sexual harassment that are the

61

experiences of myself and other women. It is my contention that I am not a crank, I am not a freak, I am not unprofessional, I am not a totalitarian fascist determined to impose my will on others, I am not sexually deprived, I do not seek revenge on men, but I am labelled as these (and worse) to my face and behind my back, because of my lack of deference and my persistent failure to accept my 'proper place' as a subordinate female in a patriarchal, competitive and hierarchical system.

It is not suggested that violence is always overt, since it usually is not, but that the potential is there and generally unacknowledged. Violence is an appropriate concept in this context, firstly because the process of subordinating women can be conceived as a form of violence and secondly, because women who resist the male domination of higher education will find their resistance is itself experienced as violent. They will be seen as unnatural, sexually undesirable, aggressive women whose personal peculiarities must account for their deviant behaviour. Academic men, and those women who are unaware that a problem exists, need to consider what it feels like to have subordination repeatedly thrust upon one, so that they can see protest for what it is, rather than as the threat of some unreasoning female assault.

The point of drawing on these experiences is to produce a reasoned interpretation of the forms of violence that are endemic in academic life, in a constructive spirit. Only when we are clear as to what mechanisms are operating and why, can we set about dismantling them and creating more egalitarian and humane academic communities.[2]

IF THE PERSONAL IS POLITICAL WHAT ARE THE POLITICS?

A common reaction to the use of personal experience is that while these experiences may be deeply felt, they are not typical and so not useful as examples. While arguing from personal experience (more than twenty years as a professional sociologist) I in no way want to set myself up as a typical female academic. The shades of positivism, however, are always with us, and social scientists seem to hanker after universal theories, which make the place of *typical* and *atypical* of key theoretical importance. While it may well be true that I am a peculiarity and my experiences, although shared by others, are not statistically typical, I set out to show that these experiences indicate structural mechanisms in academic life which *do* operate generally, and which reveal the secret sexual politics of higher education.[3]

It is not suggested that all female academics are sweet and scholarly or that all male academics are competitive and violent. Men can adopt 'feminine' behaviour patterns; women can act as 'honorary men', and there are many variations in between. Many personal styles of coping with the strains of academic life have emerged, and here I am attempting to place these personal styles in the context of an institutionalised power struggle in which violence is never openly acknowledged except as 'problems' initiated by women or other subordinates who attempt to rock the boat. Men as well as women need to be allowed to reunite their artificially separated 'male' and 'female' natures, but in the meantime men do benefit from a patriarchal system of education. If we are to identify the violence in the system and learn to do without it, we need, as Moglen has put it, to demystify the nature of academic power, and to purge it of its crippling effects (Moglen, 1983, p. 134).[4]

Personal experiences and observations *are* relevant to the sexual politics of academic life because women (and other subordinates) who do not conform to the limited roles allowed them do challenge, willingly or not, the taken-for-granted domination of the white, male, heterosexual, competitive academic establishment. This chapter argues that women alone are not responsible for the sexual politics of academic institutions, but they have played a crucial part in making them public. Some academic women may never consciously experience subordination, may opt out of career advancement, may even treat their work as an avocation for which they are grateful, but where women step out of line they receive the full force of a reaction which constitutes a specific and violent form of social control.

In order to establish these points more clearly, it is necessary to discuss the forms of violence referred to earlier, the nature of the competive academic career and the way in which the behaviour of women who do not accept their inferiority is experienced as violence against men.

VIOLENCE

The contention that violence is part of academic life obviously depends on a definition of violence that differs from many common-sense definitions. Violence is probably most often envisaged as physical assault, restraint or the use of force in interpersonal relations. It is not generally accepted that, as in Pinthus's (1982) definition, institutional arrangements themselves can be violent and intimidating:

> Violence should be understood as any action or structure that diminishes another human being; and in accepting this definition we must see that the basic structures of our society are often violent in concept. We must recognise the violence built into many of our institutions such as our schools and places of work in that they are competitive, hierarchical, non-democratic and at times unjust. (p. 2)

The exercise and experience of violence in academic life is part of the general need for men to control women and the general dependence of women on men. There is not space here to evaluate the extensive literature on these issues, and so examples have been taken of techniques of subordination which are used by academic men in order to make the point that violence can take a variety of forms. A violent academic situation is not so much an experience of fisticuffs and flying chairs as one of diminishing other human beings with the use of sarcasm, raised voices, jokes, veiled insults or the patronising put-down. There are many techniques for intimidating or silencing others, but examples of violence that are widely used in academic life for purposes of social control are verbal and vocal violence, and sexual harassment.

VERBAL AND VOCAL VIOLENCE

Skilled use of words and the voice are extremely effective means of silencing intellectual challenges and creating an atmosphere in which people are afraid to speak (the silent seminar is a clear example, and easy to blame on student apathy). Academics are verbally highly skilled and can use verbiage to confuse and intimidate others; they are also powerful users of the voice to convey sarcasm, to interrupt, to prevent interruption and to override counter-arguments. Obviously vocal and verbal skills of these sorts are not confined to academics (see Spender, 1980; Cameron, 1985; Spencer and McAuley, 1985) but they are used systematically by academics; specifically by dominant men to silence subordinates and by staff to silence students.

These verbal forms of intimidation were not generally recognised as violent until this point was made by feminists. They can be seen as rooted in insecurity and fear of intellectual challenge and are used generally against students. They are also a systematic means of controlling challenges presented by female academics while avoiding the real points at issue. Subordinates who use the same techniques, for example, of interruption or sarcasm, against dominant men will be viewed as violent, but the violence of the victim is more clearly seen in the case of sexual harassment.

SEXUAL HARASSMENT AS VIOLENCE AGAINST MEN

Recent publicity about the extent of sexual harassment in institutions of higher education has brought the existence of this form of violence to the surface. Sexual harassment is one means by which those who are not heterosexual males can be effectively subordinated, and is a widely used though often unrecognised form of violence.

Women who are harassed tend to find their experiences very painful to deal with since these are often seen as private and personal problems about which the victim is made to feel guilty and inadequate. The force of the label 'sexual harassment', and the source of its power to provoke reactions, is that it transforms these private and personal experiences into *a general problem for working women in patriarchal society*. The term 'sexual harassment' enables women to see these personal encounters as part of an institutionalised system of male domination and, having defined it as a general aspect of sexual politics, *to struggle collectively against it*. Collective struggle brings the real issues of sexual politics into the open and makes protesters vulnerable to being seen as violent.

The issue of sexual harassment, which is one of male violence against women, raises two particular problems for men. Firstly, although harassment is a form of behaviour which has a long history, the term 'sexual harassment' which labels and defines this behaviour is a recent one. Definitions of sexual harassment create great anxiety among men (and among some women) because definitions which are effective in identifying the behaviour at issue go well beyond the sort of overtly violent sexual assault of which most people would disapprove, to cover the cleavage-gazing, personal remarks, blue jokes and friendly squeezing, rubbing, patting and propositioning which are widely regarded as acceptable everyday behaviour:

Harassment may involve a wide range of behaviors from verbal

innuendo and subtle suggestions to overt demand and physical
abuse. (Brandenburg, 1982, p. 322)

This breadth of definition, which is essential for the identification of
sexual harassment, leads men to see themselves threatened *as men*,
with their normal behaviour circumscribed. It leaves them uncertain as
to what they may or may not do, and fearful of provoking reactions. As
one colleague remarked to me recently, 'I see I shall have to be very
careful what I say to you'. This is precisely the point – he will.

The second problem is that campaigns aimed at creating working
conditions for women in higher education which are free from both the
practice and the threat of sexual harassment really do intrude on the
rights of men who see students, secretaries, younger colleagues, and so
on, as sexual objects; they also intrude on the rights of any men who,
while not harassing women sexually, generally behave as dominant
males, expecting deference from women. It is hardly surprising that a
sexual harassment campaign, which is overtly concerned with women's
rights, in practice transforms male violence against women into a
female assault upon the rights of men. It is seen as an unfeminine
attempt to enforce one, prudishly-dictated pattern of behaviour on a
diversity of freedom-loving individuals. Those who object to the
intimidation of women through sexual harassment of students, sexist
jokes in staff meetings and so on, are easily viewed as revengeful,
unsexed women whose unreasoning assault is directed at men in
general and male sexuality in particular. Discussions of sexual
harassment are then very easily constructed as defences of the feelings,
rights and civil liberties of men.[5]

Women who raise sexual harassment as a public issue make the
moral confusions of academic life uncomfortably explicit, so the issue
of harassment cannot be treated as the issue it really is – an abuse of
power in the workplace. Overtly liberal men who may find no personal
contradiction in practising, or tolerating the practices of others, in
abuse of workplace sexual relations, do have problems in insisting in
public on, for example, the absolute right of teachers to solicit sexual
favours from their students. In other words, those who take the
existence of sexual harassment for granted so long as it is not
recognised as such, are usually unwilling to defend such practices
openly once they have been labelled as harassment. Sexual harassment
then has to be dealt with either by denying its existence and treating
those who assert its existence as hysterical or otherwise abnormal, or
by acknowledging its existence but denying its importance. The

importance of protecting men's rights and sensibilities precludes any effective action to stop harassment. The rights and sensibilities of those who have been harassed, and the moral responsibility of those who harass, cannot then be seriously considered.

Wherever women are effective in exposing the hidden violence of academic life, for example by questioning the rights of men to use vocal violence, or by labelling and challenging sexual harassment, their behaviour, however diplomatic (and often political inexperience leads both to lack of diplomacy and lack of efficacy), will be constructed as aggressive and intimidating, because this is how the defenders of male privilege will experience it. These experiences encourage men to label protesting women as sexually abnormal, and to legitimate the explicit defence of male privilege and domination in what has come to be termed the 'backlash'. In order to clarify this reaction, the competitive and hierarchical context of the academic career which underlies the need for violence must be examined.

INTELLIGENCE AS A SOCIAL PROBLEM

While the academic career can be seen as a competitive one, the competition is supposedly one of scholarly capacity related to intelligence, yet intelligence is admittedly a problematic term. By definition, those who achieve a place in the academic hierarchy, or even on its fringes, must be highly intelligent. These are the best brains in the country, who have passed through highly selective procedures to gain the privilege of producing knowledge and passing on the ability to think to successive generations. When one surveys one's academic colleagues, however, it is reasonable to ask what sort of intelligence is being recognised in this process.

It would seem worthwhile investigating the notion that academics are unfortunately socialised into an extremely narrow and constraining notion of intellectual achievement. Intelligence is not associated with the capacity to understand so much as with the capacity to demonstrate superiority to others. Since all cannot be superior, this notion of intelligence inculcates the necessity of demonstrating that as many others as possible *are intellectually inferior* and legitimates the academic hierarchy, since the highly intelligent will get on and the mediocre fall by the wayside. It is also a conception of intelligence which is isolated from emotion and encourages academics to develop a one-dimensional 'rational' ability, which is conceived as masculine and superior, at the expense of broader conceptions of human understanding and communication, which are seen as feminine and, therefore, inferior (see also Bleier, 1984; Gardner, 1984).

How many of us have seen a 'brilliant' visiting scholar, unable to maintain a civil conversation over lunch, or mumbling over a typescript to a roomful of yawning students? How many applicants for jobs or promotion are judged on the quantity rather than the quality of their work, or on the prestige of a referee rather than on their contribution to knowledge? How many excellent teachers are not recognised at all?

Since academic women are clearly much more highly selected than academic men, why is it not taken for granted that they are likely to be more intelligent on average than their male colleagues? Such a question is, of course, naïve. If intelligence is conceived in terms of superiority to others, then women cannot be acknowledged as the intellectual cream, let alone as having a much broader range of capability, without threatening the whole edifice of male domination:

> The creative woman poses a constant threat to the man, not simply because he is a man, but because she is a threat to the whole system that made him this kind of man.   (El Saadawi, 1980, p. 171)

In order to preserve the norm of male superiority, sanctions must be applied, and the most effective sanction is to identify the able woman as abnormal. The normal woman is one who, while admittedly able, is passive and feminine, that is, deferential to men, and who is effectively controlled by this system of deference. The woman who talks as much as a man, who presents herself as confident and powerful, who objects to being interrupted when she starts to speak, is experienced as a threat to the way academic men exercise power over women and to male sexuality. Intelligent women who demonstrate superiority simply by being themselves are then particularly likely to be seen as aggressive and sexually unnatural, because academic ability can only be judged in terms of 'superior' and 'inferior'. They must demonstrate deference and every known feminine wile if they want to remain socially acceptable.

The narrowness of the academic conception of intelligence (which has grown out of the mind/body split of earlier thinkers) also defines academics as intellectuals whose emotions are controlled by reason. This dangerous myth obfuscates an extraordinary range of passions which cannot be recognised as such. The pursuit of objectivity, although intellectually out of favour, is still, for example, the cornerstone of the examination system around which higher education is organised. It is cautiously acknowledged that academics have their violent prejudices, hence the safeguards of external assessment, but emotion and sexuality are not supposed to intrude into teaching, research or administration.

It is not suggested that academics are necessarily more passionate and emotional than other occupational groups, but that very generally they are discouraged from understanding their own behaviour or the behaviour of others towards them, and their powers of empathy tend to atrophy. These highly intelligent people are rewarded for learning destructive patterns of interpersonal communication geared to competition, domination and the attribution of failure to others, and they interpret the behaviour of others towards them in the same terms.

THE ACADEMIC CAREER AND ITS REWARDS

The academic career, which is supposed to be a scholarly pursuit of excellence, is much more accurately understood as a rat race in which most runners fall by the wayside. The rat race is run in accordance with the limited notion of intelligence which has been allowed to develop, so scholars do not normally co-operate together in a selfless production of knowledge, but compete with each other in a rush to determine who is best: they publish or perish. The problem with this race is that the course is not clearly defined so the prizes never clearly identify who is 'best'. Top rats are not, therefore, necessarily the best scholars, innovative researchers or teachers, since we have no objective means of assessing 'best', but are those who have the public trappings of rank, position and reward (see, for example, Watson, 1968). There is a contradiction between the ideals of scholarship and the anxiety-producing necessity of demonstrating that one is getting on.

The rat race is one which 'sorts out the men from the boys', and women start with considerable handicaps. Women who do not opt out of the race early on can choose to behave as much like men as possible, or to emerge as 'super rats': women who excel at everything men do, while at the same time running a home, raising children, caring, sharing and remaining feminine. Such women are indeed impressive, but hardly equal in terms of the loads they carry, and very few stagger past the finishing tape. Although some men as well as women do choose to withdraw from the rat race, they cannot be perceived by those in it as having exercised a rational choice, but are seen only as failed rats who could not take the competition. Even where women try to avoid the race, for example by putting energy into teaching, support of others and co-operation, it is almost impossible to remain an academic without being brought into the race at least to some extent.[6] It then becomes important for those for whom the race is all, that women be made aware of their proper positions at the rear.

Where women deliberately or inadvertently demonstrate their competence, they generate insecurity in those who are engaged in academic competition. This insecurity provides the motivation for taking the rat race so seriously. Even where academics appear outwardly successful they have very little inner certainty that they are 'good' let alone 'the best'. Apart from early examination successes, there is nothing in the academic career structure to reinforce an inner sense of achievement, and promotion increasingly means a shift away from research and teaching into administration. Rabbitt (1984) argues that people are not good at evaluating their own capacities:

> We think that these results mean that people cannot evaluate their own competence in any absolute sense and must always make relative comparisons. (p. 14)

Reassurance can then only come from acquiring public symbols of progress, or treating women as a subordinate category.

This lack of inner certainty is compounded by the lack of real power in academic life. Academics, for example, have little political or economic power, they can only attempt to influence those who have, or to encourage the powerless. In order to demonstrate their political prowess and intellectual abilities, they have initially to demonstrate them to each other, and this can be difficult when colleagues are divided by schools of thought, or where juniors are manifestly the more competent. This encourages the need to put others down, and for men to bolster their positions by drawing on techniques of demanding deference from those seen as subordinate. In this view of the world, women's 'successes' diminish those of men, so that academic men are drawn into a system of social control in which women are expected to defer to men.

DEFERENCE AND CONTRADICTION

The competitive career and the hierarchies of educational institutions define working situations in which women clearly do not fit. The system of deference control extends to men who occupy subordinate positions in the hierarchy as well as to women in general, but whereas lesser men who rise to dominance can be seen as normal, women can only move up the hierarchy by becoming 'abnormal'. As Whitehorn (1984) has put it, one woman is a freak, two are an outrage and three are 'they're taking over'. It is this social construction of abnormality which should be seen as a form of violence against women.

Since even deferential women are potentially threatening, it becomes reasonable to argue, for example, that all-women sub-committees are contravening the law, or at least should have male members because otherwise they carry no weight; that it is inadvisable for three female members of staff to see Professor X about problem Y because the poor man will be alarmed by a feminist delegation; that feminist ideas have no place in a course on sociological theory. Where women are clearly not deferential, and manifest their abnormality by publicly challenging assumptions such as these, they can be perceived as frightening to the extent of threatening violence by their very presence.

Through men's dependence on female deference, feminist women are constructed as a threat not just to male dominance but to male sexuality generally. The label 'feminist' has come to indicate that women are not freely available as sexual objects, hence the popularity of the word lesbian as a term of abuse. It is part of the system of deference control that men should be acknowledged as sexually powerful, and those who fail to make this acknowledgement should be treated with contempt.

These situations and the distress they cause to both men and women can be understood by seeing academic women as a contradiction in terms, and this is reproduced in generation after generation. The right to a higher education is a right that has never been freely offered; it is a right that women have fought bitterly for in the past, and one that many able girls and women still have to struggle for today. The entry of women into male-dominated institutions logically forces men to admit that there are no innate differences in ability which are relevant at the level of higher education. In the outside world, discrimination is widely practised and justified, but such discrimination, or any grounds on which it could be based, are no longer supposed to exist inside higher education. Academic men, however, are quite as emotional as they are logical and they have a good deal to lose by implementing any such admission (and innate differences in ability are still being proposed, for example, Rudd, 1984).

There is no formal sexual division of labour among academics, in the sense that there are not male and female tasks in research and teaching, so lip service is paid to equality, which is then undermined in numerous and effective ways. How many academic men have had their knee patted while discussing departmental affairs, been advised to seek therapy for their sexual problems after a stormy staff meeting, had the size and desirability of their bottom discussed in public by colleagues? These undermining tactics are wonderfully successful so long as women interpret them as evidence of their own personal inadequacies:

> We are dealing with a primitive male society in which the presence of any woman constitutes an invasion and a threat of contamination, which must be carefully guarded against by the exercise of tribal pollution sanctions. . . . Women's innocent optimism makes them take the consequent sanctions as *personal* which explains why after generations of women scholars we are still so few, so tired, so defensive, have done so much less work than we should have done. (Adams, 1983, pp. 135–6)

The missing sexual division of labour is reconstructed in terms of important/lightweight, theoretical/practical, senior/junior, intellectual/caring. Practical, caring men are losers in the rat race; important, intellectual, theoretical women must be freaks.

Effective deference control isolates women from each other by directing their behaviour, their pain and their need for approval towards significant men. It encourages women to join the rat race as unequal contenders, and then trips them up. Women who are aware of the system of deference control and the contradictions of its existence can support each other in a struggle to liberate themselves from it, but it is a male system, and if it is to be changed, then men must also acknowledge its existence.

CHOOSING TO CHANGE

My argument is not that all academic men are indiscriminately violent, but that academic institutions systematically construct non-deferential women as a real threat to men, which legitimates the subordination of women, and that men generally benefit from these mechanisms of social control.[7]

Women still differ politically over whether the struggle is against men as men or against a more institutionalised conception of patriarchy (these differences are usefully brought together in Jaggar, 1983), but it is clear that academic men have something to defend against women and women constitute a real threat to this defence, not only when they take collective action, but also as 'normal' but non-deferential individuals who do not accept their subordination. Where women see subordination as natural, or work in predominantly female departments, they are a potential rather than an open threat to dominant males. Feminism forces men to make the system of deference control overt, by allowing 'peculiar' women to see their problem behaviour as a response to a system of intimidation which is a general problem for women, and which can be challenged.

Obviously, change within institutions of higher education cannot be separated from change outside, but it is conceivable that the academic career and the examination system can gradually be redefined as a more co-operative and creative quest for knowledge, and the course laid out in terms of a much broader range of skills so that all can settle for being more like humans and less like rats. The problem is, of course, that it is men who must choose to change, since it is men who have their powers to lose, their emotions to recognise and their sexuality to reconsider; it is men who depend on deference control in order to maintain the present violent system of domination and subordination.

REFERENCES

Thanks for support to Huseyin Ramazanoglu, Vic Seidler, Mary Stiasny and Olive Till, none of whom bears responsibility for what I have written.
1. There is not space in this chapter to explore the concept of subordination fully, but it is taken in this context to mean the process of making women less important than men and the process of women treating men as superordinates.
2. Gender is not the only dimension of subordination or source of struggle in higher education. The complex and variable interrelations of class, race and gender in our power structures are insufficiently conceptualised, both generally and in the analysis of specific situations.
3. I have been much encouraged by Stiasny's (1983) excellent use of this

approach and her much fuller exposition and justification of its power and validity.

4. Domination has been adopted as a masculine form of the exercise of power, but it is necessary to identify exactly how it is that academic women are subordinated, and to recognise that women can, and often do, attempt to subordinate others. More positive ways in which power might be conceived must also be considered (Hartsock, 1983).

5. A similar argument in a different context is made by Spender (1983).

6. For comments on this contradiction see, for example, Howell (1979); the Nebraska Feminist Collective (1983); Lowe and Benston (1984).

7. For a personal account of these mechanisms from a man's point of view, see Silverstein (1974).

6 Women, Leisure and Social Control

Eileen Green, Sandra Hebron and Diana Woodward

At first sight, the areas of violence and social control, on the one hand, and leisure on the other seem to occupy opposite ends of the continuum of freedom and extreme coercion. Closer examination through feminist analysis, however, reveals that the area which is portrayed by capitalist ideology as representing the ultimate in freedom from constraint, that is, leisure, is actually one of the areas where women's behaviour is regulated most closely. The concern in this chapter is with the particular forms which this regulation takes, that is, with how social control is experienced by women in their daily lives. This entails an analysis not only of the constraints on opportunities for free time and access to leisure activities experienced at an individual level, but also of the structural context within which choices, decisions and negotiations are worked out.

Leisure within capitalism is a highly commercialised area dominated by patriarchal images which frequently represent women simultaneously as both leisure objects (Steward and Garratt, 1984),[1] and servicing agents of male leisure in the home and in the public sphere. The penalties for women who contravene the commonly accepted limits of appropriate or 'decent' behaviour in leisure venues (for example, night clubs) or public places on the way to and from those venues often involve sanctions enacted by men, ranging from verbal abuse which carries with it the threat of male violence, to actual bodily harm. This type of social control in the area of leisure reflects the generally high level of constraint which is part and parcel of normal, everyday life for the majority of women in Western capitalist society.

FEMINISM AND LEISURE STUDIES

One of the most significant and exciting developments within social science research over the last ten years or so has been the emergence of a body of feminist theory and related empirical data which documents the structure of women's lives and represents their experience in their own terms (Oakley, 1974a; Sharpe, 1976; Pollert, 1981). This has involved a lengthy and at times acrimonious critique by feminists of the existing perspectives of academic disciplines which were blind to the significance of gender, and shared a tendency to study social life in compartmentalised areas entitled 'work', 'leisure', 'family life', and so on (see, for example, Barker and Allen (eds), 1976a and 1976b; Spender (ed.), 1981). Feminist studies have demonstrated that a more illuminating approach involves investigating particular aspects of women's experience in relation to the structure of their lives as a whole, thus locating the situation of women in its wider context of patriarchal capitalism.[2]

The growing literature on gender issues in leisure has its roots in this general critique of male-dominated sociology, and forms a response to the implicit sexism of much early work in the field of the sociology of leisure. Leisure is a relatively new area of academic study and, as Dixey and Talbot have noted:

> it remains the poor relation to the sociology of work, industrial relations, the family and other well developed foci of sociological inquiry. It is only with the realisation that leisure has an important role in an industrial society undergoing rapid change due to technological innovation and economic recession that attention has been focused more squarely on it. (1982, p. 11)

Throughout the 1970s the preoccupations of the literature in this field were issues of tangential relevance to women's situation. Leisure was defined in terms of its antithesis to paid work as time largely free from external constraints, which a person could freely choose to spend as she or he wished (see Parker, 1971). This conceptual starting point led to a heavy concentration in both theoretical and empirical work on the class position, occupational cultures and associated leisure actitivies of white male workers. Women, if they featured at all, appeared as the partners of the men studied, and yet the findings were presented as axioms of general relevance and applicability (Parker, 1971; Dunning (ed.), 1971; Salaman, 1974). Parker, for example, writes:

> In considering the various categories we have had in mind men in full-time employment. Certain modifications to the scheme are necessary if it is to fit the cases of other groups. (1971, p. 29)

These 'other groups' would presumably include women as well as children, the unemployed and retired people. This assumption that minor modifications to the model would enable it to account also for the situation of women has been heavily criticised:

> It is precisely this assumption (that women form a specific offshoot from the male category which is synonymous with the neutral, general category) that constitutes what has been described as masculine hegemony. (Griffin *et al.*, 1982)

Some other genres of leisure studies work over the last decade have similarly failed to deal adequately with gender issues, albeit for different reasons. Recent Marxist analyses have emphasised the wage-relationship as the major determinant of leisure in capitalist society, leisure being seen as clearly constructed by type and hours of paid work (Stedman-Jones, 1977, cited in Tomlinson, 1981; see also Griffin *et al.*, 1982). In adopting this perspective on leisure in relation to paid employment, women's experiences were rendered irrelevant, peripheral or merely difficult to study. Whilst men are generally seen to 'earn' leisure time through paid work, the amorphous nature of women's unpaid domestic work makes it hard to identify time which is unambiguously 'free' for leisure.

Another widely-read and influential approach to leisure studies has been characterised by Clarke as 'policy reformist' and within 'a Fabian mould' (Clarke, 1981). It is perhaps best exemplified by the work of Young and Willmott (1973) and the Rapoports (1975). Both texts share an elitist assumption that the tastes and leisure interests of the middle classes will, in the course of time, become available to all. This approach tells us nothing about inequalities of gender and race, and offers an inadequate theorisation of class relations and cultures.

The growth of feminist interest in leisure studies has opened up new areas of analysis associated with the issues and perspectives with which the women's movement has been vitally concerned. Arguably the most important of these has been to identify leisure as a political issue, making gender inequalities as significant an area for study as class inequalities. It has long been noted that men and women engage in different kinds of leisure activities (see, for example, the General Household Survey, 1973). 'Official' explanations of women's low participation rates in activities outside the home have been couched in terms of women being recreationally 'disadvantaged' (Department of the Environment) or 'socially and geographically deprived' (Sports

Council and Social Science Research Council Joint Working Party on Recreational Research) (see Talbot, 1979, p. 1). Feminist analyses of leisure reject this perception of women as a neglected group whose problems are capable of resolution through piecemeal changes in social policy. They are, therefore, critical of campaigns such as that organised by the Sports Council to promote women's participation in sport, which was based on quantitative data about gender differences in participation rates, car ownership and other 'positivistic data' (Stanley, 1980). In its place, a political analysis of gender and leisure is emerging which links wider social processes and individual women's experiences:

> The concepts of patriarchy, gender relations and class are thus basic to this analysis: gender and social class provide the central structuring relations in the division of labour in patriarchal society and operate as overarching constraints on all women, but mostly with different effects. The aim [of this research] is not merely to describe the circumstances and activities of women's daily lives, but to relate these to the forces that shape their lives, define their options and scope for experience and autonomy.   (Wimbush, 1985, p. 12)

Leisure viewed in this way is not just a matter of facilities or institutions; it is an integral part of social relations, informed by and contributing to the social order (Tomlinson, 1983). Feminist researchers among others have begun to challenge the view that social class is the major division affecting access to and participation in leisure, identifying gender and also race as equally pertinent divisions structuring individual experiences.[3] Women from different class positions may be unequally constrained by income levels and resources, but they share common constraints resulting from their subordinate position to men. In applying a critical feminist perspective to research on leisure, a healthy suspicion of positivistic research methods as being inadequate in elucidating the meanings attached by respondents to their behaviour has given way to a preference for qualitative techniques. These encourage those being studied to 'tell their own stories' (Graham, 1983) and to explain their behaviour in their own terms. A number of ethnographic studies using this approach have provided rich evidence on the leisure experiences of schoolgirls and young working-class women, revealing in addition the structural absence of girls from most other ethnographic work on youth subcultures (McRobbie, 1978; McCabe and McRobbie, 1981: Hobson, 1978; Griffin *et al.* 1982).

This represents a real advance in conceptualising women's leisure. Work and leisure are no longer regarded as separate spheres but instead as a more complex set of experiences involving degrees of freedom and constraint. When the 'grey' areas between work and play become a major focus of research instead of being tacked on as an afterthought to the main model, it becomes easier to site leisure in context. Women's lack of time for and access to leisure should not be posed as a 'social problem' to be resolved through specific campaigns or social policies, but constituted instead as one aspect of the gender relations characteristic of patriarchal capitalism.

VIOLENCE AND SOCIAL CONTROL

In the remainder of this chapter it will be shown that women's access to and experiences of leisure are constrained by a wide variety of processes and mechanisms operating across those areas of social life which are often designated as separate, and divided into public and private spheres. In leisure as in all areas of life, women's behaviour is closely regulated and this regulation operates at a number of levels, taking a number of different forms.

In the context of everyday life, women make individual choices and enter into negotiations about appropriate ways to conduct themselves. However, these negotiations take place within a framework of constraints, both material and ideological. The subordinate social position of women is reinforced and maintained at one level by material inequalities and at another (though necessarily linked) level by ideological processes.[4] The forms of social control experienced by the women in this study operate across these levels and are grounded in constraints such as economic dependence, and in shared assumptions about appropriate behaviour for women. Social control is defined as an ongoing process, one element in the struggle to maintain male hegemony[5] which sets the limits of appropriate feminine behaviour.

Without resorting to a crude conspiratorial model, it is possible to identify a variety of ways in which women's lives are regulated on a day-to-day basis within the structures of patriarchal capitalism. As this study indicates, regulation is most typically experienced in negotiations with individual men and the framework within which individual women enter into negotiations over their access to leisure can be seen as a continuum or paradigm of social control. At one end of the continuum of social control are non-coercive forms, or what might be called 'control through consent' (though just how far any person with little or no power can be seen to 'consent' is difficult to see). At the other end of the continuum are those forms of behaviour which use physical violence to compel women to behave in certain ways. Between the two extremes, a variety of means of attempting to determine women's behaviour exist, involving varying degrees of coercion. Male violence has long been used as a means of controlling women, particularly wives[6] and as Wilson (1983a) has noted, it is now generally regarded as an 'extreme and unfortunate form of appropriate masculine behaviour'.

At the level of actual physical violence or the explicit threat of its use, the coercion of individual women by men has been well documented (see, for example, Dobash and Dobash, 1979; Pahl, 1978). Recently the research of feminists such as Kelly (See chapter 4 in this volume) and Hanmer and Saunders (1984), together with our own findings, indicate the extent to which many women experience forms of non-violent social control. There are two important points to be made here. Firstly, that non-coercive means of control can be backed up by both the implicit or explicit threat or the actual use of physical violence: in many negotiations between men and women, the possibility of physical violence is a known dimension. Secondly, in speaking of a continuum or paradigm, we want to move away from the concept of a hierarchy of violent and non-violent acts. Whilst not wanting to underestimate the effects of actual physical violence against women, we feel that forms of social control which involve the implicit possibility of violence frequently have the same consequences as its actual use. As Smart and Smart note in their discussion of rape as a means of the social control of women:

> It is not rape itself which constitutes a form of social control, but the internationalisation by women . . . of the possibility of rape. This implicit threat of rape is conveyed in terms of certain prescriptions which are placed upon the behaviour of girls and women, and through the common-sense understandings which 'naturalise' gender appropriate forms of behaviour.   (Smart and Smart (eds), 1978, p. 100)

In short, women who do not limit themselves to 'gender appropriate forms of behaviour' learn to expect sanction.

Leisure for women of all social classes is highly constrained by dominant assumptions about what constitutes respectable 'womanly' behaviour and is constantly overshadowed by the values of a society with a large investment in maintaining 'stable' family units. Once identified as primarily wives, mothers and daughters, women's sexual identities and social behaviour must conform to an acceptable norm.

MALE CONTROL OF THE PRIVATE SPHERE

The authority and control of men over women has long been legitimated within the areas of marriage and the family. The social and economic factors which promote women's subordination to men have been well documented (Barrett, 1980; Barrett and McIntosh, 1982). The sexual division of labour and inequalities within the labour market (Land, 1978) foster women's economic dependence on men, most typically within the institution of marriage. Materially, women are still excluded from most positions of power and influence within society (Stacey and Price, 1981) and ideologically they are firmly located within the domestic sphere. However, as Dobash and Dobash have pointed out:

> The dictum that a woman's place is in the home doesn't so much mean that she shall not go out to work, but that she should not go out to play.   (Dobash and Dobash, 1979, p. 91)

Our study has provided information about the forms of social control which effectively keep women 'in their place', experienced as negotiations over access to leisure. We would argue that women living with male partners experience particular forms of control over their leisure and indeed over substantial areas of their daily lives, and that this control has historically been understood as legitimate or even desirable (Smart and Smart, 1978). One explicit form of control over women's opportunities for leisure, particularly outside the home, is through the restriction of their access to disposable income. Jan Pahl's research on the political economy of the household unit, together with community studies (Dennis *et al.*, 1956; Whitehead, 1976; Newby, 1977) have indicated the links between income and power. Pahl asserts:

> . . . there is a substantial body of evidence testifying to the deferential dialectic in which wives are seen as subordinate to their husbands, largely because of their financial dependence . . .   (Pahl, 1984, p. 10)

In terms of leisure, a husband's status as 'breadwinner' (whether or not he is the only or main wage-earner in reality) confers 'certain prerogatives and privileges' such as authority, independence and freedom of movement (Dobash and Dobash, 1979, p. 89). If the husband is in paid work he is generally seen to have 'earned' the entitlement to have leisure time and to use it more or less as he sees fit. Not only are women not seen automatically to earn this entitlement in the same way as men, they frequently lack the economic resources and the opportunity to pursue leisure activities. Male control of household resources can be crucial in determining how women are able to spend any free time, particularly when the women themselves have no personal income. Pahl found that wives spend less money on leisure than their husbands, especially in the low income groups. It is not difficult for a husband to deny a financially dependent wife leisure outside the home; or for both partners to assume male ownership of the wage packet in such a way as to effectively deter the woman from asking for the necessary money to facilitate that leisure.

Women's responsibility for most (if not all) domestic work and child-care is a second major constraint upon leisure. Male refusal to contribute to domestic tasks or to co-operate with child-care arrangements are two of the most commonly experienced means by which men effectively restrict women's access to time and space for leisure. Thus they are able to regulate women's movement outside the home and the ways in which time is spent inside the home. Of the married women in our survey, 97 per cent do the major part of the housework themselves, and although the majority of them accept the primary responsibility for domestic work, they are well aware of the restrictions it imposes upon their opportunities for leisure. Apart from the difficulty of finding time for leisure, for many women the demands of paid and unpaid work and the obligations associated with their servicing role mean that they simply lack the energy for leisure activities:

> This is why you don't want to do things at night. By the time you've worked a full day and you've come home and cooked a meal, washed up, done your bits and bobs, there's always something to do . . .[7]

For many women, children form the central point of their domestic responsibilities and caring role. Our findings indicate that becoming a mother forms a pivotal stage in women's lives, influencing all areas, not only leisure. These changes involve altered material circumstances and also a significant change in status and greatly increased responsibilities. What seems apparent is that women's leisure patterns generally become more home-centred and largely family-orientated. For many women this sets the pattern for the greater part of their adult lives. One 22-year-old woman said:

> As soon as I had my baby I felt different, I didn't feel as though I could go to a night club.

and another summed it up by saying:

> I think your attitude changes, doesn't it, when you've got children.

Whilst children may be a valuable part of leisure, there is no doubt that women's responsibility for the care and attention which children need constitutes a very real constraint on their leisure. It is generally expected that women who are mothers will restrict their activities to those which fit well, in both practical and ideological terms, with their mothering role (Sharpe, 1984).

Women's responsibility for child-care includes the responsibility of finding someone to look after the children if they themselves will not be available (Green and Parry, 1982), whether in a context of paid work or leisure time. In many cases, where a woman's mother lives nearby she is the preferred childminder. In a similar way to the findings of Green and Parry (1982) and Martin and Roberts (1984), the majority of the women in our study felt that they had to ask their partners to look after the children on specific occasions, rather than there being a shared responsibility. Presumably this gives their partners the option of refusal. The extent to which the husbands or partners of women in the study were willing to be involved in child-care varied, but in some cases the men quite simply refused to accept any responsibility:

> I just literally had to stay at home until one of them was old enough to look after the other one or at least just for the odd hour or two, because my husband said 'Well, I don't want them'.

> . . . no way he'd have her when she was a baby. I couldn't even escape anywhere or ever go, say, just to visit relatives. He just wouldn't.

This effectively confines many women to the home for a long period, often increasing their social isolation and marking the transition to home-based leisure activities. They are then increasingly unlikely to take part in out-of-the-home activities except in their roles as wives and/or mothers.

Even when women do have access to some time and money of their own for leisure, their attempts to have any leisure time independently of their partners can be a major source of conflict, particularly when this involves women moving outside the home. McIntosh (1981) has commented on the role which women play in constituting a part of male leisure, and our findings support this. For married women, this means servicing their husbands' leisure as and when required. Many men expect their wives or partners to be available to spend time with them and will often resist the women's attempts to have some autonomous leisure outside the home. Typical comments from women in the study were:

> He thinks I should be at home all the time, especially when he is in.

> He doesn't like me to go to the health club if he is at home.

> He's very anti me going out on my own.

> He doesn't like me to go out without him no matter where I go.

Our findings indicate that men employ a range of strategies in order to regulate their partners' behaviour. A particularly prevalent form of control is the way in which male partners are able to use the women's own guilt feelings as a way of preventing them from engaging in certain behaviours. Dominant ideologies about being a good wife and mother demand that women be seen to sacrifice their own interests for the interests of the family (Oakley, 1974a), and imply that for good mothers the two should in any case be synonymous. Servicing the family is the socially recognised route through which women achieve fulfilment. Therefore, not only are women not properly entitled to time free from the demands of others, they should not *want* such time. In many cases where women in the study spoke of their 'need' to have time away from the home and family, this recognition was accompanied by feelings of guilt which are particularly acute in relation to the issue of perceived neglect of children. As one woman said:

> . . . and you feel guilty sometimes, don't you, because you've actually not ironed or not cleaned up or not read to your child in order to get an hour to yourself . . .

Male partners find it easy to regulate women's movements and participation in social activity by pointing out their responsibilities as mothers. Patriarchal definitions of gender roles ensure that men feel justified in doing this and therefore it is difficult for women to counter such male opposition, backed up as it is by the full weight of patriarchal ideology.

Other strategies typically employed by male partners during the negotiation processes surrounding access to leisure can be viewed as points along a continuum ranging from petty forms of behaviour such as sulking or 'having a face on', through to the explicit exercise of male authority, actually forbidding the woman to go out. This may be backed up by threatened or actual physical violence. Whilst our findings provide detailed evidence of non-coercive control being exercised over women, the study of battered women by Binney *et al.* (1981) and Burgoyne and Clark's study (1984) of divorce and remarriage (both based in Sheffield), have provided substantial evidence of violence being used by husbands against wives. Similarly Dobash and Dobash (1979) in their study of violence against wives, found it a common occurrence for husbands to set limits on the amount of time wives might spend away from home when engaged in any kind of social activity.

Even when women are able to go out without their partners their movements may come under scrutiny. In discussion groups made up of people involved in the provision of leisure facilities in the Sheffield area, conducted prior to the survey, it was reported to be not uncommon for men to ring up health clubs, and so on, to make sure that their wives or partners were there. In the words of one health club manager '. . . the men were terrible for checking up on them . . .' In other discussions which were held with groups of Sheffield women, individual women gave concrete examples of the ways in which they are 'policed' by their partners:

> I've been in a pub and when he's in uniform he's not supposed to come in you know, come in for a drink – and I've said I'm going in this particular pub in town and he's come in and said: 'Oh I've just come for a coke.' Never drunk coke in his life, you know, but he'll come in and have a coke. He's done that twice on me.

Our study indicates that male disapproval and displeasure is particularly marked in relation to women drinking. This issue came up frequently when we asked the women about the kinds of disagreements they have with their partners about their own personal leisure:

> He's not too keen me going drinking on my own or with friends.

> He doesn't like me to go to the pub without him.

> [He wants to know] Where I'm going and who I'm going with and how much I'm going to drink.

It seems that much of men's resistance to women's independent leisure, especially when it concerns drinking, relates to male attitudes towards and definitions of female sexuality. A considerable literature on sexuality exists, some of which documents the history of attempts to regulate women's sexuality (Smart and Smart (eds), 1978; Hartmann, 1981). As Bland, *et al*. argue:

> The control of sexuality must be regarded as a vital aspect of an analysis of women's subordination . . .   (1978, p. 165)

Contemporary Western society still clings to the premise that married women are the property of one man, their husband. However, if a woman is seen to transgress the boundaries of the marital relationship, for example by going into certain public spaces unaccompanied by her husband, the situation changes. She is seen to have given up her entitlement to the protection from any man.

Men's specific objections to women partners going out socially without them are closely associated with norms about respectability and morality. The pub has traditionally been regarded as central to masculine culture, and respectable women's access to pubs has largely been through their male partners (and has often been restricted to Saturday night in the lounge bar, for example). Although it is becoming more common for women to go into pubs unaccompanied by men, they usually do so in the company of other women rather than go alone. In line with the findings of this study, both Whitehead (1976) and Westwood (1984) have commented on the high degree of antagonism and objectification unaccompanied women in pubs and nightclubs have to endure. Such women are assumed to be 'available' and are expected to be receptive to sexual advances from men.

Women in our study mentioned their partners' jealousy at the possibility of them receiving attention from other men, and attributed their partners' restrictive behaviour to this jealousy, and to the fear that the women would grasp the opportunity to form relationships with other men. Sexual jealousy and violence have been associated through history, with men traditionally having the right to chastise, beat or divorce (and in some cases to kill) wives whom they suspected of sexual infidelity (Dobash and Dobash, 1979). The opportunities offered by many leisure activities outside the home may be regarded by a male partner as a threat to the established order, calling into question both the woman's status as 'respectable' and his own status as keeper of her sexuality, and many partners feel justified in restricting women's access to such activities.

A number of respondents in Burgoyne and Clark's study (1984) suggested that women's decisions to go to pubs, clubs, and so on, without their partners and perhaps 'with the girls' were seen by some of the women themselves and by others as possible signals of the search for a new partner. However, many of the women in our study regarded their partners' possessive and jealous behaviour as both unnecessary and unjustified, saying that they were interested in 'having a good time' and 'a laugh' with their girl friends rather than in trying to attract men:

> I weren't interested in anybody else. I thought I hope nobody comes over to talk to me, I just want to dance and to have a drink with me friend.

Given the nature of the negotiations which women have to go through because their access to any social life outside the home is such a 'charged' area, it is hardly surprising that many women simply opt out of the negotiation process altogether:

> It doesn't cause any arguments except that sometimes I just think about it, because you know I work with quite a lot of single people, they go out and I think well perhaps I could join in . . . but I don't sort of entertain it any longer.

For the majority of women this 'decision' to avoid conflict means that they forgo independent leisure.

MALE CONTROL OF PUBLIC PLACES

The control over women's leisure which is exercised at an individual level within households cannot be separated from the ways in which women's social behaviour is regulated in public places. Fundamental to this is the question of a woman's right to occupy certain public spaces (Imray and Middleton, 1983). As one woman put it, 'It's still OK for a man to go anywhere, virtually, but there are still no-go areas for women.'

Women's proper place has traditionally been seen as the domestic sphere, with the public sphere being monopolised by men who have a range of strategies available for maintaining their control of public spaces and indicating to women that they are not welcome there.

Women in this study were given a list of public leisure venues including pubs, wine bars, social clubs, cinemas, theatres, discos and nightclubs, sports or health clubs. The majority of women said they would not feel comfortable going to such places alone. A smaller number of women, particularly older women, said they would not feel comfortable going there even with other female friends. Most of the women felt that it is still not socially acceptable for a woman to walk into a pub on her own:

> The general expectation is that if you go there by yourself, you want to be picked up.

> I suppose for a man it would be much more easy to go into a pub and start chatting and I still think for a woman to actually do the same they would be looked at as though 'Oh well, is this a prostitute?'

A considerable number of women said their discomfort arises partly from this assumption that unescorted women in leisure venues are 'asking' to be picked up, and partly from unwelcome male attention associated with this belief:

> It's really uncomfortable, because you just get stared at, passes made.

> It's quite acceptable for any man just to walk up to you and start talking to you . . . it's very irritating.

The social control of women in the public sphere and the exclusion of women from certain public spaces can take a number of forms. Women in our study reported a range of behaviour used by men, from silent disapproval through a variety of joking and ridiculing behaviour and sexual innuendo to open hostility. This supports Whitehead's (1976) study of sexual antagonism. What is crucial here is the knowledge that underlying these strategies is the threat of physical violence. Should non-coercive means of control fail, men can take the option of using physical coercion, and women know this.

Men not only dominate public places but also control access to them. One of the most severe restrictions on women's leisure time activities is their fear of being out alone after dark. Many women are afraid to use public transport after dark or late at night, whilst for others it is having to walk to bus stops and wait there after dark which deters them. The findings of the second British Crime Survey state that half the women interviewed only went out after dark if accompanied, and 40 per cent were 'very worried' about being raped (Hough and Mayhew, 1985). When women in our survey were asked about the limitations on their free-time activities, the most common reply was 'not liking to walk alone after dark' with similar comments from many women in the discussion groups, such as:

> I do it, but I think your nerves are always on edge . . . I've known of so many women that have been attacked.

> That fear is always there.

Despite statistical evidence that violent attacks upon women are most likely to take place within their own homes the majority of the women we interviewed regarded the possibility of physical attack in public spaces as a very real threat:

> You feel as though there are more attacks on women.

> I think there's more likelihood of a woman being attacked than a man.

Deeply held norms about 'appropriate' places for women to be are reinforced by the fear and actuality of male violence. Women are deemed to be responsible both for their own behaviour, and for the behaviour of the men they come into contact with. Police comments upon and media coverage of reported sexual attacks highlight the distinction between legitimate and illegitimate violence against women. They frequently focus upon the time and place where the attack took place, with women being seen as particularly culpable if they are unescorted in public places after dark:

> A lot of it is still attitudes: that if you're on your own, you're fair game, you know, whatever you're doing, and especially for some reason once it's dark.

Women who are on their way to and from leisure venues, wearing normal evening wear, can also be represented as displaying their bodies in a provocative manner, thereby inviting unwanted sexual advances, including violent attack.

WOMEN CONTROLLING WOMEN

In discussing the ways in which women's leisure is controlled or constrained, we need to recognise that this process is not the simple 'policing' of one gender by the other, but a complex process operating across a number of levels. A consideration of social control would be inadequate without some mention of the way in which women themselves may regulate the behaviour of other women. This takes place within the framework of dominant definitions of femininity and domesticity, manifested at the level of common sense as shared assumptions about being a good wife and mother.

Delamont's (1980) review of a number of community studies notes the support women receive from their women friends or kin to lighten their domestic burdens, but these female networks can also be powerful reinforcers of the system of patriarchal control. There may be quite severe censure for women whose behaviour is deemed to fall outside the bounds of 'normal' respectable behaviour with gossip or ostracism acting as effective means of control. Whitehead (1976) for example argues that newly married women and young mothers are particularly subjected to this kind of control, as they are often isolated within the home from opportunities for social contact, in the workplace or the pub. For many women, being 'a good wife and mother' is one of the few avenues available to them for securing respect and approval. The censure of women whose behaviour is deemed to fall short of the ideal enhances the moral virtue of the critic, as well as reinforcing traditional norms (Delamont, 1980).

In addition to directly regulating or coercing women to comply with patriarchal norms of acceptable behaviour, men also benefit from women engaging in a certain amount of 'policing' of this kind amongst themselves. Indeed, it could be argued that this type of control, based on the acceptance of dominant (male) definitions, is particularly effective: in so far as women are seen to be controlling each other, the patriarchal nature of the control is obscured. This type of control often renders the use of more transparent repressive forms unnecessary.

CONCLUSION: THE NORMALITY OF SOCIAL CONTROL OVER WOMEN'S LEISURE

In this chapter we have attempted to identify how women's access to and use of free time is regulated. Much of the social control of women's behaviour, relying as it does on norms about respectability, being a good wife and mother and so on can to a large extent be regarded as control through 'consent' rather than through 'coercion'. However, it is worth reiterating that should this form of control break down, men have a range of more directly coercive methods available for regulating women's behaviour both inside and outside the home.

For many women, the primary site of regulation is within the household: in order to enjoy leisure activities, particularly those located outside the home, women have to negotiate with male partners for their consent (and perhaps also for a share of the household income). When men offer resistance, this is largely upheld and legitimated by ideologies about women's (lack of) entitlement to personal leisure and assumptions about appropriate behaviour for women. Women's leisure is also constrained outside the home in leisure venues and on the way to or from them. It is by no means unusual for women to be harassed by men in pubs or other public places. Women who are unreceptive to male advances may be verbally abused, threatened with physical violence or subjected to its use. Our findings clearly indicate that many women's fear of male violence outside the home leads them to circumscribe their behaviour.

What is important is that male social control of women is unexceptional; a part of normal, everday life. Generally, this control is seen as natural and legitimate, particularly within marriage, with husbands being historically entitled to govern their wives' behaviour and to punish improper conduct. Furthermore, it is widely accepted that women should live under threat of male violence. As accounts from the police and the media on violence against women – as well as public comments – indicate, women are required to guard their behaviour closely, to ensure that they are not actively encouraging attack. The women we interviewed recognised that they themselves and women in general are not free to come and go as they please. If they attempt to do this they can be labelled as irresponsible and 'asking for trouble'. This has clear implications for how, when, where and with whom leisure time is spent, and is a major factor in promoting and perpetuating gender inequalities in leisure.

REFERENCES

1. A fascinating account of the experiences of women in the music industry by Steward and Garratt includes interviews with female vocalists ranging from Helen Shapiro to Elkie Brooks, most of them expressing great unease with the narrow stereotypes to which they were expected to conform. As Steward and Garratt comment

   > Women's bodies are used to sell their own music in the same way they are used to sell records made by men, guitars, hi-fi speakers, and any other consumer item. (1984, p. 56)

2. An excellent early example of this approach is Oakley's study of housewives (Oakley, 1974b) which, although concerned primarily with documenting women's accounts of the management and experience of housework, provides insights into the nature of the constraints which prevent women with young children from enjoying leisure, and includes a comprehensive critique of sexism in sociology texts.

3. We recognise that race is an important source of inequality, and regret the ethnocentric focus of our current study of leisure and gender, based as it is on a sample of predominantly white women drawn from the electoral roll.

4. A full examination of the ways in which ideology 'works' to reproduce existing social inequalities is beyond the scope of this chapter. A useful discussion appears in Barrett (1980).

5. Whilst originally developed by Antonio Gramsci to theorise the nature of class relations, hegemony has more recently been used by feminists to describe gender relations. Hegemony refers to the process whereby inequalities are maintained through legitimation rather than through enforcement or coercion. It involves the 'organisation of popular consent to the views of the dominant class' (Barrett, 1980). We are using it here in a similar way to Bland *et al.* (1978) who state: 'We use the concept for two reasons: it "includes the ideological but cannot be reduced to that level" . . . it also involves the notion of "consent" to domination by the subordinate group'.

6. See, for example, Dobash and Dobash (1980) on the rigid patriarchy of the early Romans.

7. Where not otherwise referenced quotes are from on-going work in our current study of leisure and gender jointly funded by the Sports Council and the Economic and Social Research Council.

7 Flashing: Its Effect on Women

Sandra McNeill

Criminologists and psychiatrists have interviewed and examined flashers. Criminologists, psychiatrists and sexologists have theorised about flashing; they have even theorised about its effects on women. This chapter sets out to examine those effects by recording conversations with women.[1] Victim studies, sometimes called 'victimology', have been the subject of much controversy, not to say notoriety, because of the tendency of the (usually male) authors to blame the victim.[2] Here I have not set out to 'study the victims' but to attempt to see flashing through the eyes of women who were flashed at, and to examine the effects on women's lives as they define and experience indecent exposure.

These effects, notably fear of the streets or of dark or empty places, and the ensuing limits set on women's access to public places frequently blends in with existing confinement. This should not be seen as minimising the effect of flashing along the lines of 'well, women are not safe on the streets anyway'. Women are protesting against such confinement.[3]

It will, of course, require further study, but the effects of spacial confinement are probably more wide-ranging than has been previously suggested. Studies of the effects of racism, notably that by Simpson and Yinger (1965), point out the damaging effects on blacks caused by the spacial confinement resulting from the segregation laws in the southern states of the USA. One effect was that blacks who 'accepted' segregated, 'black-only' sections of buses and so on, also tended to accept lower wages for blacks. In other words, if unequal treatment is 'accepted' in one area of life it is likely to carry over into other areas also.

While there are no laws explicitly denying women free access to public places at all times, in practice their freedom is curtailed by men who attack them, men who threaten to attack them, insufficient law enforcement against these men, and a tendency for the media to trivialise all incidents except the most serious ones – and these they sensationalise. It is against this background that flashing is examined –

the most minor and most common sexual offence against women, classified as a criminal offence.[4]

INDECENT EXPOSURE AND EXHIBITIONISM – A HISTORY OF FLASHING

Flashing has two histories, one as a criminal offence, the other as a medical condition. Section 4 of the Vagrancy Act, 1824 makes it an offence for a person 'willfully, openly, lewdly and obscenely, to expose his person with intent to insult any female'. 'Person' was subsequently clarified to mean the penis (Working Party on Vagrancy and Street Offences, 1976). Rooth (1971), currently the UK chief clinical expert on flashing, tells us, 'Contemporary accounts in Hansard suggest that the measure was introduced in response to an epidemic of flashing in London parks'. The very careful wording was designed to protect men who may simply have gone into the park to urinate.

Although suspected of being vastly under-reported, flashing is the commonest sexual offence. The English law of 1824 is the first record of it as a legally defined crime. The first attempt to medically classify it as a disorder was by a Frenchman, Laseque, in 1877 (Rooth, 1971). He coined the term 'L'exhibitionism' and noted the following characteristics:

1. It was only done by men.
2. They described it as experiencing sudden powerful urges to expose their genitals.
3. There was little attempt to avoid capture.
4. There was no erotic or obscene gestures or any attempt to enter into a relationship with their victims.
5. The exposers found their own behaviour inexplicable.

R. P. Snaith comments: 'What he described was a certain kind of flasher. Most do try and avoid arrest, many do make obscene gestures, and some assault as well.'[5] But there is the origin of the myth – the myth that flashers are harmless, that is, they will never do anything but flash. This myth is still prevalent although Gebhard (1965) found that one fifth of convicted flashers admitted to previous sex offences involving force.

Much of what is written about exhibitionism becomes null and void once it is realised that the writers have predefined it as 'the expressed impulse to expose the male genital organ to an unsuspecting female *as a final sexual gratification'* (Mohr, 1964, p. 116), or 'the term exhibitionist is confined to those exposers for whom genital display to members of the opposite sex *is an end in itself* ' (Rooth, 1971, p. 521) (my italics). They can then reiterate that these men never assault once they have eliminated *by definition* those who do.

The other element of myth in Laseque's definition is that of 'sudden powerful urges'. Subsequent writers have suggested that the 'irresistible nature' of the behaviour 'annihilated the will' and freed the subject from legal responsibility for his acts (Rooth, 1971). Mohr is another propounder of the uncontrollable urges theory 'in spite of the fact that on some occasions the act may appear to be premeditated and carefully planned' (1964, p. 20).

The classification of flashing as a *crime* in England in 1842 could be related to the diminishing power of the local gentry in controlling people's behaviour. In the nineteenth century, local magistrates, with wide powers, gradually conceded authority to a central state judicial system with more fixed penalties. With the growth of large towns the previous system of 'talkings to' or penalties at the discretion of the local squire/justice of the peace, became inefficacious.[6] Flashing was classified as a crime, along with other crimes committed by vagrants – those who had no roots in the locality. Men usually flash at women who do not know them. It is an act generally committed by 'strangers' and its increase in the large city of London was the motivating force behind the new law.

One explanation for the classification of flashing as a *medical disorder* could be the diminishing power of the church in controlling people's behaviour. This was not unconnected to other changes in society, as the power of the vicar in a small community was linked to the power of the squire. As the church lost its power to regulate sexual behaviour by designating certain practices sinful, that power began to be wielded by the medical profession, who designated certain practices as sick. As part of this process, all the perversions were described in detail and classified, their aetiology explained, and treatment recommended.

The key work in this vein was Dr Richard Von Krafft-Ebing's *Psychopathia Sexualis*.[7] Krafft-Ebing believed that civilisation is attained when man controls his passions, and confines his sexual activity to coitus within monogamous marriage. All else is perversion. He described all the perversions in detail using examples and suggesting causes. When it comes to flashing, he uses the limited 'exhibitionism' definition – exposure with a flaccid penis, no other act attempted. He sees flashing as being like other sexually violent acts against women, but as the man is impotent he can only commit 'silly' acts. He exposes because of an uncontrollable urge, for which he needs medical treatment. (Krafft-Ebing takes the same view of men who rape, commit lust-murder, and so on.)

Foucault (1979) noted how the religious 'confession' was adapted by the medical profession, even before the development of psychoanalysis. But it's nature changed: it was no longer a 'test' but a 'sign' – something to be interpreted: 'The sexual domain was no longer accounted for simply by notions of error or sin, excess or transgression, but was placed under the rule of the normal and the pathological (which, for that matter, were the transposition of the former categories)' (Foucault, 1979, p. 67).

WHAT MEN THINK ABOUT FLASHING

When I began this research I thought that references to flashing would be rare. In earlier research on rape, classified as a serious sexual offence, I had discovered that prior to 1970 there were very few references. The word 'rat' occurred more frequently in indexes than did the word 'rape'. Not so with flashing. The reason for this is that flashing was and is classified as a sexual perversion but rape generally is not! Since all who write about sex have theories about sexual perversions, they all include a reference to flashing. The theorists fall roughly into two groups: psychologists and sexologists. The first includes most psychiatrists/psychoanalysts/behaviour therapists. They pursue two questions: why do they do it and how can we cure it? 'Exhibitionists display their genitals in order to get a sight of the other person's genitals in return' (Freud, 1953, p. 57). It is not surprising that Freud considers flashers to be slightly mad, since this reciprocation never occurs. Fenichel (1945), another psychoanalyst, develops this further. He thinks that a man shows off his penis to get the woman to show her penis in order to prove that there is no such thing as people without penises. Flashing then, is a symptom of the 'castration complex'.

So why do men develop this behaviour? According to most psychoanalysts, 'to understand the exhibitionist, one must first understand the woman of his life – the mother'. Rickles (1950) describes these mothers as suffering from 'penis envy'; a condition believed to be normal in women so long as it is kept within bounds. He lists types of blameworthy mothers: some are 'masculine' and 'brusque', which is a sign of immaturity; others are 'over-feminine' and 'clinging vines'. Either way, they all 'castrate' their sons, who respond by flashing. (Rickles mentions in passing that mothers of schizophrenics are similar to this.)

If it is not the mothers to blame, it is the wives and 'co-joint marital therapy', that is, treating the wives as well as the offenders is practised widely in the USA and at London's Maudsley Hospital. The Maudsley, like most UK medical establishments, is not forthcoming about its treatments. Macdonald's (1973) analysis of American treatments says that as the first stage, the wife must accept that she is involved (that is, to blame). Rooth (1971) thinks that 'dominance and mastery over women' is the reason why men flash. The treatment of wives appears to be based on the idea that the wife must be made to be subservient, so the man will not need to attack other women, a theory not borne out by studies of serious sexual assaulters.[8]

Other explanations of flashing include remnants of phallus worship and pride in the genitals. But some men expose with flaccid penises and men with different lengths of penises expose. If the penis is large, he is showing it off and if it is small, he is exposing due to his inadequacy (Rooth, 1971). Since men with different kinds of mothers and different lengths of penises expose, perhaps the answer is to construct a typology. Rooth distinguishes between two types of exhibitionists: type one is an inhibited young man of otherwise good character. He exposes with a flaccid penis and does not masturbate. Type two is 'sociopathic': he exposes with an erect penis, is highly excited, shows a 'marked sadistic element' and may have other sexual disorders . . . well you get the picture, a kind of drooling fiend. Having distinguished the two types he concludes, 'Although one does meet exhibitionists who fit the type one or type two category, the majority have features of both'.

Psychiatrists disagree strongly over what causes flashing, whether flashers are 'harmless' or liable to assault and, of course, over how to treat them.[9] Where the psychiatrists agree is on the fact that there is something wrong with these men and that they need treatment. Not so the second group of theorists, the sexologists. Ellis (1933) defined exhibitionism as a 'remarkable form of erotic symbolism'. What does this mean? To discover *that*, one has to digest whole chunks of Ellis's theory of sex and the perversions, in seven volumes. According to Ellis, the perversions are simply slightly exaggerated forms of normal male sexuality – all part of a continuum. Therefore there is nothing much wrong with them – indeed, he often seems to frankly admire those who engage in the perversions – note the name he coins for them: 'erotic symbolists'. This may have been connected to the fact that Ellis himself was a urolagnist – he 'got off' by watching women urinate. However he does not really seem to approve of flashers:

> We must regard exhibitionism as fundamentally a symbolic act based on a perversion of courtship. The exhibitionist displays the organ of sex to a feminine witness, and in the shock of modest sexual shame by which she reacts to the spectacle he finds a gratifying similitude to the normal emotions of coitus. He feels he has effected a psychic defloration.   (Ellis, 1933, p. 163)

The idea that flashing occurs as a result of some primeval courtship instinct seems to have been much in vogue in the 1940s. The following illustrative quotation is from Arieff *et al.* (1942):

> Clifford Allen has been enlightening in his discussion on sex perversions from a phylogenetic point of view and quotes the following investigators to confirm his theory . . . Zuckerman has noticed many of the perversions in growing monkeys . . . Another exhibitionist behaviour is the sex dance which the male primate indulges in prior to copulation . . . The Polynesian also exhibits self in his sex dances . . . Allen classes the performances of voyeurs with exhibitionism, ie scopophilia–exhibitionism, as instinctive. Following this thought Baker describes the newt in breeding season . . . In the mating of all animals exhibitionism plays a part to some degree.   (p. 527)

This analysis with its equation of men and newts, to say nothing of Polynesians and monkeys, may strike us as somewhat absurd. But one treatment still advocated for flashers is based on the assumption that flashing is an attempt at courtship and can be cured by teaching socially acceptable dating procedures.[10] The largest offender study, that by Mohr in 1964, compared flashers to normal men and found them to be no different (Mohr, 1964). But before then Kinsey had found that sexual offences were statistically normal male behaviour (Kinsey, *et al.* 1948).

Stoller, a current American sexologist, takes an unusually broad definition of sexual perversions. He notes that:

> at the core of the perverse act is the desire to harm others . . . Hostility is evident in murder that sexually excites, mutilation for excitement, rape

sadism, enchaining and binding games . . . and also in non-physical or whatever sadisms like exhibitionism, voyeurism, dirty phone calls or letters, the use of prostitutes and most forms of promiscuity. (Stoller, 1976, p. 56)

While he clearly feels unhappy about it, he thinks this behaviour is perhaps natural and inevitable in the human male: 'Can anyone provide examples of behaviour in sexual excitement in which in human males at least, disguised hostility in fantasy is not a part of potency' (1976, p. 88).

All these writers see flashing as some natural offshoot of male sexuality, which they take as being biologically inevitable. Other writers, while not specifically examining flashing, see sexuality as something learned. Finkelhor, in examining the sexual abuse of children notes that it occurs more in some societies than in others. He concludes that in examining this sexual behaviour we must examine society as a whole and 'not just the outcome of the idiosyncrasies of certain individuals, families or sub-groups' (Finkelhor, 1979, p. 30). The conclusion of the sexologists, implicitly or explicitly, is that since flashing is inevitable, women should just learn to tolerate it.

This chapter is not primarily concerned with why men flash, however, but rather with its effects on women. It is useful for men that the form male sexuality takes acts as a type of social control over women. Could this behaviour be part of the mechanism by which a powerful group maintains its power?

WHAT WOMEN THINK ABOUT FLASHING

Incidence

The study consisted of interviews with 100 women. The sample comprised twenty-five students (occupants of a residence block), twenty-five women attending a woman's liberation conference and fifty women from a door-to-door survey in Leeds.

The first finding is that out of 100 women interviewed, sixty-three recalled having seen a flasher and forty-three had done so more than once. Out of 233 incidents only 14 were reported to the police, by eleven of the sixty-three women, three women reporting twice. In general, those who reported were treated sympathetically, but were given the impression that the police did not really take the offence seriously:

> It happened on the hill going up to the women's college [residence]. There were three women's colleges at the top of a hill. Men parked in their cars all the way down the hill . . . [she describes the first time one of them flashes at her; she noted the car number and make and reported it to the Bursar who called the police]. The police never caught him, though they had the car number and sort of car. Which is odd. So I don't think they took it as seriously as they made out. All they needed to do was park a car at the spot and they could have collected them in droves.

The main reason given for non-reporting was that the women did not believe the police would treat them seriously.

Of those who had seen flashers, half said the first incident occurred when they were under sixteen. Twenty per cent said the first incident occurred when they were under ten.[11] Analysis of the incidents confirmed findings of previous studies (of offenders) in so far as most incidents took place in the afternoon. Most incidents took place in the street, followed by in the country, or in a park. About half the incidents occurred when the women were alone and in almost all of the remaining times they were with another woman/girl or a group of women/girls. The women were engaged in perfectly normal everday activities, for example, 'going home', 'out shopping', 'going to college', 'waiting for a bus'. The men were usually total strangers. They were of all ages. Some also masturbated. Some were quite nude. Some jumped out at women from a hiding spot, others tried to engage them in conversation before exposing. In only nine incidents did the man do or attempt to do anything other than expose himself. One of these was an attempted rape.

INITIAL REACTIONS

Using the interviewees own words the first emotional reactions to the incidents were tabulated. Fear, shock and disgust were the most common reactions, followed by (if taken together) giggles/funny/ amusement. Anger or outrage mentioned alone came next – but where interviewees mentioned 'mixed' reactions, anger frequently rated as the second, for example 'fear and anger' or 'shock and anger'. Some women felt guilt/shame/humiliation. And three women reported no reaction, for example, 'I just ignored it'.

Obviously, an analysis or any theorising based purely on simple word coding would be quite inadequate. For instance, those who reported 'giggles' may also have felt shock and vice versa – to point to just the most obvious example. So the first question to be asked is: why do women have different reactions? Not only did women have mixed reactions to the same incident but, more noticeably, some women had different reactions to different incidents; it depended on the circumstances. Women reported fear and panic in situations where they perceived they were more at risk. Factors involved were: Were they on their own? Were they in a deserted place? Did the man do anything other than expose his penis? Men masturbating was perceived as a danger sign. If the man fitted a stereotype of 'the flasher', that is, an old man in a dirty raincoat, he was not perceived as dangerous. Some studies, for example that of Mohr (1964), suggest that the main influence on the women's reactions is her psychological state of health. My finding is that the main influence is a fairly realistic personal assessment of the possible danger to herself in that situation:

> It was on a Girl Guide Patrol outing (eight girls aged 10–11 plus patrol leader). We were climbing Box Hill in Surrey. We saw a bloke totally nude. I was quite frightened but there were eight of us. It was a real effort climbing the slope. We had to carry on past him and it seemed to get steeper and steeper. But after, it seemed quite amusing. As one girl said 'He looked like Tarzan'.

> I was walking home from school. I was crossing the bridge. A bloke came towards me. Wanking. He had an erection. I have never been so scared in all my life. I thought . . . I thought I was going to have to hit him . . . He's going to murder me. He leered, wanking away. I thought he was going to grab me. The bridge had very steep walls. I felt hemmed in by him.

> I was walking down Epsom High Street going to drama group. It was 7.30 at night but it was a busy street. In a doorway was an old bloke. It was classic. The dirty raincoat thing. Opening his coat like in the films. His trousers were open and his penis all shrivelled up hung out. I laughed and walked on. (Three incidents recalled by the same woman)

When asked if she thought flashers were harmless this woman replied:

> The first guy, I don't know. The old guy, he was pathetic. I think he is a hospital [mental] patient. There are three mental hospitals nearby. You see nutty folk on the corner. I don't think it would do any good to send him to prison. But the second guy. When I saw his face, I think he was

really pleased he was frightening me. He was doing it to frighten women. Getting a sexual thrill from frightening women – doesn't it lead to other things? Maybe he would get a kick out of rape.

It seems that women's initial reactions are based on the threat of violence perceived.

THE FEELINGS BEHIND THE REACTIONS

Fear

The original question I set out to answer was 'what do women fear?' and the answer was a surprise. Every researcher has hidden or conscious expectations, which a survey can confirm or confound. Before this survey began I assumed that the fear would be fear of rape, and indeed in general discussion of flashing in the second part of the interview, many women linked it in some way with rape. But at the time of the incidents women don't fear rape: *women fear death.*

One woman recalled a man approaching her and exposing himself in the middle of Woodhouse Moor, Leeds. She looked around and saw she was alone:

Respondent: I thought 'Oh my poor mother'.
Interviewer: Why did you think that?
Respondent: Well, she had always warned me, you know, to beware of strange men. I thought, "How awful for her . . . when she hears I have gone like that."
Interviewer: You mean murdered?
Respondent: Yes. I know it might sound silly, but there is this strange man. And he has done that. *You wonder what he is going to do next.*

Time and again women mentioned 'what he was going to do next' as the reason for their fear. And at the back or the front of their minds was death.

It may be relevant to note here that the general door-to-door survey was conducted in Leeds, where for the previous two or three years women had been under particular threat from the man known as the 'Yorkshire Ripper'. So perhaps fear of death came more quickly to mind. But many women 'comply' with rape because they fear death, which is the ultimate threat. The flashing incidents served to *remind* women of this threat.

Shock

Shock was closely linked to two other emotions; on the one hand giggles, and on the other anger/outrage:

> It was a shock, we were not particularly scared. We got the giggles. Partly nerves. It was very unexpected.

> He was flashing at me. He only had a shirt on. It was a shock and I was furious that I couldn't walk along the road without somebody doing that to me. An incredible interruption to my pleasant Sunday morning going-for-the-papers feeling.

The incidents where women reported 'shock' tended to be at the other end of the scale from the incidents where fear was the main reaction. Women often reported 'shock' when they were in crowded public places, or when with large numbers of other women. These incidents, however, still often left women disturbed or unsettled because of the invasion of their private space.

Disgust

This reaction barely needs comment:

> After two minutes I felt he wasn't really paying attention to what I was saying or where I was pointing. I realised he was playing with himself. At which point I withdrew my head from the car window. He drove off. I felt really sick. My stomach went in a knot. So pathetic you know. I didn't like the way he was playing with himself . . . so disgusting. I felt I had been insulted.

As indeed she had been.

Several of those who mentioned disgust gave graphic descriptions:

> . . . it was flaccid and really revolting. We both felt quite sick. It was hanging and dangling about the place. Just quite revolting. We were both incredibly shocked. And really really angry . . . I've seen men you know, coming out the gents, with it accidentally out, not properly put away. But it's completely different. He was definitely doing it AT us. Staring with a superior expression on his old face. The old FUCKER.

He was saying, 'I might be an old slob but I've still got more power than you have. I've still got this. I can keep you under control.

Some of those who mentioned disgust, like the above woman, felt they had to justify it ('I've seen men you know . . .') for fear of being seen as prudes!

Giggling

As mentioned above under 'shock', giggling is a nervous reaction. The few cases of genuine amusement at the time occurred when the flasher fitted the commonly-held stereotype.

Anger

Interestingly, a greater number of women who had already had a previous experience of flashing reported anger as their main emotion, when, that is, they were not in situations likely to produce terror, such as being alone with the man.

Guilt/Shame/Humiliation

Most of the references to guilt and shame were from childhood memories and may not refer to 'initial' reactions.

Interviewer: What was your reaction?
Respondent: I don't know . . . because I blanked out and . . . but it left a feeling of shame.

One woman who felt embarrassed and humiliated at the time, later felt very angry:

I was just waiting at the bus stop. I wasn't doing anything. He was the one doing it. Why should I feel embarrased? I was totally humiliated.

It is likely that if this woman ever sees another flasher her reaction will be one of anger.

No Reaction

Three women reported 'no reaction'. Several women, however,

commented that this was the reaction 'you were supposed to have'. In view of this, it is worth noting how few of the women's initial reactions matched the attitude they are *expected* to have. However, many women who were shocked/frightened/angry, said that if they told their friends they did so in a blasé manner.

EFFECTS ON WOMEN'S LIVES

Eleven of the women reported that the flashing incidents had no effect on their lives. Among them was this student:

> Interviewer: What about reporting it to the police?
> Respondent: By the time you contact them . . . he's gone anyway . . . If I'd been attacked I would have reported it to the police . . . I mean . . . if I had reported it I would have had to see it as an attack. And I don't want them to make me worried. I'm not going to let that affect my life. I'm not going to stop going out.
> Interviewer: Did it affect your attitude to men.
> Respondent: It makes you wary of any man on the tubes at night. Or suspicious-looking men around anywhere.

This shows how a woman can minimise the incident in order to minimise its effects. Her reporting 'no effects' was probably part of that process.

Localised Effects

Some women reported 'only' a localised effect; that is to say, the restriction of their lives was confined to a particular area or activity, for example, walking in the park:

> One woman was flashed at, aged fifteen, as she played tennis with a friend in the early evening. She stopped playing tennis.

> One women had seen three flashers, one in the country one on the edge of town near the country, and one in Epsom town. She reported that the first two incidents had stopped her walking alone in the country: 'Yes, it put me off and I've always felt it since. There are lovely country places . . . but the flashing made me scared of open country places.'

> One woman flashed at while hitch-hiking has not hitched a lift since.

One woman was flashed at while with a friend, as they collected their coats in college after an evening class. Not frightened at the time (her initial response was 'giggling'), she later began to think, 'What if I had been alone?' And from then on got her boyfriend to collect her from evening class. She said, 'But I do miss going for a drink after with the other girls. But I can't go now my boyfriend collects me.'

One woman said that as a result of being flashed at, 'I would never walk in districts like that on my own'. She also tries to avoid being out 'at pub closing time'.

One woman who had a flasher/peeper moved home and would never consider living in a downstairs flat or a house as she does not feel safe in them.

Half the women in the study reported a localised effect.

Of course, many women's lives are restricted in the above ways from 'general' fear of male violence. So the direct effects of flashing become hidden, invisible or unexceptional. It is likely that if the above restrictions were put on men's lives there would be a public outcry. Imagine a lad having to give up football at the age of fifteen. Or a man who loves the country not being able to go for country walks. Or a youth who gives up hitch hiking. Or a man deprived of drinking with his mates. Or a man who feels unsafe in certain areas and at certain times so lives under partial curfew. Or a man who has to move house as he feels unsafe. Of course, sometimes men do have to move house – particularly because of racist attacks. This is not taken seriously either, perhaps indicating that black men, like all women, are only here on sufferance.

The finding of this survey – that most women's lives were restricted by their experience of flashing – will come as no surprise to many people. Anthony Storr, in *Sexual Deviation* (1977), writes:

There are, nevertheless, a few women who constantly find that men are exposing themselves to them. These repeated shocks, however, do not have the effect of deterring them from taking solitary walks on heaths and commons were exhibitionists are known to lurk; and the woman who complains that this experience often happens to her may generally be justly accused of seeking it out. (p. 93)

Feminist Sheila Jeffreys commented on this:

The real effects of flashing then are *expected* to be a restriction of the freedom of women. The legacy of flashing in childhood is anxiety and fear, of strange men of open spaces. In adulthood the message is the same.[12]

General Effects

As well as recording specific localised effects, the women in the study were also asked if the flashing had contributed to more general fears such as fear of open spaces or of going out alone after dark. Thirty per cent of the women said the flashing incidents had not affected them because they did not go out alone after dark, or take solitary walks in the country. Forty per cent of the women who had been flashed at said the flashing added to fears about going out alone. The process appears to be that women have a general wariness about going out alone, due to past experiences, what they have read in newspapers, and so on. Flashing reminds them of this threat and the result is further restrictions on women's movements.

Not every incident of flashing resulted in women feeling unsafe only in *deserted* places. One woman who was flashed at in a crowd reported that it made her afraid of being in crowds. In some cases women did not actually stop going out on their own, but they were still affected:

> It made me much more wary about walking around on my own. I never wanted to admit to being frightened. I was determined to be independent and prove myself as capable as any man and all that sort of thing . . . So I'd still walk home alone at night but I'd have to grit my teeth, force myself not to run.

This last quotation illustrates a connection between accepting a restriction, any restriction, on your freedom and the effect this would have on you seeing youself as in some way inferior.

One general effect of flashing is to undermine women's confidence. The woman quoted above was determined that it was not going to confine her movements but it had still affected her. By way of comparison, here are comments taken from conversations I had with two men during the 'Ripper' scare. They reported that a woman had glanced back at them as they were walking down the road, then hurriedly crossed to the other side: 'Oh she must have been thinking I might be the Ripper'. When it was suggested to them that they might take care NOT to walk closely behind women in the street, the suggestion was met with total outrage: 'I am just on my way home from the pub. I don't want to be constantly worrying about who I am walking behind.' This very minor restriction to their freedom of thought and action was totally unacceptable to them.

Flashing affects women's lives. For some it means a serious restriction on movement or independent social contact. For others, the incident is just one of many reminders of the necessity to be vigilant, switch off a relaxed mood and concentrate on getting home safely. The fact that public places and open spaces are not 'theirs' to be in safely is a lesson women learn at an early age. Should they forget, there are men prepared to remind them. The act of flashing reminds women both of the threat and to whom these public places belong – men.

These restrictions on women's freedom of movement and social participation are no longer acceptable. Shortly after my door-to-door study was done, a flasher was seen in the area. Immediately, spray-painted slogans appeared: 'Flasher do not expose yourself to women's anger'; 'Watch out Flasher about'; 'Flasher beware. We will get you. Angry Women'. The flasher has not been seen since. Perhaps this is what is meant by community policing?

REFERENCE

1. A. M. S. McNeill, *Flashing – It's Effect on Women* (unpublished dissertation, Social Administration Dept., University of York, 1982). A copy is also held by The Feminist Library, Hungerford House, Victoria Embankment, London WC2.
2. See the criticism of victimology in Clark and Lewis (1977). Also the ongoing debate in the American journal, *Victimology*.
3. rhodes and McNeill (eds) (1985).
4. See Radzinowicz (1957) and Rooth (1971).
5. R. P. Snaith, MD is Senior Lecturer in Psychiatry at St James University Hospital, Leeds. These and other quotations are from a lecture he gave at Leeds University in October 1980. Dr Snaith is the psychiatrist to whom flashers are referred in the Leeds area. Quotations are reproduced with permission.
6. See D. Hay, *Crime, Authority and the Criminal Law* (unpublished thesis, University of Warwick, 1975), quoted by D. Philips in V. A. C. Gatrell *et al.* (eds), *Crime and The Law, The Social History of Crime in Western Europe* (London: Europa Publications, 1980).
7. Dr R. von Krafft-Ebing, *Psychopathia Sexualis* (New York: Putnam, 1965). First published Germany 1886.
8. See, for example, West (1976).
9. This became clear during discussion at a meeting at Leeds University following a talk by R. P. Snaith, MD.

10. See, for example, Macdonald (1973).
11. Chapter 11 of the dissertation upon which this chapter is based (not included here), examines the effects of flashing on girl children.
12. See S. Jeffreys, 'Indecent Exposure' in rhodes and McNeill (1985).

8 You Can't Commit Violence Against an Object: Women, Psychiatry and Psychosurgery
Diane Hudson

AUTHOR'S INTRODUCTION

I have worked in the area of mental health for fifteen years. Since 1977, I have been systematically gathering information on leucotomised patients with whom I have come into contact. All the clients mentioned attended a rehabilitation day centre over a ten-year period. Their case reports were read and they were interviewed in order to understand how a leucotomy could affect their lives and functioning, and why such drastic treatment was deemed necessary. The client group was composed of ten women and one man, out of which a sample has been chosen to be considered more fully.

In this chapter it will be argued that psychosurgery as a mode of treatment in psychiatry is directed predominantly at women in order to modify behaviour felt by the women's relatives, husbands, psychiatrists, and often by the women themselves to be undesirable. In the case studies it was seen that some women had experienced physical violence at the hands of men – this included sexual and physical abuse by fathers, rape by strangers and battering by husbands or co-habitees. Little or no attempt was made by the psychiatric professionals to take account of the causative factors in women's lives. A woman's response to the often violent behaviour towards her by the men in her life was interpreted as a psychotic illness by the medical profession. Attempting to avoid confrontation was interpreted as 'apathy and passivity' and diagnosed as depression. Confronting the violence became 'hostility and aggression' and a diagnosis of personality disorder was given.

All the women in the case studies experienced the 'threat of violence', as discussed by Hanmer (1978) which forced them to comply with a code of behaviour felt to be desirable by others. This threat of violence is seen at its clearest in the stance taken by the psychiatric profession towards the women in their care. The threats included long-term psychiatric hospitalisation, electro-convulsive therapy, and, at the extreme end of the spectrum, leucotomy. Running parallel to the threatening environment is the construction by doctors of the women's acceptance of the role of psychiatric patient, which is in turn reinforced by the women's families. When women receive a psychiatric label, their definitions of reality are dismissed as skewed or invalid. This enables the men in their lives, husbands, fathers or psychiatrists, to define reality for them. Controlling the woman's behaviour in this way is possible due to the subliminal fear of violence that all women experience and which confines their behaviour into channels acceptable by men. This can be experienced as unease, a concern to behave properly in case one is laughed at or ridiculed. Fear can be activated by actual violence to the woman, or by her knowledge that violence can occur in particular situations. The triggers of fear or unease may be used by the psychiatrist as he moves through a repertoire of behaviours in relation to his female patients; he will be father, husband or son and each role will evoke a different response from the woman. All women share an inherent awareness of male-defined 'no-go' areas, but women with psychiatric labels are told they are sick, therefore their perceptions are no longer valid. Flitcroft (1978) points out that if a woman returns to the casualty department too frequently with her injuries, her status changes from 'sick' to sickening and she is referred to the psychiatric department. Dismissing the women's perception of reality and labelling her as a disordered personality enables the medics to shape her acceptance of her new psychiatric role, and to offer radical modes of treatment.

LEUCOTOMY: THE FACTS

Leucotomy is an operation on the healthy brain tissue of someone suspected of suffering from a mental disorder in order to change or influence their behaviour. The operations were called lobotomies in 1888, when Dr Gustav Burckhardt performed the first operations on a woman in her fifties, who was diagnosed as suffering from schizophrenia. Dr Antonio Egaz Moniz coined the word 'leucotomy' forty-five years later, when he designed an instrument like a slim apple-corer, which he called a 'leucotome'. Moniz used a neurosurgeon called Dr Almeida Lima, and their first patient was a middle-aged woman diagnosed as an 'agitated-depressive'. Lima bored holes in the woman's skull and injected two cubic centimetres of pure alcohol into the holes produced in the brain by pushing in the leucotome and twisting it, exactly like coring an apple. If an entire frontal lobe of the brain is severed and removed, the operation is known as a 'lobectomy'. Present-day operations use other techniques to destroy brain tissue, such as freezing, introducing hot wires to burn brain tissue, and inserting radioactive 'seeds' which destroy the surrounding matter gradually. The favoured technique is 'free-hand' surgery, whereby a scalpel is inserted into the brain, via a hole bored through the skull, and moved to and fro, severing tissue. This technique was used in over 40 per cent of operations before 1976 (Mitchell-Heggs and Barraclough, 1978).

STATISTICS

Despite the drastic nature of these operations, great difficulty was experienced in obtaining any reliable statistics about them. Through a Parliamentary question the number of operations performed over a twenty-year period was requested, with a breakdown into age, sex, diagnoses and hospitals performing the operations. Three months later Sir George Young informed the House of Commons that the Department of Health and Social Security 'only had realistic figures for 1979 and 1980' and 'held no complete information on diagnoses centrally' (*Hansard*, 6 July 1981). It was known that between 12 000 and 15 000 operations had been performed in the UK from 1942 onwards (Valenstein, 1980; Breggin, 1972), but I could obtain no official statistics to verify this. The picture that was being presented was one of haphazard record-keeping and inefficiency.

A summary was produced of what had been learned so far. After fifty years of psychosurgery in the United Kingdom, the DHSS had no reliable statistics. Tooth and Newton (1961) discovered no consensus among doctors regarding diagnosis, methodology or site of operation. Twenty years later, Mitchell-Heggs and Barraclough (1978) discovered the same lack of consensus, and old-style, free-hand operations still being performed in 40 per cent of cases, despite technological advances:

Surgeons were making 16 different types of lesion in 14 different sites in the brain . . . It is disquieting that the same site in the brain is the target for treating quite different disorders, and different sites are operated upon for similar or identical disorders.   (Gostin and Knight, 1980)

The Brook Hospital is the major UK centre for psychosurgery – fifty out of a total of sixty-two operations were carried out there in 1980 (*Hansard*, 6 July 1981). Dr Bridges, the physician in charge, 'frankly admitted he had no statistical proof that the operation worked. "We do think we know what we are doing within the limits of medicine – and medicine can be very vague sometimes"' (*Guardian*, 3 April, 1981).

During the fifty-year history of psychosurgery in the UK, 'there had never been any monitoring arrangements, guidelines, controls or regulations concerning this treatment' (Gostin and Knight, 1980). Research papers published by physicians involved in psychosurgery have been castigated for 'anecdotal testimonies of dramatic cure, bizarre assessment procedures, unsophisticated and casual methods of follow-up and amateur statistics' (Carroll and O'Callaghan, 1982).

Research of such appalling quality that it did not meet the guidelines laid down for animal research was accepted and published by the British Medical Journal (Clare, 1976, p. 310). Valenstein (1977) reviewed 153 research papers on psychosurgery worldwide, and applied a sliding scale of 1 to 6 for scientific merit. Most of the articles (published between 1971 and 1976) received a rating of 5 or 6. 'A rating of 6 is assigned to those reports that present only a descriptive information . . . it is unlikely that an animal study with a rating of only 4 would be accepted for publication' (Valenstein, 1980, p. 150). For example, one woman suffered 'no or little changes in intellect and discrimination ability': the evidence to scientifically prove this was a sample of her post-operative knitting (Winter, 1972, as quoted in Valenstein, 1980).

Within this morass of information one fact stood out; more women than men had been treated by psychosurgical operations since they began in 1888. In 1947, the UK Board of Control reported that out of 1000 patients, 65 per cent were women. Tooth and Newton (1961) discovered that 60 per cent of leucotomy patients up to 1954 were female. Post-1970, in the USA, Valenstein reported 56 per cent of all operations were on women. In 1981, *Hansard* reported that eighty-eight women and forty-four men, received these operations. The preference for women as patients was sometimes taken to extremes: In 1970, a Canadian hospital refused to allow surgeons to operate upon male patients because of 'the unfavourable publicity given to lobotomies . . . But they were allowed to operate on women, 17 in number' (Breggin, 1972).

An excess of women in mental illness hospitals has led authors to assume that this accounts for the greater number of operations on women (Carroll and O'Callaghan, 1982, p. 261; Valenstein, 1980, p. 101). However, an examination of the DHSS statistics (see Table 8.1) proves illuminating.

Table 8.1   Resident patients by sex and age, 1978–81 (estimated numbers and age)

	Age	Male	Female	Excess
1978	35–64	16 835	13 896	2 939 male
	65+	12 210	27 952	15 742 female
1979	35–64	15 645	13 397	2 248 male
	65+	12 190	27 590	15 400 female
1980	35–64	14 535	12 381	2 154 male
	65+	12 181	27 756	15 575 female
1981	35–64	13 825	11 776	2 049 male
	65+	12 099	27 570	15 471 female

SOURCE: Figures for 1978–79 from In-Patient Statistics in *Mental Health Enquiry for England 1979* (HMSO). Figures for 1980 and 1981 were calculated by taking the numbers in the various age ranges given in the *Mental Health Enquiry for England 1981* (HMSO), and using the 1979 percentages.

The table shows an excess of women over men in mental hospitals in the 65+ age group, but these patients are a small proportion of those operated upon. An examination of the Tooth and Newton report of 1961 (covering the period 1942–54) shows that women aged over 65 received only 3.06 per cent of the total number of operations. We have no reason to believe that the proportions of the elderly receiving operations are any different today.

From 1978–81 there were fewer women than men resident in mental hospitals within the age range 35–64 years, yet this is the age group most likely to receive psychosurgery. If women do not predominate in the mental hospital population in the relevant age group, then the theory that men are as likely to be selected for psychosurgery as women is wrong.

PSYCHIATRY AND WOMEN

Psychiatry is increasingly becoming biologically determinist, particularly with regard to women. Biological determinism locates defects within the individual; these defects can be excised by controlling individuals, leaving their social environment unchanged (Rose, Kamin and Lowentin, 1984). In this context criticism has been levelled at leucotomy being used as the controlling factor, as in the case provided by Knight (1973) and quoted in Clare's discussion of psychosurgery (1976), of a woman married to a sadist. She developed obsessional tidiness and depression and was given a leucotomy. Clare (1976) has suggested that the correct response would have been to operate on the sadistic husband. Sometimes the leucotomy affects only the operatees' attitude to their difficulties: Rose *et al.* (1984) quote the case of a woman who obsessionally tidied her house and was profoundly depressed by this behaviour. She was operated upon yet a short time afterwards she began the compulsive housework again. But there was a difference: '. . . now, instead of being depressed as she cleaned, she was quite cheerful about it' (pp. 190–1).

Psychiatry has its roots in biological–determinist theories, such as craniology, phrenology and notions of IQ, which 'scientifically prove' women's inferior brain capacity (Chorover, 1980; Darwin, McGrigor and Allan, 1869 quoted in Rose *et al.*, 1984). In the twentieth century, it is psychiatry 'which upholds the sexist tenets of women's fundamental defectiveness' (Gray and Leeson, 1978, p. 92). Inge Broverman *et al.* (1970) investigated the stereotypes psychologists use to define a mature, socially competent, healthy woman. The results were that therapists rated a healthy woman as passive, more emotional, less independent and more excitable than men. They then asked for a description of a healthy, mature, socially competent adult; no gender was specified. The resulting description was identical to the traits given as those of a healthy mature male – independent, unemotional and active rather than passive. Feminine qualities were seen as inherently mentally unhealthy (Nairne and Smith, 1984). This led Goldberg and Huxley (1980) to observe: 'A middle-aged woman whose marriage had broken up would be more likely to have her disturbance detected than a young professional man, even if they had the same number of symptoms.' Barrett and Roberts (1976) point out that middle age in women is seen by doctors as a psychological problem.

Another explanation for the female preponderance in leucotomy operations is differential diagnosis (Valenstein, 1980, p. 102; Carroll and O'Callaghan, 1982, p. 93). But diagnostic trends have changed dramatically since the advent of psychosurgery. Women were overwhelmingly diagnosed as schizophrenic in the years 1942–54 (Tooth and Newton, 1961, p. 5 Table II). Twenty years later, 85 per cent of the diagnostic categories resulting in leucotomies were depression, anxiety states and obsessional disorders (Mitchell-Heggs and Barraclough, 1978, p. 1592). This allowed one researcher to state: 'If there is an over-representation of women subjected to psychosurgery . . . it might simply be because affective disorders are over-represented in that sex' (Flor-Henry, 1981, p. 311). The discrediting of leucotomy as an effective treatment for schizophrenia (Staudt and Zubin, 1957 quoted in Carroll and O'Callaghan, 1982), may have led to: '. . . a deliberate shift in psychiatric disorders deemed appropriate for psychosurgery' (Carroll and O'Callaghan, 1982).

THE CASE STUDIES

The sample of clients in this study comprised ten women and one man. Each was identified by a letter of the alphabet. Seven of the women had received leucotomies, as had the man. Of the remaining three women, one took part because of the problems with her leucotomised husband, one received electro-convulsive therapy instead, and the last killed herself after a leucotomy had been discussed with her. Apart from two of the women, one diagnosed as mentally handicapped and the other as schizophrenic, all the other diagnoses were of depression. The man had been operated upon in the 1950s for schizophrenia, in the 'heyday' of psychosurgery. He had been an engineer prior to surgery, but post-operatively he was unable to feed or wet-shave himself. He remained in hospital for twenty years following the operation, unable to converse when asked to talk about a particular topic or in a particular order, and he talked mainly rubbish. He was the only leucotomised man ever to have been referred to the rehabilitation centre in fourteen years.

Descriptions of the causative factors in depression read like role definitions for the leucotomised women in the centre: 'Learned helplessness' (Seligman, 1975), manipulative behaviour (Forest and Hokanson, 1975) and an inability to arouse sympathy without also arousing aversion (Freden, 1982).

'Women are assigned a fixed position geared to other people' (Freden, 1982)

Four women had been assigned this 'fixed position' geared towards their husbands and families, and the sole meaning in their lives stemmed from their husbands. When, due to the violence or unfaithfulness of the husbands, the meaning in their lives was destroyed, they became depressed (Bart, 1974; Freden, 1982).

For example, following the birth of her daughter, A became convinced that her husband was having an affair. She became 'obsessed' with her daughter, not allowing her out of her sight. After a suicide attempt, A was persuaded by her husband to accept the leucotomy being offered for the depressive and obsessional behaviour, in order to save their marriage. Whilst A was in hospital recovering from the operation, the husband filed for divorce and moved A's closest friend into the marital home. A was given access to the daughter by the court but, when A visited, she wasn't allowed into the house. The presents she bought her daughter were returned and, when A's husband informed her he was moving several hundred miles away, A killed herself.

Various authors have pointed out that women are expected to be passive and dependent on men, while also acknowledging that this is not conducive to mental health (Broverman *et al.*, 1970; Fabrikant, 1974; Neulinger *et al.*, 1970). C was diagnosed as 'reluctant to accept authority' when she found it difficult to relate to a male psychiatrist after disclosing involvement in a long-term stable lesbian relationship. Her lesbianism was interpreted as a personality disorder for which she received drugs and ECT. She was diagnosed as 'hostile and aggressive' towards the stepfather who sexually assaulted her when she was thirteen, and was dead from an overdose at twenty-seven, when warned that, unless she conformed, she would become a long-term hospital patient. She confided, just before she died, that a 'brain operation' to help her had been discussed. She perceived this as a threat rather than as a mode of treatment and the fear instilled by this threat probably contributed greatly to her suicide.

'Lobotomised women make the best housekeepers' (Freeman, quoted in Shutts, 1982)

Four women were diagnosed as depressed due to their inability to make normal relationships with men. Of the four, two were married. D had been subjected to years of mental cruelty by a husband variously described as 'abnormal' and a 'rigid personality'. E was physically beaten for years by her husband, sustaining many broken bones. Both women received leucotomies to enable them to continue within the confines of their marriages. This course of action is advocated by Sargant and Slater (1972):

> A depressed woman, for instance, may owe her illness to a psychopathic husband who cannot change and who will not accept treatment . . . [women] patients of this type are often helped by anti-depressant drugs. But in the occasional case where they do not work, we have seen patients enabled by a leucotomy to return to the difficult environment and cope with it.

The two unmarried women, F and G, were both sexually assaulted when children, F by her father, and G by strangers. Both women were offered leucotomies by their male social workers to alleviate their 'abnormal distrust of men'. F had reported the rapes by her father, but because the social worker felt that the father's behaviour was 'somewhat excused' due to F's resemblance to her dead mother, no action was taken. F refused the leucotomy, but accepted ECT for the depression caused by her inability to effect any change in her life.

G had witnessed her father beating her mother constantly, and was sexually assaulted twice as a child. Her distrust of men led to allegations of lesbianism from her family, and after a suicide attempt, she accepted the offer of a leucotomy. She was twenty-three years old. The violence in this woman's life was ignored prior to the operation. Her early experience of male violence and sexual molestation left her with a deep distrust of men, and she refused to take part in 'normal' heterosexual relationships. She perceived these as being little different from being attacked. Her refusal to join the dominant culture was seen as the problem, rather than acknowledging that there was anything amiss with the male world around her. Her lack of response to her male social worker was construed by him as further evidence of a psychiatric illness, rather than as a response to his maleness.

FINDINGS

'Depressive symptomatology, particularly in women, is much improved by leucotomy, irrespective of precise target' (Flor-Henry, 1981)
Depression is linked to a lack of control over one's life, and a parallel lessening of self-esteem. All of the seven women operated upon for depression were still depressed post-operatively. There was no

attempt by the professionals to change the women's circumstances. The violent husbands were still in the home to which the women returned and no marital counselling was considered. As a result, all the women felt they were defined as abnormal, and that was why they received treatment. A realisation that nothing had changed, despite undergoing major surgery, deepened their depression. Most responded with passive withdrawal, but one woman had six post-operative admissions to hospital with 'agitated depression'.

'. . . having a leucotomy does not mean that the original symptoms will not return' (psychiatrist's letter, case notes)
The original symptoms not only returned post-operatively in all the women interviewed but they were overlaid with new problems. Two women developed temporal lobe epilepsy, a common side-effect (Shutts, 1982), four made suicide attempts and one actually killed herself. Five women became grossly overweight due to the 'orality' reported as a side effect of some operations (Valenstein, 1980). All reported some loss of memory, and all described the frustration they felt at the lack of recognition of their sacrifice in having the operation. One woman became aggressive, but turned the aggression on herself. She expressed a sense of worthlessness by overdosing, allowing her teeth to decay and refusing to take medication for her asthma. She was eventually admitted to hospital as a long-term patient when thirty years old.

'I was in such a state I would have consented if they'd wanted to cut off my head' (Mind Out, 1980, No. 41)
The majority of women interviewed alleged that they were not warned about possible side-effects from the operations, but despite this, most said they would not have been worried. The opportunity to alleviate their depression overrode all other considerations. It is this aspect which makes it difficult to assess whether patients understood the implications of the surgery offered when they consented to it. The Mental Health Act, 1983 includes the 'safeguard' of informed consent, but, as Gostin has pointed out, informed consent presumes that the patient is given information by doctors that (s)he can understand. Even when careful explanations are given as at the Brook Hospital where the majority of operations are performed, most patients 'admitted they hadn't understood the explanations given before their operations' (Gostin and Knight, 1980). The assumption is made that the quality of the doctor/patient relationship will result in the

information necessary for informed consent. But, as one patient who allowed her operation to be televised said:

> Nobody in their right mind would have taken a gamble like that. But I wasn't in my right mind. I'd been on sedatives for months; I was used to doing what the doctors told me; I would have signed my own death warrant.   (Margaret Chapman, 1980)

The 'thank-you syndrome' is evident in the concept of informed consent. The 'thank-you syndrome' allows the doctor to presume he knows best, and the patient will say 'thank-you' at the end:

'If I were desperately depressed, I would want the doctor to decide for me . . . even if I didn't understand the implications' (Dr Bartlett, neurosurgeon, 1980)

AUTHOR'S CONCLUSION

As a practitioner, I started out by believing that leucotomies were a last resort treatment for aggression and given predominantly to men. I also believed that the operations ceased in the late 1950s. During my research into psychosurgery, I discovered that none of these beliefs are true.

After relatively short periods of medication or ECT, twice as many women as men receive leucotomies. In the 1950s to 1960s, diagnoses were deliberately changed in order that new treatments could be tried. (Hare, 1974). The operations are continuing (admittedly to a lesser extent), but twice as many women as men continue to receive psychosurgery. As this is not due to the excess of women in psychiatric hospitals, I am left with an inescapable conclusion: women are being preferentially selected by psychiatrists for psychosurgical operations, the reasons for which I have tried to illustrate.

Psychiatry reflects a societal confusion of the physical brain with the abstract concept of 'mind'. Psychiatrists are known as the 'doctors of the mind', and are trained as doctors first and foremost. Even though it is recognised that psychiatric training often produces a 'trained incapacity' to distinguish between normal and deviant (Offer and Sabshin, 1975), psychiatry has traditionally elected to champion the status quo, to be the arbiter between normal and deviant. This is seen at its clearest in relation to women. The 'norm' is the male projection of the female role and any other presentation will at best be tolerated and at worst treated as deviant.

'Force and its threat is used to maintain power differences over many oppressed and exploited groups . . .' (Hanmer and Saunders, 1984)
The ten female cases cited above have in common some form of physical, sexual or psychological abuse by men. This exercise of individual power, reinforcing the idea that establishes the normality of the abuse of women by men is further reinforced by psychiatry, which reflects social, cultural and political biases. Many men are violent, but not all women respond with depression, therefore the problem lies with the individual woman's abnormal response and not with the behaviour of the men around her. There is an aspect of coercive, institutionalised violence inherent in psychiatry. The woman is labelled sick and treatment is offered, but if she refuses this help, she may be returned to a physically violent home as untreatable, or her behaviour may be interpreted as stemming from an intractable psychosis and leucotomy may be advocated.

Returning to Hanmer's (1978) discussion of violence as the use of force and its threat to mould women's behaviour, the case studies show that this is the reason why the women acquiesced to a psychiatric assault upon their brains. They had all experienced the use of force at the hands of men prior to their admission to hospital, and understood that the power of men could be reinforced at any time.

Acknowledgement
An important acknowledgement is due to all the women patients who have undergone experimental surgery in the guise of medical science, and in particular to the women whose case histories were discussed in this chapter.

9 Typical Violence, Normal Precaution: Men, Women and Interpersonal Violence in England, Wales, Scotland and the USA

Elizabeth A. Stanko

Victimisation surveys note that individuals commonly fail to report criminal incidents to the police. Only about one-third of all serious crime is reported to the police in the United States and England, Wales and Scotland (Bureau of Justice Statistics, 1983; Chambers and Tombs, 1984; Hough and Mayhew, 1983 and 1985). Researchers have noted that failure to report crime involves assessments of individuals about how 'private' they feel the dispute is; the fear of reprisal for reporting the matter to police; the feeling that the police would not think the matter serious; that, even if reported, nothing could be done to resolve the matter; or that despite its statutory seriousness, the matter was not important enough to report to the police (Bureau of Justice Statistics, 1983; Hough and Mayhew, 1983 and 1985; Chambers and Tombs, 1984). As such, reporting of serious criminal events to the criminal justice system also reflects the confidence of individuals in the authority of the police to resolve disputes involving criminal matters.

At the same time as citizens' reporting of crime remains low, fear about criminal victimisation remains high. This fear about criminal victimisation, researchers suggest, focuses around issues of personal safety, particularly safety from various forms of violent personal criminal behaviour – robbery, assault or rape (Hindelang et al., 1978; Maxfield, 1984a; Skogan and Maxfield, 1981). Furthermore, criminologists speculate that this fear for one's personal safety is centred around concern about violent crime, generally associated with outside, street crime – the type of crime the police are supposedly more responsible for preventing (Rubenstein, 1973).

It is this concern about the fear of crime which has become a target for policy-makers in both the US and Great Britain (Hanmer and Stanko, 1985). In the US, for example, 45 per cent of respondents expressed concern about being alone at night on foot in their own neighbourhoods (Hindelang *et al.*, 1978). Respondents to recent crime surveys in Scotland, England and Wales also expressed concern about personal safety outside their own home and within their own neighbourhood (Hough and Mayhew, 1983 and 1985; Chambers and Tombs, 1984; Maxfield, 1984a). This fear undermines the confidence of individuals in the police as protectors and sustainers of an orderly society. As governmental officials and law makers focus on the danger violent crime poses to a 'free' society, combating fear of crime among citizens becomes an important area for concern.

Police, government policy-makers and citizens alike conceptualise fear of crime as associated with individual citizens' concern about being outside, alone and potentially vulnerable to personal and harmful confrontation from criminal violence. As such, fear of crime affects the lives of both women and men: it is characterised as a feeling involving a diffuse sense of anxiety or unsafeness when one is alone, particularly when one is alone and walking on the street after dark, and which may affect a person's lifestyle choices and mobility.

The purpose of this chapter is to explore the role that gender – a significant variable within a gender-stratified society – plays in our understanding of criminal victimisation, men's and women's fear about it and the implications of this fear for understanding male violence to women – one process of the social control of women in a male-dominated society. While researchers acknowledge that violence among the familiar and familial – 'inside' crime – is under-reported in government sponsored victimisation surveys, they focus their analysis of the findings on 'outside' crime and fear among citizens about the violence of strangers. This focus has additional significance for understanding how criminal violence and fear about it affects men's and women's lives. Women's fear of criminal violence is reported in officially-sponsored victimisation surveys, but, as will be discussed later, not their experiences of violence. It is the growing body of knowledge about male violence, largely collected by feminist researchers, which shows that women's experiences of criminal violence continues to remain hidden (Hanmer and Saunders, 1984;

Russell, 1982 and 1984; Stanko, 1985). This chapter puts forward the argument that contemporary discussions about fear of crime omit many of women's experiences of criminal violence and distort our understanding of the importance of male violence within women's everyday lives.

FEAR AND RISK OF VICTIMISATION

Who, according to national crime surveys, is most likely to be victimised by interpersonal, violent crime? When government-funded crime surveys assess risk, men, not women, have a greater likelihood of being victimised by interpersonal forms of violence. Compounding the risk are the variables of age, race, income, residence and marital status. Young, single, black, Hispanic or Asian poor men who live in urban areas have the highest likelihood of being victims of interpersonal violence and have the greatest probability of sustaining injury as a consequence of that victimisation. Hindelang *et al.* (1978), Skogan and Maxfield (1981), Hough and Mayhew (1983), Gottfredson (1984) and Widom and Maxfield (1984) suggest that this population is typically victimised by individuals with similar demographic characteristics. Exposure to victimisation, these authors further suggest, varies according to the lifestyle of the victim (Hindelang *et al.*, 1978, p. 122).

Criminal violence, largely robbery and assault, is one part of male-to-male interaction, particularly for young males who are single, spend several evenings out a week and engage in social drinking (Maxfield, 1984a; Gottfredson, 1984). Male violence to men, at least as the results of crime survey data in the US and Great Britain indicate, takes on the appearance of 'exchanged' blows rather than predatory crime. Moreover, predatory crime, not exchanged blows, is most commonly associated with 'fear producing' situations (Maxfield, 1984a). While men are more likely to be robbed by strangers and assaulted by non-strangers, young men's lifestyles – socialising activities, bravado and greater mobility outside the home – seem to affect their risk of victimisation.

In contrast to men's higher risk of criminal victimisation, young and middle-aged men report feeling reasonably safe or very safe on the streets alone after dark. While fear increases with age and area of residence (Maxfield, 1984b), overall, men's reported fear is much lower than women's. Men's reported fear of personal victimisation is approximately one-third that of women's (Hindelang, *et al.*, 1978; Skogan and Maxfield, 1981; Hough and Mayhew, 1983; Maxfield, 1984a; Chambers and Tombs, 1984). So while men of all ages appear to be at greater risk of criminal victimisation than women, on the whole they report feeling safer than women. 'Young males are at risk,' states Maxfield, 'but their lower fear may be the product of either reckless disregard for their own well-being (not unknown among the young), or a self-assured confidence that neighbourhood streets hold no dangers for them' (Maxfield, 1984a, p. 13).

On the other hand, women, as a gender class, constitute a 'low risk' population with respect to interpersonal violence, at least according to the results of government-sponsored victimisation surveys. Just as with men, the risk of victimisation varies with age, income, race, residence and marital status. The demographic characteristics of women's assailants are generally similar with one major exception: women are not the targets of other women, but the targets of male assailants who may also sexually victimise them. In their analysis of the 1982 British Crime Survey data for England and Wales, Widom and Maxfield (1984) found that one in four of women's assailants were other women, and approximately one in three assaulted women were assaulted by female assailants (p. 14). The majority of women's assailants, however, on both sides of the Atlantic, are men.

Criminal violence for women takes on elements of sexual violence and, according to victimisation surveys, women's assailants are as likely to be strangers as people known to them. Rape as a crime of violence primarily affects women and women's consciousness (Gordon *et al.*, 1980; Griffin, 1971; Beneke, 1982; Russell, 1973, 1982 and 1984; Brownmiller, 1975; Stanko, 1985). So too, rape is often the action of acquaintances, lovers, relatives, husbands or friends – men known to the raped woman. And while women are less likely to be robbed or assaulted than men, when women *are* assaulted, they are as likely to be assaulted by acquaintances or relatives as by strangers. While researchers do acknowledge that data on interpersonal violence between acquaintances or relatives tends to be under-reported by respondents, what *is* reported shows, in fact, that two-thirds of all assaults on divorced or separated women were committed by acquaintances and relatives; half of all assaults on never-married women and 40 per cent of assaults on married women were committed by relatives or acquaintances. If one were to look solely at spouse or ex-spouse assault committed in the US, 95 per cent of those assaults were committed by men on women (Bureau of Justice Statistics, 1983,

p. 21). While women's assailants, as reported by official sources, include many men who are known to them, stereotypical images about criminal violence remains focused on violence occurring outside, on the street and typically from strangers.

In contrast to the 'low risk' of women to recorded criminal victimisation, women's fear of criminal victimisation – a fear which has been examined in terms of their feelings of safety while walking alone at night in their neighbourhoods – is significantly higher than men's. As noted earlier, one complicating factor for women is that interpersonal violence is commonly violence from known male assailants, creating, perhaps, a fear of known (and presumably safe) environments as well as a fear of violence in familiar (but presumably unsafe) environments – their own neighbourhoods. As with men, women's fear varies according to age, race, residence, income and marital status. Yet women's fear crosses the boundaries of all these variables. Despite their reported low level of risk of victimisation, young and old, women constitute the group most fearful of crime in the US, England, Wales and Scotland. Overall, the most significant predictor in understanding fear of crime is being female (Balkin, 1979; Hindelang *et al.*, 1978; Dubow *et al.*, 1979; Riger and Gordon, 1981; Maxfield, 1984a and 1984b).

Explanations of the gap between men's and women's reported fear of crime focus on issues related to gender experience and gender role expectations (Balkin, 1979; Clemente and Kleiman, 1977; Bowker, 1981; Riger and Gordon, 1981; Riger *et al.*, 1978; Hindelang *et al.*, 1978; Lewis and Maxfield, 1980; Maxfield, 1984a; Skogan and Maxfield, 1981). Similarly, researchers continue to speculate about the differing levels of men's and women's fear of crime. Men's fear of crime, as every researcher examining victimisation and fear recognises, does not seem to match their risk of, and experiences of, reported criminal victimisation. Since men are at greater risk, should they not also be the most fearful? Why do men, the more common recipients of reported interpersonal violence, not report being wary of dark streets at night, or of having feelings of insecurity? Is it simply a case of cognitive dissonance? Is it, as some researchers have speculated, that men are simply reluctant to report fear (Clemente and Kleiman, 1977) – a speculation squarely located in one gender expectation: men's bravado?

Perhaps men, as a gender, feel less vulnerable to interpersonal violence and more physically secure than their female counterparts. There is, however, one exception. Residing in 'high crime' neighbourhoods, Maxfield (1984b) has recently noted, may affect even young men's feelings of fear. In areas where 'crime problems are regular features of the neighbourhood environment, measures of physical vulnerability are less important in predicting differences in fear among individuals' (Maxfield, 1984b, p. 233). For young men, characteristically the least fearful group, living in 'high crime' areas may reduce their feelings of immunity from criminal victimisation.

Even in high crime areas, however, men's fear of crime remains low in comparison to women's fear. As speculated earlier, what men report as instances of interpersonal violence is related to their lifestyles. Men who wish to avoid certain forms of assault – pub fights, for example – might simply avoid violence-prone drinking spots (Gottfredson, 1984). So, too, men who wish to avoid sites of victimisation – particularly if they live in 'safe' neighbourhoods, can do so by avoiding 'dangerous' places. But to what extent is crime avoidance part of men's everyday context? It may be for those living in a 'high crime' area because other factors reflecting social and economic disadvantage might mitigate against being able to avoid victimisation. Is fear, however, a part of advantaged men's lives?

In order to advance our understanding of interpersonal violence and fear of crime, the issue of men's fear and victimisation needs to be explored through the question of 'maleness' rather than the current taken for granted-gender-neutral approach to criminal victimisation. As mentioned earlier young, minority, poor men who live in urban areas have the highest rates of interpersonal victimisation; they also share demographic characteristics with those who are most likely to victimise others. Yet many questions about male interpersonal violence still remain. The dynamics of male-to-male interpersonal violence may differ from male-to-female interpersonal violence, and for that matter, female-to-female and female-to-male interpersonal violence. To what extent is male-to-male victimisation a result of male predatory behaviour; a result of male fighting; the failure of male compromise; or a solution for men's disagreements? Might the fear-producing consequences of that victimisation differ from the way men define their victimisation? These and other questions remain as speculation in current research knowledge about men's fear of crime.

In explaining women's fear of crime. Skogan and Maxfield (1981) suggest that the fear that women and the elderly feel is a perception of their social and physical vulnerability. To Skogan and Maxfield (1981), physical vulnerability concerns 'openness to attack, powerlessness to resist, and exposure to significant physical and emotional consequences if attacked'; social vulnerability involves 'daily exposure to the threat of victimization and limited means for coping with the medical and economic consequences of victimization' (pp. 77–8). Fear of criminal victimisation, then, may be a logical assessment of women's and the elderly's ability to physically defend themselves in the face of (most commonly) male assailants, and when women and the elderly are victimised, they are more frightened as a consequence (Skogan and Maxfield, 1981, p. 78).

It was Griffin (1971) who linked this 'powerlessness' and 'daily exposure' to one significant reality of women's lives: the fear of rape. As such, for women, fear is the invisible barrier which surrounds them in all aspects of their everyday lives. The work of Riger, Gordon, LeBailly and Heath (and various combinations thereof) attributes women's fear of crime to their fear of rape (Riger and Gordon, 1981; Riger *et al.*, 1978; Gordon *et al.*, 1980; see also Hough and Mayhew, 1985). The authors note that women's fear is proportionate to their subjective estimates of the risk of rape (Riger and Gordon, 1981, p. 86). Estimates of risk do affect women's everyday strategies to protect themselves from possible confrontation with potentially violent men. Women's assessments of risk include their perception of risk, linked with their perceptions of physical competence and the degree of what Riger and Gordon term as 'women's attachments to their communities'.

According to Riger and Gordon (1981), women's strategies for avoiding victimisation involve both social isolation – not going out at night because they are concerned about safety – and adopting 'street savvy' – the variety of precautionary strategies many women already adopt when they are out alone at night. Two out of five women respondents in Riger and Gordon's study indicated that they used isolation tactics, while three out of four reported frequently using a variety of precautionary strategies. Moreover, the use of these strategies will vary depending on how safe women feel their daily context to be. Heath (1984) notes that the media contributes to women's everyday context of safety. The media's role in disseminating information about murder and sexual assault can effect women's fear of crime, particularly in situations where there may be acute danger. During the 'Yorkshire Ripper's' reign of terror in the North of England, for example, women stepped up their use of both types of protective tactic. In Dallas, Texas, in the spring of 1985, where five women were murdered within a six-month period, women were flocking to self-defence courses and many were reported to be buying handguns for protection. Fear, elicited by the all-too-common serial killers of women, immediately translates into everyday lifestyles where women alter shopping, travel and social habits.

Throughout the work of Riger *et al.*, however, is the undercurrent that fear of rape is still a subjective risk, a perception, not an assessment of real risk or real experience. While they do query the available objective data on rape victimisation (Riger and Gordon, 1981, p. 76), Riger *et al.* found that only 11 per cent of their 367 respondents (which included sixty-eight men) reported rape and sexual assault. Reported experiences of victimisation, then, still do not match the levels of fear reported by women. But we know that women do not always report experiences of rape and sexual assault, even to researchers (Russell 1973, 1982 and 1984; Clark and Lewis, 1977; Hanmer and Saunders, 1984).

Rather than informing us about officially recorded levels of risk of victimisation and fear of crime, women's fear of crime may alert us to the unrecorded instances of threatening and violent behaviour by males and thus give us far more information about the structure of gender and violence in a gender-stratified society. If women commonly encounter threatening and/or violent behaviour from men who are strangers *and* from men known to them, how can they predict which man will be violent to them and in what instance? Moreover, disarmed by friendship or kinship, women's ability to protect themselves against familiar and familial interpersonal male violence is reduced. One study, for example, of women who were raped and those who avoided a rape indicates that women were more likely to avoid rape when the rapist was a stranger! (Bart and O'Brien, 1984).

The gap between women's fear of crime and the objective, official estimates of women's experiences of interpersonal violence is not an anomaly for feminists working in the area of violence to women. Even casual analysis of official data on interpersonal violence underscores what women working in rape crisis centres and refuges for battered women have heard so often: physical and sexual violence are common experiences of many women. Russell's study of 930 women in San Francisco, California, for example, found that there is a 26 per cent probability that a woman will be the victim of a completed rape at some time in her life (Russell and Howell, 1983, pp. 690–1) and that there is a 46 per cent probability that a woman will experience a completed or attempted rape in her lifetime (p. 692). She further found that 50 per cent of the women who had been attacked at least once had experienced attack from different assailants. Russell's data further shows that women's subjective estimate of their risk of rape may indeed be an objective risk, not a perception of risk.

British researchers, Hanmer and Saunders (1984), provide us with further clues as to women's experiences of threatening and violent male behaviour. Interviewing 129 women in a door-to-door survey, Hanmer and Saunders used a format similar to that of victimisation surveys, except that they asked women to describe situations of 'violence' which they had experienced, witnessed or overheard involving women in the past year. Fifty-nine per cent of these women reported at least one instance of male violence they had either experienced themselves, had witnessed or had overheard.[1] What threatened women most was the inability to predict the outcome of a disturbing event. A 'flasher' intimidated and threatened women because of the fear of potential violence, as did men who followed women down a street.[2] Moreover, instances of sexual harassment – 'cat calls' while walking on the street – also created feelings of insecurity. So, in addition to the probability of rape in women's lives, the probability of being sexually harassed while walking on the street or while at work is extremely high (MacKinnon 1979; Stanko 1985). These daily, commonly taken-for-granted experiences of women contribute to the hostile and intimidating atmosphere wherein women are presumably supposed to feel safe.

While women's fear remains an anomaly of perception for criminologists and policy-makers, understanding women's fear of crime – which might also be read as *women's fear of men* – entails understanding the ever-present reality of women's experiences of men's threatening and/or violent behaviour. Could not women's fear of crime be, in many ways, a recognition that women feel unsafe by virtue of their femaleness, to men by virtue of their maleness? If so, do women then expend greater time and energy making themselves feel safer? The fact that women's assailants are characteristically male, and frequently known to the women, is another factor aiding our understanding of interpersonal violence of men to women. Can women feel safe around strangers when those familiar to them have already harmed them? Russell's (1982) survey, for example, indicates that women currently in violent relationships are more afraid of sexual assault outside the home (p. 221) and thus fear the unknown more than the known violence. Another key factor for women is knowing whether outside agencies will intervene in situations of male violence: women commonly predict that those in decision-making positions in the criminal justice system will consider the victimisation event itself to be a non-criminal matter (Hanmer and Saunders, 1984; Stanko, 1985; Hanmer and Stanko, 1985; US Attorney General's Task Force on Family Violence, 1984). *In effect, women's feelings of fear may relate to their tacit understanding of the likelihood of experiencing male violence and the lack of protection they receive from those around them, and in particular, from those in positions of authority to protect them from abusive situations.*

PRECAUTION AND FEAR

Another way of examining the differences in men's and women's perceptions of personal safety and fear of crime is to explore the use of precautionary strategies used by individuals to increase the feeling of security. Precautionary strategies are, for women and men, mechanisms for coping with feelings of insecurity. Researchers note that in addition to the cognitive effects of fear of crime, behavioural changes might also occur for individuals afraid of victimisation (Riger and Gordon, 1981; Tyler, 1980). Assessments of personal vulnerability to criminal victimisation, Tyler (1980) found, are strongly related to crime-prevention behaviour. Precautionary strategies of individuals who fear crime, for example, might include the installation of additional locks on their property; the avoidance of certain 'high crime' areas; the 'insurance' of a companion when leaving or returning to one's home; the carrying of keys between one's hands; the self-assured walk on the outside of the pavement and the avoidance of poorly-lit spots on the street; the purchase of a watch dog, and so forth.

With respect to perceptions of personal vulnerability, Perloff (1983) notes that individuals who have been victimised tend to perceive themselves as more vulnerable than before. How victimised individuals cope with victimisation, she suggests, relates to whether they 'feel "uniquely vulnerable" (more vulnerable than others) or "universally vulnerable" (equally vulnerable as others)' (p. 41).

Do feelings of unique vulnerability and universal vulnerability vary by gender? If we read the use of precautionary strategies as one indication of universal vulnerability, most of the research indicates that women feel more universally vulnerable than men. While, on the whole, individuals who have experienced some form of victimisation have a greater tendency to change their behaviour to avoid future victimisation, many victimised men do not seem automatically to alter their behaviour to protect their *physical* safety. Preliminary evidence from this ongoing research indicates that men are more likely than women to take additional measures to protect their material possessions – their cars or their belongings – rather than their persons, even if they themselves had been physically threatened or assaulted. Moreover, physical competence and confidence seem to influence male respondents' feelings of safety. Be it bravado or be it an accurate assessment, the male respondents feel that in general they can physically match any single assailant. If the male respondents did express concern for their physical safety, they reported being wary of groups of assailants – situations where they would be physically outnumbered. Riger and Gordon (1981) have also found that men's perceived immunity to victimisation is reflected in the minimal use of precautionary strategies to avoid victimisation.

Precaution, particularly for women in structurally more vulnerable situations, may be the only way to approach living in a world which is potentially, and actually, dangerous for women. Goldstein (1984), for example, in an examination of violence within drug addicted women's worlds, notes that most women addicts in his study reported at least one experience of attempted rape or robbery that took place when they were buying drugs. As a precautionary strategy, women either employed other drug users to buy their drugs or teamed up with a male friend for protection when buying drugs (p. 13). While not all women live in such dangerous surroundings, some evidence exists that women who adopt non-traditional ('unprotected') lifestyles are more likely to be victimised than women living in traditional ('protected') lifestyles (Widom and Maxfield, 1984).

Another common strategy for women – particularly those following more traditional lifestyles – is to use 'safe' men for protection from other men. This strategy is not always successful. Firstly, it is not always possible to distinguish 'safe' from 'unsafe' men. If, however, women do find 'safe' men, it is virtually impossible for them to be protected twenty-four hours a day. And from the experience of women in supportive, loving relationships with 'safe' men who have encountered violence from male strangers, we know that these women must take time to sort out 'safe' male behaviour from that which was harmful. 'Like other victims,' states one women. 'I had problems with sex, after the rape. There was no way that Arthur could touch me that it didn't remind me of having been raped by this guy I never saw' (MacKinnon, 1983, p. 646, note 23).

It is the social context of womanness that continually reminds women of their universal vulnerability. And as additional information about sexual and/or physical abuse comes to light, we know that womanness also is likely to involve the experience of sc•ne form of male threatening and/or violent behaviour in a woman's lifetime. No doubt, for women, one typical result of an experience of victimisation is the adoption of precautionary strategies aimed at avoiding future victimisation. Whether it be sexual assault (Burgess and Holmstrom, 1974; Janoff-Bulman, 1979; Russell, 1982; Scheppele and Bart, 1983; Bart and O'Brien, 1984), physical assault (Hilberman and Munson, 1978; Walker, 1978), or sexual harassment (MacKinnon 1979; Farley 1978; Stanko 1985), women adopt precautionary strategies as a way of living in a male-dominated world.

Women and men adopt precautionary strategies very differently – regardless of whether they have been victimised or not (Riger and Gordon, 1981). Few men – if any – turn to women for protection against women, or men. It seems that women – more so than men – continually monitor the threat of danger around them from men (particularly strangers) – regardless of age, class or race. Women must observe men for potential danger, a price of subordination (Goode, 1982). As one way of explaining the continual use of self-protective strategies for women, Beneke (1982) suggests the following exercise for men:

> Walk down a city street. Pay a lot of attention to your clothing; make sure your pants are zipped, shirt tucked in, buttons done. Look straight ahead. Every time a man walks past you, avert your eyes and make your face expressionless.

It is the connection between the use of precautionary strategies, gender and social control that is most useful in understanding the dynamics of 'fear of crime' and criminal victimisation. Why do women, more so than men, exercise elaborate precautionary strategies to avoid interpersonal violence in their everyday lives? Are they merely exaggerating risk or have they, as some have speculated, successfully avoided victimisation because of their precautionary strategies (Balkin, 1979)? Are women, as others speculate, 'overly afraid' (Dubow, 1979)? Is their fear a rational assessment of risk (Hough and Mayhew, 1983)? Or does the gap in women's and men's reported fear arise because of gender expectations: women are more willing to admit to being afraid (Clemente and Kleiman, 1977)? Many unanswered questions remain, but it is possible to begin to frame them within an understanding of gender and gender stratification. While we continue to ask why women, who reportedly occupy a position of low risk to interpersonal violence (Skogan and Maxfield, 1981), fear dark streets and feel unsafe alone at night on the street, perhaps we should direct our inquiry to the reality of 'risk' and the long-term consequences of learning what it means to be universally vulnerable, a subordinate, in a male-dominated society.

REFERENCES

1. See also, Jill Radford, 'Policing Male Violence – Policing Women', Chapter 3 in this volume.
2. See also, Sandra McNeill, 'Flashing: Its Effects on Women', Chapter 8 in this volume.

10 Legalising Woman Abuse

Lorraine Radford

LAW AND SECONDARY ASSAULT

Man's violence against women has only recently been reborn as a concern worthy of academic debate or public recognition. Although the problem has an extensive history, pressures for change did not gain much significance until the second wave of feminism was awarded some repute a mere fifteen years or so ago (Dobash and Dobash, 1979; Schecter, 1982). Although we have begun to uncover the extent of physical and sexual abuse, to estimate incidences and assess the adequacy of remedies, there is still much work to be done, particularly in the area of the law.

Technically, the law no longer excludes women victims from its sphere of influence. Yet the traditional struggle to gain women's rights offers no guarantee that the problem giving rise to legal need will be solved by the mere creation of an Act of Parliament. In recent years, new Acts of Parliament (such as the Domestic Violence and Matrimonial Proceedings Act, 1976 and the Domestic Proceedings and Magistrates Court Act, 1980) have been implemented specifically endorsing legal recognition of the problem of assaults between spouses or cohabitees. Although the legislation on domestic violence improved the formal legal rights of women in violent situations, the actual improvement of their position is far from impressive (McCann, 1985). The law may assign individuals rights or remedies yet these are of little use if both the courts and police fail to enforce them. Winning a legal case is of small benefit to a victim if the offender is not prevented from continuing the assaults: a woman may 'win' a case in court under one of these Acts but her actual gain may be little more than symbolic. Powers formally won in law can soon be whittled down in practice to a level of minimum significance.

Rape, incest, sexual harassment and battery remain in many quarters of society 'problems denied'. It is almost routine for women in refuges to complain that their experiences of victimisation have been trivialised, ordained unimportant or turned back on themselves by 'helping' agencies. This refusal to recognise a woman's experience can appear to many as a secondary assault. Despite formal legal recognition of her need for protection, a woman who is raped, assaulted or battered by a man may find herself victimised again by police, state and medical agencies. Perversely, it can be *her* actions or behaviour and *her* responsibility for the offence, rather than the offender's, which is judged.

Feminist research has begun to expose the extent of this secondary victimisation and to challenge institutionalised 'victim blaming' (see Binney *et al.*, 1981; Pahl, 1985). For many acts of violence and sexual assault upon women, the man's behaviour may be seen by the courts not only as non-criminal but understandable, normal or even an irrelevant concern. Violent assaults in the home become 'just domestics'; rapes, the understandable response of a man led on by a woman dressed provocatively; sexual harassment, the normal behaviour of virile males. Some dissatisfied victims have recounted their experiences of law (Binney *et al.*, 1981; Griffiths, 1981; London Rape Crisis Centre, 1984; Meredith, 1979; Pahl, 1982) but at present there is not sufficient research into women and the law to show how frequently victim-blaming occurs. To assess adequately how the law deals with women as victims, extensive research is needed at all levels of definition from Acts of Parliament and decisions of the higher courts to the informal organisational practices and interactional relationships at the grass-roots levels of the professions, legal actors and victims.[1] The emphasis in this chapter will lie with just one aspect of the process, the adjudication of behaviour in reported decisions. These are the decisions reported from the higher courts (the House of Lords, Courts of Appeal, High Courts, and so on) and published in official law reports such as the *All England Review* which form the basic units of what lawyers call 'case law'.

Stanko (1985) has drawn our attention to the relevance of assumptions about gendered inequalities to the labelling by law or society of men's behaviour as 'normal' or 'abhorrent'. By looking at how men as a powerful group maintain their positions of privilege, the belief that violence against women is a social problem involving only a few disordered individuals, rather than a problem of society, can be countered.

This chapter is based on the conviction that the process of defining what is acceptable or unacceptable behaviour for men and women warrants attention alongside studies of the incidence of male violence and the lack of support for their victims. For ease and brevity of discussion the focus will be upon the legal adjudication of conflicts of the most common type – those between intimates, men and women in the family situation.

Some form of judgement of the behaviour between intimates is relevant to a variety of legal cases. Loose principles governing the level of physical damage and apprehended dangers required to qualify as a victim in order to obtain legal relief vary in accordance with statutory guidance, the principles developed in case law and judicial practice. The behaviour cases which form the basis of the discussion which follows include all the reported decisions traced from 1969 to 1985 where a woman applied to the law for protection as a result of a husband's, ex-husband's, cohabitant or ex-cohabitant manfriend's violence or unacceptable behaviour. Over 300 cases were traced where behaviour (excluding the sole complaint of adultery) was held to be a major factor in the discussion. The cases included divorce, injunction, nullity, custody and property disputes plus the occasional criminal and damages case.[2]

Reported decisions are basically legal texts compiled as ritualised forms for both teaching the law and carrying it out. One crucial assumption made here is that language is of primary importance in structuring reality. Women are subjectified as victims in the process of defining the boundaries of appropriate male and female behaviour in language. Judges, magistrates, solicitors and other legal actors have their own jargon, technical words, ways of seeing 'truth' from 'falsity' and of judging evidence which enable them to name some women as victims and others as not. The intention in this chapter is to discuss reported decisions as texts with social, cultural and symbolic value. The concern lies with how the problem of domestic violence is constructed in legal discourse. Simply, discourse can be defined as the framework within which explanations are sought. More formally, the working definition of discourse used here refers to a linguistic unity or group of statements, constituting and delimiting a specific area of concern, governed by its own rules of formation with its own modes of distinguishing truth from falsity.

For lawyers, reported decisions are the 'good policy' cases which serve as teaching texts for trainees, solicitors, barristers or judges. Legal dogma holds that practitioners search through these cases, sorting out the precedents and principles to guide them in winning cases for clients. The specifically micro-legal content of these texts (what the law dictates at the present time) is, however, disregarded here in preference for an analysis of the cultural ordering of the problem. The focus is upon the legal profession as a culture which is none the less part of the social world. It is, therefore, the ordinary aspects of these texts rather than their legal details which will be discussed here. No attempt will be made to examine the adherence, or not, to particular legal precedents or to search for the loopholes of practice.

Legal texts are notoriously mystifying. There is a tendency to develop precise formulations of words to embody past and cover present or future conflicts over meaning which only legal experts can understand or manipulate. Evidences, especially from experts, are supposed to clarify meanings yet in practice they can serve to isolate the law's sphere of debate even further from the understanding of ordinary people. By careful and laboured debate, by examining various truths, a reported decision may appear to be laboriously fair. Adherence to rules and precedents, largely a matter of convenience or routine, is also, however, affected by personal interpretation. Whilst rules are important to the law, they should not be treated as isolated from the 'outside' world.

By focusing on language, it is not intended to discover the beliefs of individuals. Ambiguity is central to the law. As texts, reported decisions are dogged by language which is fragmented and contradictory, therefore quotes of what judges said about the men and women involved have not been selected in order to prove the fairness or bias of an individual judge or of the law as a whole. These cases may tell us little of what happened in court. At best, they tell us merely what a judge thought worth saying for reporting purposes, and even this is filtered by the person who wrote up the case for publication.

In legal texts, the dogma of individualism always has some importance. There are different facts, different parties to a dispute and different experts involved (doctors, social workers, probation officers, welfare officers, and so on). Many reported decisions reinforce the uniqueness of a case by including at some point a history of variable length or at least reference to the specific details recorded elsewhere. This may take the form of merely citing the 'bare bones' or 'skeleton' background – the ages of the parties to the dispute, the number, ages or sexes of the children, the length of marriage, cohabitation or relationship, a brief statement as to its happiness and a reference to the problems or events leading up to the present case. The following extract is a fairly mundane example:

This is an appeal from an order which was made by Mr Recorder

Balstrom at the Maidstone County Court on 12 November 1981. The order which the recorder made was what is now called an ouster injunction against the husband . . . The facts, very briefly are that these parties have been married for a long time, I think over 20 years. They have four children, of whom the youngest is 7. On 23 June 1981 the wife obtained a decreee nisi against the husband in undefended proceedings on the ground of his conduct . . .   (*O'Malley* v. *O'Malley*)[3]

The history may be truncated because details have been minimised for brevity's sake or to protect an individual's privacy (these reports are available in public libraries to anyone who wants to read them). In some decisions the history is merely referred to as 'dealt with elsewhere' in a lower court or in chambers. Judgements can assert that the facts 'need not concern us here', have been 'adequately covered' in the various evidences or are the types where 'the least said, the better'. In *Shemshadfard* v. *Shemshadfard*[4] for example, the particulars were disposed of as follows:

There are a number of specific allegations on which the [wife] relies. I need only mention that one of them concerns false allegations of adultery and prostitution and a number of others which set out complaints of physical violence of a severe degree.

Occasionally, however, the historical details can be set out at great length. In *Mitchell* v. *Mitchell*[5] for example, the whole of the wife's particulars about her husband's behaviour drawn from the written evidence (her affidavit) are reproduced. These historical discussions often include extraneous material. Decisions may contain details as to the race, age, education, social status or appearance of the parties which formally bear little relevance to the legal issues subsequently defined. The following are just a few examples:

. . . the wife is an attractive woman who dresses well . . .   (*Foley* v. *Foley*)[6]

. . . the husband, who is obviously a man of considerable energy and ability . . .   (*Griffiths* v. *Griffiths*)[7]

. . . the victim of the conduct (. . .) was Leak's wife, a slightly built young woman in her early twenties . . .   (*R* v. *Leak*)[8]

. . . the parties who are Ghanaian by origin, were married on April 2 1973 . . .   (*Ansah* v. *Ansah*)[9]

Both parties have strong temperaments. The husband originates from Southern Ireland. The wife from Northern Ireland. (*Bateman* v. *Bateman*)[10]

The histories may contain statements of sympathy for one or other party or merely assert that the case is distressing for all concerned. The actual details included, although important for confirming the individuality and difference of each case, are, none the less, arbitrarily selected and greatly dependent upon the whims of the particular judge. Whether or not the facts of the history presented 'match' the explanations of events subsequently offered, some reference to the history of the dispute serves a crucial function in providing a grounding for the rest of the discussion.

Discourse sustains relations of domination by making explanations appear natural or inevitable. Legal intervention into the cocooned realm of the family must generally be justified in terms of the relationship between the parties and between the parties and the court. The specific discursive strategies discussed in this chapter, while not offered as exhaustive nor the only ones available, have been chosen because they vary most in the way in which the 'position' for judgement is established. As explanatory frameworks, the first three strategies are 'sex blind'. Technically, they could work for both men and women victims, to their advantage or their detriment. The last strategy described is gendered as it is built upon the differences between men and women. The judgements researched, therefore, did not always conspire to effect a secondary assault on victims by nature of their being specifically women. What all four strategies have in common is the tendency to judge so called 'domestic violence – that which occurs between intimates and which is almost always violence from man to woman – as less serious or less dangerous than other attacks. Whilst the concerns of the law encompass the domestic abuses by men by acknowledging that some men are wife beaters, these men are treated in the texts as dangerous only to their wives and not to society at large. This has the effect of limiting the help wives receive from the court. The following analysis exposes how this occurs.

Warring

A common opening in legal judgements is the vindication of responsibility and demonstration of judicial impartiality effected by constructing the scenario of the family at war. Here the parties' disputes have resulted in the creation of a mass of competing claims, a welter of 'tangled litigation', which has hampered the court in its attempts to reveal the truth. The explosive or warring family is a familiar metaphor employed in criminal and custody cases. The judgements of these may be packed full of references to couples 'locked in conflict', fathers 'obsessed with love' acting badly because they are trapped in a spiralling battle of matrimonial dispute. One noticeable feature of this type of judgement is the detailed reproduction of past events using suitably militaristic terminology. It is not uncommon for them to contain descriptions of husbands 'storming in', as though invading a foreign country rather than the front room, 'enlisting' accomplices or making preparations for 'attack'. The wives hide behind a 'smokescreen' of excuses or act like 'time bombs', thereby precipitating their husbands' 'explosive' conduct. The children are invariably referred to as 'objects' in a struggle, they are 'seized' to be used as 'pawns' or 'armoury' in the battle between parents.

Presenting the evidence in a judgement in a particular way can make it easier to assert that both parties were equally implicated in the family war. Reported decisions can differ considerably in the order of presentation of various evidences from the parties involved or from experts. One can, for instance, tell the wife's story first and then move on to the husband's or vice versa. In warring cases a common technique is to weave together descriptions of the two parties' actions so that the image of two individuals both fuelling each other's behaviour becomes more powerful. In *R* v. *D*[11] for example, interwoven with the description of the husband's 'bad' acts lies the history of the wife's fight back and resistance. Her repeated applications to courts in England and abroad, her flights to Eire and New Zealand to find the child he had violently removed, her removals to secret addresses, calls to the police and screams for help in the streets are recounted as part of the history of bitter matrimonial dispute. By presenting the history in this manner, it is much easier to assert that the conflict was 'mutual' even if evidence only of the man's violence is offered, as in this case.

Expert testimony can be presented to endorse the view that a couple are at war. In fact, in some of the cases it appears that the court bowed down in favour of expert, non-legal opinion. It can be the social workers', probation and welfare officers' evidences which are quoted to provide insight into the difficulties arising from 'mutual bitterness'.

Where neither party can or will 'move sideways' it is difficult for all the professions involved to establish where the 'truth' lies. Use of these linguistic techniques is not, however, essential for decisions addressed to the warring family. Warring basically relates to the court's position in relation to the truth of the individual facts of the case. Warring means that the bitterness of the conflict between the parties makes it impossible for the court to get at the real facts of the case. Instead of attempting to decide just who did what, the question invariably becomes, 'should the law intervene and how should it do so?' The disputed behaviour serves as a foundation upon which to erect issues of public importance and negotiate the relationship between the law and the family. This can act as both a justification for legal intervention and a safety valve against overzealous concern.

Warring families are generally those whose disagreements go beyond 'mere matrimonial conflict' by impinging upon 'public peace and public conscience'. Just when matrimonial conflict becomes in this sense extraordinary poses great difficulty. The judgements seldom spell out what the term 'public' means. Is it the world outside the couple's home? Is it the rest of the population, excluding them? Is it the legal profession? The ways in which the warring family may offend the public differs a great deal in the judgements. They can cause a waste of resources (high legal costs, waste of professionals' time, and so on); be harmful to the children's interests (exposing the children to divided loyalties, using them to hurt the other parent, and so on); expose the local population to danger (use of explosives, and so on); or merely offend some ordained moral standard supposedly found in the public conscience. No matter what the public happens to be, defence of the 'public' is crucial to a judge's role. This means that intervention can only be justified if it is in the public interest. Whether or not it is in the interests of the man or woman in the warring situation is largely incidental.

By separating individuals from the public, non-intervention – bowing down to the status quo or vindicating responsibility to a higher authority or to parliament – can also be legitimated. In some of the reported decisions this resulted in the law virtually washing its hands of the problem, saying, 'we are powerless to intervene', 'we have no jurisdiction', and so on. The belief that family violence is seldom of public importance is reaffirmed by setting the terms of the debate on the basis of this distinction between individuals battling it out in the isolation of the family and those who battle it out in public.

The Conflict of Passion

A different kind of family 'war' is the conflict of passions. Here the discussions emphasise the allegations of mental unkindness between men and women who 'taunt' each other or generally 'carry on'. It is not so much the battleground which forms the scene in these cases as the dramatic, soap-opera-like qualities of the domestic situation. Violent behaviour between intimates resulting from an outburst of passion is virtually never viewed as the dangerous type. Incredibly, in passion dramas the need for justice can shift from the victim on to the offender. The behaviour, if not justifiable, is at least an understandable response to the other party's actions. In the passion scenario, individuals will use violence if their love for another is threatened, even if this means using violence against the very object of those affections. For the judgements confronted by a conflict of passions, the court's job is to do justice by examining the facts in order to draw the interventional line between behaviour which is understandable and that which is not.

Feminist work has highlighted how violence against women is used as a controlling strategy. Reported decisions may also emphasise the domineering rather than the violent aspects of behaviour between intimates but, unlike feminism, the concern is more with explaining it than with challenging it. As in all good soap operas, these decisions treat the allegations of misbehaviour as sensationally distorted. Most often the trouble is found to be sexual in nature – jealousy, flirtatious wives who go out who-knows-where, and so on. In *Mitchell* v. *Mitchell* for example, the whole of the women's particulars as to the husband's behaviour are reproduced.[12] The husband's behaviour is said to have included domineering his wife, timing how long she was out shopping, excessive jealousy, objections to her going out to see friends or relatives, physical assaults, screaming or swearing, threats to kill, threats of violence, 'insistence' on sexual intercourse, locking his wife out of the house, ignoring her for long periods and belittling her in front of her sister. Yet only the domineering aspects of the husband's behaviour are discussed in the judgement. The victim, rather than the aggressor, appears to be on trial as it is her performance as wife, mother and sexual servicer which is scrutinised.

Domination, even violent domination, is legitimated in the passion drama if motivated by love and used for the good of others. With ultimate illogicality, the use of domination or control against a member of the family can be deemed to be a justifiable technique in order to save the family as a whole. It was frequently explained in the texts as part of a man's efforts to 'keep his family together'. The husband can become, as in the Mitchell case above, the 'good father' struggling for family stability, and the wife the one who disrupts it. His trying to bring her into line with a modicum of force gets treated as quite understandable.

In the passion drama, the law aims to do justice by hearing the other side of the story. This means that allegations of violence made by victims must be regarded with the utmost scepticism. Like the warring situation, behaviour arising from a conflict of passions is deemed to be the result of an interactional drama between spouses. Unlike street crimes, muggings, murders of police officers, and so on, the behaviour of the victim and aggressor are linked. The passion drama is not as hopeless as the warring family situation as there may well be a possibility of forgiveness and repair. Intervention by the law is calculated not on the basis of the public and private divide used for the warring situation, but by judgement as to whether the present relations between the parties require 'outside', that is, legal, intervention.

Judgements need to qualify intervention into intimate relations carefully as intrusion of the law into the family is seen to be disruptive. If it looks as though a couple can sort out their problems without the law being involved, non-intervention is the probable outcome.

Medicalising

Boundary disputes between law and medicine will no doubt be familiar to anyone who reads the murder cases which make the news. Law and medicine have at times hit the headlines as a result of conflicts about who should take charge of offenders who are either 'mad' or 'bad'. In reported decisions of non-murder cases of violent assault between intimates, however, disputes as to whether the aggressor was 'bad' or 'mad' are rare. These offenders cannot be 'bad' if, at the most, they are a 'danger' only to a victim with a high level of tolerance, that is, a partner in a domestic situation. Instead of being 'mad' they are considered to be 'anti-social' or 'eccentric'.

There are many situations of violent or aggressive behaviour where no doubt, one party to the dispute can be found to be suffering from a sickness. In cases of medicalised behaviour, however, sickness attains utmost importance. Rather than being an effect of or aggravation to an unhappy domestic situation, it becomes the sole cause of the upsets between a couple. In the case of *White* v. *White*,[13] for example, the woman's affidavit is quoted in the judgement as saying that the husband's refusal to take his medication led to an *increase* in the intensity of his abuse and violent behaviour. By promptly dropping the qualifying word 'increase' however, the remainder of the judgement presents the argument that the sole cause of the man's behaviour was his refusal to take medication. Medicalising allows a shift in attention from the family or couple in a state of turmoil on to the tumultuous individual. Unlike the conflict of passions and warring situations, where the judgements centre upon the violent event (whether it was justified, a threat to the public, and so on), with cases of medicalised behaviour the concern lies with assessing the responsibility of the aggressor. The behaviour becomes a personal affliction instead of being an interactional condition. This does not mean, however, that the victim's response is entirely irrelevant. Her domestic closeness to the offender is crucial in assessing the seriousness of his condition.

One big attraction of medicalising is that it can be done with or without expert medical diagnosis of the aggressor. Even when a medical opinion exists, it is possible for a judge to offer his own diagnosis, either in preference or in addition to the expert view. In Re: K[14], for example, the judge, after describing the doctor's opinion on the cause of the husband's violence as attributable to 'paranoid schizophrenia', moves on to offer his own diagnosis:

> [the wife and doctor] attributed his violence to illness, a brain tumour or paranoid schizophrenia. I should add also that he was a persistent and heavy drinker and may well have suffered in his intellectual capacity and power of self control as a result.

Medicalised violent behaviour is the uncontrollable type with preferably an entirely physical cause.

No doubt there are many conditions of illness, physical or mental, where it can be extremely difficult to isolate factors aggravating violent tendencies from their cause, should this be the concern of professionals. In the domestic situation, the choice of the aggressor's object of attack – a wife – may be regarded in court as a mere chance result of the illness. Preoccupation with the aggressor's illness is not muddled by consideration of possible pre-illness relations between the parties. If a wife, rather than a neighbour, employer or close friend, is attacked it is just 'bad luck'. Here is how the judgement in the case of *White* v. *White*[15] describes the husband's decision to try to kill his wife:

> On 30 September 1982 . . . he was intending to kill himself by jumping

from a balcony when he heard a message from God telling him not to kill himself but to kill his wife instead.

In non-murder cases of medicalised behaviour, cure of the unhappy situation can lie with medicine alone or with medicine helped by the law. In assessing the need for legal intervention, however, the victim's level of tolerance is crucial. In the decisions researched there is a preference for non-intervention, as violence or aggressive behaviour from a known party – a husband in a domestic situation – is regarded as more tolerable and less frightening than an attack by a stranger. It is the peculiarity or oddness of the aggressor's behaviour which is emphasised, not the dangers posed to the victim. Tolerance by a victim is assumed by judgements minimising the effects of the aggressor's violence so that it appears to be little more than irritating. This can be effected in a number of ways – by referring to the past behaviour as merely 'annoying', 'embarrassing', 'eccentric' or a 'nuisance' to the wife; by offering extracts from written evidences which highlight the oddness of the behaviour rather than the dangers it poses; by adding medical testimony about the need of the aggressor for medication rather than by focusing on the need to protect the victims, and so on. Paradoxically, it is even possible to present part of the victim's own evidence on the state of health of her partner in order to justify a lack of intervention of her behalf.

Yet it should not be assumed in medicalised cases that non-intervention is an inevitable conclusion. While sicknesses are open to cure, and hence their results often tolerable in the domestic situation (especially for wives), some may be incurable. The law may then intervene if the victim's ability to tolerate long-standing behaviour goes beyond the requirements of duty. In *Thurlow* v. *Thurlow*,[16] a rare case concerned with the unreasonable behaviour of an incurably epileptic wife, it was stated that legal intervention was necessary as:

> This husband has conscientiously and courageously suffered the behaviour of the wife for substantial periods of time between 1969 and July 1972 until his powers of endurance were exhausted and his health endangered.

In medicalised cases of domestic behaviour, emphasis upon responsibility for the offence – where it lies in relation to the control/loss of control standard – turns the entire legal problem around. The main difficulty is not what to do with the offender, but how to help the victim.

Protecting

In their protective guise, the decisions did not seek to explain specifically the man's behaviour, his justification or responsibility for the offence, but rather its effects in terms of the sufferings of the victim. To legitimate legal intervention, the judgements generally made some reference to the man's behaviour in terms of the 'damage done'. For example:

> There seems to have been a good deal of violence between the appellant and the respondent and more recently, in February, the respondent . . . made a series of assaults on her as a result of which she sustained scratching, bruising and other injuries. He also behaved in such a way as to drive her out of the flat of which she was a tenant and deprive her temporarily of the care of the boy . . . The situation as it existed before 6th March was of such a grave character that this court ought to do all it can by way of interlocutory relief to protect the appellant and her child. (Re: *W*)[17]

The amount of physical, mental or sexual abuse the women suffered varied from judgement to judgement. To assess her suffering, the question of primary importance became 'can she put up with it?'. To gain legal protection from domestic violence, a woman must earn her victim status. So judgement is centred upon her desserts as wife, mother, dependant or weaker being.

There were two main ways in which the victim could earn protection, both of which were treated in the judgements as evidence of the woman's vulnerabilities. The first assessed her material inequalities, the second her reasons for not leaving the domestic relationship sooner.

The first variety of explanation works around physical, biological or 'sex role' differences between the parties. Some of these differences are special vulnerabilities afforded only to women, others vulnerabilities of either sex. The amount of damage a violent act causes is dependent upon the parties' relative ages, abilities or disabilities, muscular strength, size, and so forth. Direct reference to a woman's vulnerability resulting from domestic or sexual inequality was occasionally made, generally by reference to her maternal condition:

> . . . the family doctor dealt with the situation in which the parties were living. He said [the son] had become very difficult to deal with and was spending a great deal of time in his bedrom, and the situation was causing the wife mental illness. (*Phillips* v. *Phillips*)[18]

> this unruly incident by the husband . . . caused her . . . at 1.30 in the morning, when she was in the precarious conditions of 2 months pregnancy, to leave the matrimonial home. (*Bergin* v. *Bergin*)[19]

> the appellant has the right, through and for the infant Cordelia, to go back to the flat and have the father excluded. (*Davis* v. *Johnson*)[20]

Sexual inequality, whilst it may be acknowledged, often becomes the inevitable result of 'natural' differences, so that even when controlling an individual man's abuse of power, men's power over women as a whole gets a boost.

Victims 'outside' the family generally run from attack, so agencies such as the law have problems in explaining why fit or young women do not do the same thing. During the 1970s, however, it seems that the legal profession 'discovered' battered women. References to a 'battered wife' in the judgements generally invoke some sympathy. The battered wife is regarded as being more vulnerable as a result of her resource, housing and financial, shortage. But problems arise if women have not been previously so labelled by, for example, going to a refuge. One familiar puzzle is trying to decide how, after several years of marriage, a woman can 'suddenly' decide her partner's behaviour is intolerable.

One much-criticised explanation in the more recent texts, at times leading to a reversal of previous decisions, is that women do not leave because they are 'used to' abuse. In rough families, generally seen to be the poor, rough treatment can be mistaken in some parts of society for behaviour which is a normal part of married life. In Mrs Bergin's case[21] the magistrates concluded that she accepted her husband's violent behaviour 'as part of their married life'. 'Brutalised' individuals are supposed to tolerate or even become accustomed to circumstances which would offend those with 'refined sensitivities'. As Lord Ormrod put it in *Rennick* v. *Rennick*,[22] 'Families of this kind do tolerate an extraordinary amount of ill-behaviour remarkably well'.

Yet, whilst a woman's vulnerabilities can be dependent upon her social (class/race) position, her status as a wife may work to her advantage. Some of the protective judgements are rife with statements of sympathy for wives who have made strenuous efforts to save their marriages or to 'cover up' for their husbands. Mrs Bergin, for example, won her case on appeal and the judgement contains the following statement of sympathy for her plight:

> It is not for every assault that a wife would wish to go to the police to get her husband into trouble . . . The wife appears to have covered up for the husband . . . on one occasion she mentioned to Mrs Hindmarsh (her neighbour) that one of these injuries had been caused by walking into the garage door, and Mrs Hindmarsh pointed out that this lady did not have a garage. It is now quite clear that she was merely trying to make the marriage work and for about 12 months she put up with this violence from her husband. (*Bergin* v. *Bergin*)[23]

Judging a woman's request for relief in law from a protective framework is by no means governed by chivalry, however. Legal relief in the texts is handed out rather like a means-tested benefit. Not only must women 'earn' protection as victims, but they are likely to 'abuse' the legal system by making false claims. Judging the effects means also policing the protective framework by hunting down incidents of merely trivial upsets. A woman's claims for relief in 'trivial' cases brings strong condemnation from the law (see *Richards* v. *Richards*[24]). Judging the effects of the man's behaviour in subjective terms of the woman's vulnerabilities as wife, mother, dependant or weaker being can lead to conflicting and contradictory conclusions, many well-known to practitioners and legal academics. When, for example, is a woman a 'wife'? What happens when her vulnerabilities as 'wife' conflict with her children's interests? The individualistic emphasis upon the victim – her weaknesses, her poverty, her marriage-saving or motherhood, and so on – as a guide to intervention means essentially that protection from assault or abuse has to be earned by women, not granted by men.

CONCLUSION

This discussion has been concerned with the ideological aspects of the law and domestic violence. The reported decisions which form the focus of the discussion are not typical examples of the law's treatment of women victims. They are at best, the 'good policy' cases of the legal profession. Because of this, we can only infer their implications for the everyday practice of the law.

It has been argued that the judgements offer a variety of explanatory frameworks when dealing with violence against women in a domestic situation. Three features of the legal texts researched – individualism, privacy and minimisation – ensure that no two cases read the same. No victim blaming consensus can be found, therefore, in these 'good policy' cases of the law. The texts vary as to where responsibility for the behaviour lies (victim, aggressor, both or neither) and as to whose behaviour should be judged. In discussing these texts it was not intended to provide a theory of law and violence against women. This has been largely an experimental analysis. Rather than resort to sweeping statements about how the law or legal profession should be reformed, by way of conclusion, there are threads to be drawn out from the previous discussion which offer possibilities for further research.

The way in which the problem was debated in the texts does much to support the conclusion that intervention by the law, although regarded as possible and, in some cases desirable, should be minimal. In the legal judgements, although 'hard cases' may occasionally exist (where the conflict goes beyond mere matrimonial dispute, for example) violence against women in a domestic situation was seen to be largely a welfare issue. It was something found in 'problem' families or families with problems, rather than the outcome of power inequalities between men, women and children. It appeared not only natural but just, that legal intervention should be guarded. In the judgements read it was held to be unjust to use the essentially coercive law against 'sick' men, unjust to oust 'good' fathers from their homes, unjust to use the law against victims of passion, unjust to allow individual women to make 'exaggerated' claims in order to win benefits from the courts.

No doubt one can counter such charges by pointing out that it is, likewise, unjust that abused women die or spend years 'putting up with' or fleeing from a man's violence. But it may be more fruitful to attempt to find a way out of the constraints of a debate which have been, in a sense, preset.

Although it is unlikely to provide a solution to the problem of male violence, legal intervention could do a great deal to alleviate the difficulties of abused women. Apart from the protective cases, in all the decisions examined there was a preoccupation with the *cause* of the behaviour rather than a concern for its *effects*. A shift in emphasis from the cause of behaviour to its effects, not just in terms of physical damage but including mental cruelty to women, their fears and restricted access to the outside world could be well worth exploring. Such an approach may provide an answer to the question – how can the law protect women?

REFERENCES

1. This work has begun. See particularly Atkins and Hoggett, 1984; T. Faragher, 'The Police Response to Violence Against Women in the Home' in Pahl (ed.), 1985; McCann, 1985; Pattullo, 1983; Radford, 1982; Smart, 1984.
2. Only recent cases have been referenced here. The standard form of legal citation has been used. The first figure refers to the volume of the *All England Law Review*. The second is the page number.
3. *O'Malley* v. *O'Malley* [1982] 2 All ER 112.
4. *Shemshadfard* v. *Shemshadfard* [1981] 1 All ER 726.
5. *Mitchell* v. *Mitchell* [1983] 3 All ER 621.
6. *Foley* v. *Foley* [1981] 2 All ER 857.
7. *Griffiths* v. *Griffiths* [1974] 1 All ER 932.
8. *R* v. *Cogan, R* v. *Leak* [1978] 2 All ER 1058.
9. *Ansah* v. *Ansah* [1977] 2 WLR 760.
10. *Bateman* v. *Bateman* [1979] 2 WLR 377.
11. *R* v. *D* [1984] 1 All ER 574.
12. *Mitchell* v. *Mitchell* [1983] 3 All ER 621.
13. *White* v. *White* [1983] 2 All ER 51.
14. Re *K* [1985] 1 All ER 403.
15. *White* v. *White* [1983] 2 All ER 51.
16. *Thurlow* v. *Thurlow* [1975] 2 All ER 979.
17. Re *W* (a minor) [1981] 3 All ER 401.
18. *Phillips* v. *Phillips* [1973] 2 All ER 423.
19. *Bergin* v. *Bergin* [1983] 1 All ER 905.
20. *Davis* v. *Johnson* [1973] 1 All ER 841.
21. *Bergin* v. *Bergin* [1983] 1 All ER 905.
22. *Rennick* v. *Rennick* [1978] 1 All ER 817.
23. *Bergin* v. *Bergin* [1983] 1 All ER 905.
24. *Richards* v. *Richards* [1983] 2 All ER 807.

11 'Provoking Her Own Demise': From Common Assault to Homicide

Susan S. M. Edwards

INTRODUCTION

The processing of domestic violence, from homicide to common assault, within the civil and criminal justice process, reflects the reluctance of a largely male magistracy and judiciary to protect women. Women's experience of the so-called remedies to violence within this context falls very short of expectations. Indeed, women are frequently perceived as 'provoking their own demise' and assaults against their person are very much seen as 'victim precipitated'. These and other ideologies very much influence and colour the legal process, resulting in great injustice to women victims.

In considering violence against women in the family context it is specious to draw a line between domestic violence as if it were trivial, and grievous bodily harm and spousal homicide as if they were two quite distinctly separate species. They are not. Instead, they are often one and the same event and when placed along a continuum of violence are distinguished only by, among other things, the force and number of blows, the speed by which the victim was conveyed to hospital and the skill of the medical team. The issues raised in this discussion derive from a far wider consideration of the way in which particular gender ideologies are assimilated within the socio-legal process.

Within the fabric of our understanding of domestic violence we find that the state legitimates and to a great degree normalises the cult of masculinity. By the same token, the state, through its treatment of victims of rape and victims of domestic violence, reinforces the expected and desired acquiescence, passivity, total conformity and subjection of women to men and their corresponding acquiescence with the appropriate gender role. These two competing constructs constitute the social and legal backcloth against which domestic violence assault is constructed and understood. As Greenblat (1983) shows most clearly, cultural norms perpetuate the acceptance of the hitting of wives; and as Dobash and Dobash (1979) have shown, the 'marriage licence becomes a hitting licence'. Masculinity is frequently exonerated, even in perverse forms. From male sex offenders to male violent offenders, violent behaviour is often seen as an extension of the cult of masculinity. Through ideologies and social constructs, through the lack of civil and criminal remedies and their interpretation, which often fails to give women adequate protection, we find that male violence is frequently, if covertly, legitimated. In effect, men are awarded the right to chastise and to castigate along with the right to consortium within marriage. These 'rights' of men are upheld in various statutes within family, civil and criminal law. Remarking on the male right to consortium, for example, in the case of *R* v. *Clarence* (1888, 22 QBD) the presiding judge argued: 'The sexual communion between them is by virtue of the irrevocable privilege conferred once and for all on the husband at the time of the marriage . . .'. Women, on the other hand, are expected to be 'good sweet maids'. Women who contest male power are seen to deserve their lot and the law through discretion has correspondingly held out little protection. Engels (1972) captured the scenario of women's subjection when he wrote:

> In order to make certain of the wife's fidelity and therefore the paternity of the children, she is delivered over unconditionally to the power of the husband; if he kills her, he is only exercising his right. (p. 22)

Unequal treatment is perpetuated through this sexist organisation of society and its corresponding legal institutions. Whether as victims or as offenders, the treatment, reparation and restitution women receive is determined by the degree to which they conform to, or deviate from, the appropriate gender role. Women victims of rape, as Edwards (1981) and Adler (1982 and 1984) show, are assessed for the degree to which they conform to sexually appropriate models.

As Adler (1984) argued, judges continue to be prejudicial in terms of admitting past sexual history within the trial process. In exercising their discretion regarding Section 2 of the Sexual Offences Amendment Act, 1976, they are, in effect, giving a judgement. In the investigation process, Chamber and Millar (1983) found that the police are less likely to believe the drunk woman, the unchaste woman and the woman with some kind of sexual past. In their study, for example, eight out of nine women, all known prostitutes, who complained of rape got no further than making a complaint at the police station. The remaining one had her case later turned down at the Procurator Fiscal stage. McLeod (1982) found that known prostitutes complaining of victimisation received quite different treatment in the legal process, from that offered to non-prostitutes. Within the area of domestic violence, Dobash and Dobash (1979) and Stanko (1985) found that the investigatory stages and later court process were also guided by notions of class, race, status and gender.

MARGINALISED AND TRIVIALISED

Assaults against wives or against cohabitees, whatever their class or background, historically have been marginalised and trivialised. Either they are ignored totally or they are diverted (Dobash and Dobash, 1979) to the civil or to the lower courts (Wasoff, 1982). The introduction of the Domestic Violence and Matrimonal Proceedings Act in 1976 and in 1978 the introduction of the Domestic Violence and Magistrates Courts Act, facilitated this diversion whilst being publically acclaimed as a watershed in extending the protection of women from violent assault to the civil domain. Domestic violence assault, when reported, is either trivialised and dealt with as a civil matter, or if dealt with as a crime, is considered a minor offence within the criminal process. Research shows that domestic violence, in particular, is under-recorded and under-reported. Binney et al. (1981) found that most women did not report their experience to the police, an observation widely confirmed throughout the literature on the subject (Dobash and Dobash, 1979; Hanmer and Saunders, 1983 and 1984; Horley, 1985) and further supported by Chapter 3 in this volume. One of the major reasons for under-reportage is the feeling on the part of complainants/victims, that the 'police response' is not a sympathetic one. If the incident is reported it frequently goes unrecorded or is listed as 'no crime' or played down, and if convictions are secured, sentences are inadequate. Women, for multifarious reasons, are reluctant to report incidents to the police. Those who do may find that the police regard domestic incidents as 'not real police work' The Times (10 April 1983) reported the preparation of proposals by Assistant Commissioner John Dellow for shedding domestic disputes along with 'stranded people, lost property and stray animals' as issues which could be dealt with by other agencies. In those cases where a woman wishes to prosecute a crime sheet may be made out. At a later stage the investigation may be dropped, allegedly because of lack of evidence or because the complainant wishes to withdraw the charge. In those few cases where proceedings are continued the charge brought may be of a lesser nature than if the assault had been between non-intimates. 'Criming down' is a not unknown feature of police investigation practice, but in domestic violence it may lead to serious cases being dealt with less seriously by the courts. Stanko (1985) argues:

> Decisions to arrest or not to charge a suspect with a crime, decisions to charge a suspect with 'disorderly conduct' rather than assault, or decisions to refer 'incidents' of male violent behaviour to the social services instead of the criminal court all affect how men's threatening or violent behaviour comes to be defined as criminal or non-criminal behaviour. (pp. 103–4)

Despite evidence to the contrary, the courts continue to reiterate and mouth the principles of equality and justice in such cases (Binney, *et al.*, 1981; Pahl, 1982 and 1985). In *Buchanan*, 2 CAR(S) (1980, p. 15), a case of wounding with intent on a cohabitee, it was decided that violence in a domestic context was not to be treated in any way differently from violence generally. It was declared that 'the courts must impose sentences appropriate to the gravity of the offence despite the domestic background', and a two-year sentence of imprisonment was upheld. Similarly in *Giboin*, 2 CAR(S) (1980, pp. 99–101), it was asserted that wives should get equal protection:

> An assault by a man on his wife should not be brushed aside as due to emotional upsets or jealousy; wives are vulnerable at the hands of violent husbands, and there is no reason why a man should not be punished in the same way for assaulting his wife as he would be for assaulting any other person.

However, it seems that in spite of these judicial utterances, there is a general reluctance in practice to deal with such cases or to deal with them with any kind of equity or consistency. Wasoff (1982) found that cases of domestic violence in Scotland in 1981 were systematically treated much less seriously by the criminal justice system than were a comparable sample of non-domestic violence cases. Domestic violence cases were allocated to lower courts and given lower penalties. Only 3 per cent of the sample quoted were found guilty and the overwhelming tendency was merely to fine. Bedfordshire police, in their own investigation in 1976, found the following dispositions for a sample of 288 cases reported: of seventy-three proceeded with, only eight received a prison sentence or a suspended sentence, whilst thirty-one were fined or bound over, five received probation, seventeen received a conditional or absolute discharge and twelve were dealt with in other ways.

TOWARDS QUANTIFICATION OF VIOLENCE AGAINST WIVES

Statistics reveal that a high proportion of homicide is between family members and against wives in particular, a fact borne out by studies internationally. Von Hentig (1948, p. 292) in his analysis of 1931 data, found that of those victims of homicide related by marriage/cohabitation, 14.3 per cent were husbands and 61.5 per cent wives. Wolfgang (1958), conducting a larger study, used data from criminal records of violent crime in Philadelphia, USA, between 1948 and 1952. Of the homicide cases, 41.7 per cent of the female victims were wives, 21 per cent were lovers and 6 per cent close friends; whilst 11 per cent of male victims were husbands, 6 per cent were killed by lovers and 34 per cent by close friends (see Dobash and Dobash, 1979, pp. 15–18). More recently, Willbanks (1983, pp. 11–12) followed through all 569 homicides that occurred in Dade County (Miami), Florida in 1980 to the final disposition in court. Of 569 homicides, only forty-seven female offenders were involved. This is similar to homicide figures for England and Wales: in 1982, of 520 homicide suspects, fifty-six were female. Bell (1984 and 1985) in a study of police response in Dade County, USA found that in domestic disputes, wives were victims in 71 per cent of the disputes, husbands in 8 per cent, mothers in 4 per cent, fathers in 2 per cent, children in 7 per cent and other family members in 8 per cent. Whilst McClintock (1963, pp. 38 and 250), in his examination of violent crimes in the UK which result from domestic disputes, found that 41.7 per cent of all offences of violence recorded were committed against another family member and of those, 60 per cent were between cohabitees and married couples.

Gibson and Klein (1961) in their study of criminal homicide in the UK from 1955 to 1960, found that for over 40 per cent of women victims of homicide the suspect was the husband and in 25 per cent the suspect was either a close relative or lover. Homicide statistics in England and Wales for the period between 1972 and 1982 consistently reveal that between 21 per cent and 29 per cent of all victims have been acquainted either as a spouse or cohabitant, former spouse or cohabitant, or as lover or former lover. The categories form 21 per cent of all homicides in 1972, 27 per cent in 1973, 26 per cent in 1974, 28 per cent in 1975, 29 per cent in 1976, 27 per cent in 1977, 27 per cent in 1978, 29 per cent in 1981 and 25 per cent in 1982. Figures for 1982 are as alarming as they are illuminating. Out of a total of 576 cases recorded in *Criminal Statistics*, 1982 as homicide, a total of 143 were between spouses, lovers or former lovers, cohabitants, or former spouses or cohabitants. In the spouse/cohabitant/former spouse/former cohabitant category, 104 victims were female and twelve victims male, a ratio of nine females to one male killed.

Figures for common assault, assault and grievous bodily harm tend to be less certain and less reliable. With regard to the *Criminal Statistics*, there is no way of identifying domestic cases within the category of summary assaults (common) or from other indictable offences recorded variously as assaults, other woundings, murder, attempted murder, threat and conspiracy. Violence against wives and cohabitees is generally absorbed into all these categories. The figures are as follows for those initially proceeded against. In 1983, 1811 men and 542 women were proceeded against for common assault, 367 men and 34 women were proceeded against for assault. For the offence of wounding, 56 859 men were proceeded against compared with 5010 women, and for attempted murder and murder respectively 60 and 364 men were proceeded against compared with 5 and 48 women. We do not know, however, what proportion of these categories of male violence involved known or family female victims.

Cases of violence against wives are also diverted into the civil justice process. Under the Domestic Violence and Matrimonial Proceedings Act, 1976, Section 1, 367 injunctions were refused in 1983, 2501 were granted with a power of arrest (Section 2) and 7952 were granted without a power of arrest. In 1984 figures show 380 injunctions refused, 3568 granted with a power of arrest and 10 562 without that power attached. Courts still refuse to grant injunctions and when they do, only a quarter are in any way made effective through a power of arrest. Police officers consistently remarked during my research into police responses to domestic violence that without a power of arrest 'an injunction is not worth the paper it is written on'. Statistics on domestic proceedings in magistrates' courts began to be collected systematically in 1983. In that year 7700 applications for a protection or exclusion order were heard in accordance with provisions in the Domestic Violence and Magistrates Courts Act, 1978. About 65 per cent of the applications were granted and about 30 per cent withdrawn.

In almost half of the cases in which an order was made, the court considered there was imminent danger of physical injury and made an expedited order.

VIOLENCE AGAINST WOMEN – SOME IDEOLOGICAL CONSTRUCTS

Violence against wives and cohabitees is processed within the civil and criminal systems in accordance with a number of factors. These considerations influence the use of discretion by the police to investigate, to record, to prosecute and the use of discretion by the sentencer to mete out an appropriate sentence to the violent offender. Some of the key factors influencing discretionary action are:

(i) the physical severity and visibility of the injuries sustained
(ii) the degree to which women conform to or deviate from appropriate female roles of wife, mother, homemaker
(iii) the degree to which women are seen as responsible
(iv) the degree to which women are thought to have provoked their own demise either by:
  (a) being sexually inappropriate, that is, having friendships or relationships with men outside marriage, being bisexual or lesbian
  (b) being inappropriate in terms of gender, that is, bad mothers, bad cooks, bad housewives
  (c) challenging either the gender assumptions of their expected roles or challenging male domination.

Physical Severity of Injury and Role Conformity

As in rape and other forms of victimisation of women by men, the severity of the attack is and always has been a primary factor in establishing credibility of the complaint and corroboration of the allegation. In addition, race, class, status and gender conformity influence the exercise of discretion by the police in the decision to investigate reported incidents and to offer protection to women. Smith and Klein (1984) found that class was a factor influencing the tendency of the police to arrest. Moreover, if the behaviour of the woman is deemed by observers as inappropriate, she is held responsible. This factor has always been present and is a justification and rationalisation of the male right to chastise. For example, Whatley (1617) wrote that beating a wife was only justified in circumstances of 'the utmost extremities of unwifelike carriage', thereby justifying wife-beating when a wife stepped out of line.

The Degree to which She is Deemed Responsible

The responsibility of a wife for assaults upon her person is seen very clearly in the interpretation of both the criminal and the civil law, particularly family law, concerning divorce, cruelty and violence. In the case quoted in Edwards (1981), where a man forced himself sexually on his wife, Lord Dunedin, in normalising the exercise of violence, said:

> If the wife is adamant in her refusal, the husband must choose between letting his wife's will prevail, thus wrecking the marriage, and acting without her consent. It would be intolerable if he were to be conditioned in his course of action by the threat of criminal proceedings.   (p. 35)

When wives are seen to hold the present and future behaviour of husbands in their own hands, they are held responsible for his behaviour. Wives who make divorce applications on the grounds of cruelty as Atkins and Hoggett (1984, pp. 129–30) point out in the case of *Meacher* v. *Meacher* (1946), have been told that it is not cruelty for the husband to beat the wife if she disobeyed his orders not to visit her relations. *She is seen as having it in her own hands to prevent a repetition* (!) [my emphasis].

Provoking Her Own Demise

Whether women suffer violent sexual or violent physical assault, they are monitored for the extent to which they are thought to have provoked their own demise. As Atkins and Hoggett (1984) point out, 'the most insidious concept of all to emerge from the court cases however, is provocation' (p. 129). The earliest reported case held that 'a wife was not entitled to divorce for cruelty unless it appeared that she was a person of good temper and had always behaved well and dutifully to her husband' (cited in *Taylor* v. *Taylor*, 1755). The notion of a wife deserving assault or chastisement if she challenges male authority was reaffirmed in *Wallscourt* v. *Wallscourt* in 1847 when it was declared: 'If a wife violates the rules and regulations of her husband (provided they are not absolutely absurd or irrational) he has a right to complain of it'.

From the stage of the police investigation to the court trial the notion that women provoke their own demise has guided the judicial process. Women are seen to provoke their own demise if considered sexually non-conforming. Mr Justice Bristow, summing up in the trial of one Peter Wood said of the woman murdered:

> Mary Bristow with an IQ of 182 was a rebel from her middle-class background. She was unorthodox in her relationships . . . Those who engage in sexual relationships should realise that sex is one of the deepest and most powerful of emotions, and if you are playing with sex you are playing with fire.   (Pattullo, 1983, pp. 14–15)

Similarly, research by Mike Chatterton (1983) identifies the way in which models of the appropriate wife, husband, gender identity and behaviour shape police response to domestic assault. Chatterton notes that in one case an officer had arrived at a decision not to arrest in a domestic dispute because 'there was dirty breakfast crockery on the table'. The house was in a filthy state generally and the husband had been 'working his balls off to earn extra money for the family'. These examples of inappropriate female and appropriate male behaviour had some bearing on the action, or lack of action, taken by the officer. In situations where women are not conforming to the appropriate model of motherhood and wifehood, women can only be blamed for any assaults against them.

Many writers continue to emphasise and insist on the justice of considering such factors. For example, William Clifford, formerly Director of Australia's Institute of Criminology, writing in *Justice of the Peace* (1984) says:

> . . . In cases of domestic violence, rape or assault generally, there are sometimes degrees of responsibility for what actually happens. There might have been provocation or unnecessary risk taking, which the court can never totally ignore, if they are to do justice and not merely apply the law.

These themes amongst others are identified in the work of Straus (1977), and Jackson and Rushton (1982), as influential in the legal process, not only in assault, but also in spousal homicide cases. The influence occurs both in the processing of the defence case and in mitigation and sentencing. As Greenblat (1983) argues: '. . . much interpretation of wife beating historically has been based on ideas of the wife's precipitating acts and the husband's rule following response' (p. 236).

FROM COMMON ASSAULT TO MURDER

From cases of common assault to woundings to the ultimate of violence – homicide – the female victim in both theory and practice is frequently monitored for the extent to which she provoked her own demise. The concept of provocation, although not a defence, can be taken into consideration when deciding sentence in common assault, assault occasioning actual bodily harm and grievous bodily harm. There is every reason to believe that mitigating pleas on the behalf of counsel for the defence become preoccupied with apportioning blame through so-called victim precipitation. At the extremes of this violence, men kill women as a continuation of their abuse while women kill husbands often in self defence and out of fear of another assault. The interpretation of the law provides a defence for a husband who loses his 'self control'. The wife is often excluded from using this partial defence since she, in delaying her response, will find no legal justification of her behaviour available to her. Given the precise legal conditions required to satisfy the defence of self defence and of provocation, the female defendant who suffers years of violence and torment from an abusing husband and who, in the midst of this suffering, kills him whilst he is incapacitated by drink or sleep, will find that the law holds out no 'partial defence' capable of encompassing her definition of the situation.

It is by no means an accident that women are expected to tolerate and endure a far greater degree of provocation on the part of an unfaithful husband than the husband whose wife is unfaithful. In the latter case the courts are much more ready to accept provocation as a defence and the sentence passed is usually lenient. Women are 'victims' of unequal power relationships existing within the microcosm of the family structure and within the wider fabric of the social structure. They are victims of a legal system which offers them little real remedy or protection from violent assault. For example, the legal conceptualisation of homicide defences contain such a male-orientated construct of legitimate response that women frequently find themselves cast into the dramaturgical role not of self preservers or self defenders, but either of cold-blooded heinous killers, or of the mentally ill whose responsibility is diminished.

In the context of spousal homicide we are chiefly concerned with the rarely-used excusing condition of self defence and the partial defence of provocation and diminished responsibility, which effectively reduce a charge of murder to one of manslaughter. Provocation as a partial excuse is operative only with regard to homicide and, like diminished responsibility, it presents one of the more controversial aspects of criminal law. Provocation developed largely to combat the problems associated with the fixed penalty for murder. A successful defence of provocation depends on evidence of:

   (i) a sudden and temporary loss of control
  (ii) an action which immediately follows the provoking act
 (iii) a reasonable relationship between provocation and retaliation.

First, evidence of a sudden and temporary loss of self control immediately before the fatal act is required if a plea of manslaughter is to be accepted. The jury must take into account both the prior events and the relevant characteristics of the defendant which may result in loss of self control. Secondly, a defence of provocation succeeds where the defendant's action is committed suddenly as a result of the provoking act. There is some disagreement upon this. In *Duffy* (1949, 1 All ER 932), there is a strict understanding of provocation, '. . . a long course of conduct causing suffering and anxiety are not themselves sufficient to constitute provocation'. There are, however, departures from this strict application and it is important to identify the features, or ingredients, of the cases which deem such a departure apposite. Following *Duffy* once again (where the woman defendant subjected to brutal treatment from her husband kills him when he is asleep), Justice Devlin, advising the jury said, 'You are not concerned with blame here – the blame attaching to the dead man'. When a male defendant stands trial, however, all too frequently the blame attaching to the dead woman becomes a crucial part of a defence of provocation. There is no legal guidance with regard to interpretation except that of experience, which by definition is informed by individual and sexist bias regarding what kind of behaviour might amount to provocation. Legal texts and case law give some indication of the parameters of what has been said or done which is more or less likely to pass as provocation. Not surprisingly, the texts refer to the 'gender specific' situation of adultery. Smith and Hogan (1978) write: 'To taunt a man with his impotence or his wife's adultery may be cruel and immoral, but it is not unlawful and may surely amount to provocation' (p. 308). This is the classic or typical situation considered the most likely to provoke and in the court's view deserving of the greatest sympathy. It is noteworthy that a husband's adultery has never been mentioned as sufficient to provoke a wife in similar circumstances. The degree of provocation to her is possibly considered low or negligible in law and by the court. Thus case law clearly enshrines a gender bias regarding what passes as provocation.

Another condition to be satisfied if a defence of provocation is to be successful, is that of the relationship between the provocation received and the subsequent retaliatory action which must be reasonable. English courts concern themselves with the 'mode of resentment', that is, the method of retaliation – whether a knife, fist or gun is used – which must be proportional to the provocation received. If the various conditions are more or less met and the defence of provocation successful, the implications for sentencing are great. Mitigating excuses affect the length and type of disposal, but the gravity of provocation remains the preponderant factor in the court's assessment.

WOMEN'S DEFINITIONS PRECLUDED

The precise legal predicament of women who kill husbands is the subject of considerable international research and comment; Ward *et al.* (1969), Tweedie (1975), Fiora-Gormally (1978), Schneider (1980), Rittenmeyer (1981), Scutt (1981), Bacon and Lansdowne (1982), Wasik (1982), Durham (1984), Radford (1984), Edwards (1984 and 1985), amongst others. Much of the concern and criticism focuses on the more controversial issues affecting women's attempts to use the defence to homicide. This includes consideration of the restrictive nature of the homicide defence, the interpretation of what passes as provocation according to the 'reasonable man', and the proportionate retaliation standard.

First, it is necessary not merely to meet the legal rules and conditions, but to satisfy the judge/jury that any 'reasonable man' may act in the same way. Such discretionary judgements are firmly based in background expectancies and perceptions of what men do when provoked and what things are likely to provoke men. To further expand this point, women do not always act in the heat of the moment and not at least against those physically stronger. It is unlikely that women will act in the heat of the moment towards the men who are physically abusive towards them over a period of years and are twice their size and strength. Instead, a woman may wait, attacking or killing him sometime later, when he is incapacitated through sleep or drink. Within the framework of the law, the delay and lapse of time between his last violent assault or provoking act and her fatal response more readily constitute premeditation than provocation. As Scutt explains (1981):

> The man's social conditioning and physique enable him to lash-back and to come within the bounds of a mitigating defence. The woman's social conditioning and physique preclude her from reacting in the same way, and thus tend to preclude her from gaining the benefit of that rule of mitigation.

Secondly, gender ideologies penetrate even further in the concept of 'reasonable man'. What comes to pass in minds of reasonable men as provocation is influenced by background expectancies, understanding of situations, concepts of what is appropriate and inappropriate behaviour, and what certain persons, individuals and genders may be expected to tolerate and endure.

Thirdly, the requirement that force must be equal and apposite is based on a notion of appropriate male physical response and physical capability. Thus, on the few occasions when women do retaliate, it may not satisfy the proportionate retaliation test. For example, few women can box, spar or land a good punch and few women are physically able to defend themselves from the violence of a husband. The commission of the violent crime or the 'mode of resentment' by women is less likely to involve battery. Frequently it involves only one assault which may or may not be fatal. Ward *et al.* (1969, p. 120), in a study of women homicide offenders, found that their victim was helplessly drunk or otherwise incapacitated in 61 per cent of cases. In 28 per cent of cases the victim was not incapacitated and in the remaining 11 per cent no information was available. Willbanks (1983, pp. 11–12) in a study of 569 homicides found similarly that victims of female offenders were more likely to have been drinking. Female offenders were more likely to kill the victim in the home, less likely to use handguns and more likely to use a knife. The result is that women's self-defensive or retaliatory action is more likely to be perceived as cold-blooded and premeditated.

MALE–FEMALE HOMICIDES AND PROVOCATION

It seems reasonable to argue in the light of our previous discussion that, as far as male–female homicide is concerned, what passes as provocation in the everyday sense, that is, those things said and done and the factors influencing mitigation of sentence, reveal a clear gender bias. In the case of Wright (*The Times*, 14 October 1975), where the defendant killed his wife with a hammer as she lay in bed, the court was successfully persuaded by the defence, *inter alia*, that he had to contend with his wife's 'Saturday night and Sunday morning activities' with boyfriends. This amounted to provocation as a defence to manslaughter and also served to mitigate sentence. Similarly in the case of Asher, the defendant was found guilty of manslaughter by reason of provocation and given a six-month prison sentence, suspended for two years. In neither of these cases was provocation preceeded by an act of the victim. The defendant was portrayed as a model husband devoted to his children whilst the dead wife, unable to speak for herself, was portrayed as a 'flirt' a 'two-timer' and someone who 'made up to other men' (Radford, 1984, p. 88). In such cases women are seen as responsible for taunting men and such men are regarded as justifiably provoked. In cases where the provocation is considered great, as in cases of adultery by the wife, sentences have been lenient. Adultery by the wife nearly always amounts to a provocation defence. Sentencing may be for several years if the degree of provocation is considered low, and negligible if degree of provocation is considered high, as in the following case. In 1984 John Wilkes walked free from court after the murder of his wife. Mr Justice McCowan said at Shrewsbury Crown Court, 'The wife insulted, abused, threatened, lied to and goaded her husband for many months.' Convicted of manslaughter, Wilkes was put on probation for two years. The popular press in typical vernacular reported: 'A tormented husband who killed his cheating, spendthrift wife walked free from court yesterday . . .' (*Daily Mirror*, 9 October 1984).

WOMEN ON TRIAL – THE BATTERED WIFE

The courts are becoming increasingly aware that the definition of provocation is severely restrictive and that in some cases the notion of cumulative provocation, the situation so often confronting the battered wife, should be taken much more into consideration in sentencing. Wasik (1982) defines cumulative provocation in this way:

> Typically it involves a course of cruel or violent conduct by the deceased, often a domestic setting, lasting over a substantial period of time, which culminates in the victim of that conduct, or someone acting on his/her behalf, intentionally killing the tormentor.   (p. 29)

There are some recent cases which begin to reflect the court's unease with the predicament of the woman homicide offender who has suffered years of domestic violence, though many judgements remain unsympathetic and harsh. In the Scottish case of *Greig*, the appeal judge surmised:

> There were various expedients open to a woman regularly subjected to rough treatment by her husband, but a licence to kill was not one of them . . . We cannot hold that the sentence imposed was excessive – indeed it may well have been higher.   (Pattullo, 1983, p. 10)

However, in 1983 in Glasgow Freda Paterson was put on probation for two years after admitting stabbing her husband to death. She had been beaten regularly by her husband, who twice broke her jaw and fractured her ankles and her wrists (*The Times*, 27 July 1983). Again, in England Celia Ripley shot and killed her husband after suffering several years of violence and abuse. He had broken her nose and ribs, threatened to shoot her and forced her to take part in distressing sexual practices. She was convicted of manslaughter on the grounds that she was provoked and at the time was suffering from diminished responsibility. She received a short term of imprisonment (*Guardian*, 1 November 1983). A more recent case at Manchester Crown Court where Pauline Wyatt stood trial for the manslaughter of her husband again illustrates how so often women who kill husbands have previously been abused for many years. He had degraded and abused her and finally made threats to kill her and the children. At this point she said she could take no more and shot her husband whilst he was asleep in bed (Manchester Crown Court, 22/23 November 1984). In *Tickner* (Old Bailey, 16/18 July 1985), there was again a history of violence. Finally, the wife stabbed her husband during a row and she received a probation order. When their own physical abuse in the marriage is proven over a long period of years, women may receive comparatively lenient sentences. But it does seem that women must experience extremes in degradation, violence and humiliation before they may be protected or defended. And whilst women homicide offenders who kill violent husbands are so few (twelve in 1982), thousands of women are regularly abused without any assistance from remedial agencies or the legal framework. Whilst the court on occasion may show some sympathy towards the actions of a battered wife, it is unlikely that women will be able to bring successful cases of provocation where men are adulterous. In the case of *Davis*, for example, as reported in *The Times* of 29 July 1985, the accused wife claimed that her husband told her that he had another woman and that he wanted to leave her. She was jailed for killing her husband. The partial defence of diminished responsibility was allowed, but not provocation.

CONCLUSION

This chapter began with the argument that it was specious to draw a line between domestic violence assault and spousal homicide because whatever the degree of violence, notions of race, class and gender, female appropriate behaviour and duties, male domination and rights, influence discretionary decisions in the civil and criminal process at each and every level. Gender ideologies extend even further to the discretionary treatment of women in housing and custody battles that occur on the break-up of a relationship where there is domestic violence. These ideologies go beyond mere crime, affecting other resources and restitution to the victim. As the revised scheme of the Criminal Injuries Compensation Board (1983) states:

> The board will scrutinise with particular care all applications in respect
> of sexual offences or other offences arising out of a sexual relationship,
> in order to determine whether there was any responsibility, either
> because of provocation or otherwise, on the part of the victim . . . (para.
> 9)

One of the main problems, as many will agree, is the reluctance of the police to get involved and to prosecute (Dobash and Dobash, 1979, p. 207). This is because it is considered likely that a wife or cohabitee may decline to prosecute, or if proceedings are instigated, she may withdraw her allegation at some later stage. Wasoff (1982), however, found that this outcome was no more or less likely in domestic than in other cases.

With the new powers of arrest and provisions for evidence created by the Police and Criminal Evidence Act 1984 will women be more protected or conversely, more at risk, from violent assault? Under the Police and Criminal Evidence Act, 1984, spouses become compellable witnesses. The decision of *Hoskyn* v. *Metropolitan Police Commissioner* (1978: HL 2 All E.R. 138, p. 160) is now reversed. In this case their Lordships decided by a majority that though competent, the wife could not be compelled to give evidence. Lord Wilberforce justified this decision on the grounds of the 'identity of interest between husband and wife' and because 'to allow her to give evidence would give rise to discord and perjury would be, to ordinary people, repugnant'. The position set out in Section 80 of the 1984 Act confirms the dissentient view of Lord Edmund-Davis in the Hoskyn case:

> Such cases are too grave to depend simply on whether the injured spouse is, or is not, willing to testify against the attacker. Reluctance may spring from a variety of reasons and does not by any means necessarily denote that domestic harmony has been restored . . . It may well prove a positive boon for her to be directed by the courts that she has no alternative but to testify. But be that as it may, such incidents ought not to be regarded as having no importance extending beyond the domestic hearth.

The new provisions must be taken together with the impact the Crown prosecution system will have on such cases. Following the Prosecution of Offences Act, 1985, it will be up to Crown prosecutors to decide whether a case should proceed or be discontinued, what charges to bring and the mode of trial (Section 10(1)(a) and (b)). However, since it is up to the police whether to instigate proceedings, the discretion still lies with them. They may make decisions which go against the wishes of the victim and leave women more vulnerable to further abuse. However, without a corresponding confrontation of the sexist attitudes displayed by the police and the courts to female victims of assault any change in prosecution policy and arrest powers will be unlikely. So long as women are blamed for the violence which they sustain, so long as some women are considered less worthy of protection on grounds of race, sexuality or class, and so long as violence towards women remains a male prerogative, women will be victims of repeated common assault and ultimately homicide.

Acknowledgement
I would like to acknowledge the assistance of Dorothy Mukasa in the typing and preparation of this chapter.

12 The Response of the British and American Women's Movements to Violence Against Women

R. Emerson Dobash and
Russell P. Dobash

In charting the discovery of the problem of wife abuse, the building of a social movement, and the formulation of responses in Great Britain and the USA, it is only possible in this chapter to touch upon some of the most important events and issues within the larger struggle for change. In both countries, the battered women's (BW) movement emerged from the broader women's movement and has formed a significant part of it since the early 1970s. The accomplishments of the BW movements during the last decade involved numerous crucial struggles over the recognition of the problem, recognition and legitimation of grass-roots activists, definitions of causes and solutions and construction of pragmatic and direct ways of working within these movements as well as with outside agencies. It is important to stress that the achievements have been gained through continuous struggle and confrontations, although this chapter will concentrate more on the outcome than the process by which it was achieved.

DISCOVERY OF THE PROBLEM AND EMERGENCE OF THE MOVEMENTS

The BW movement began in Britain in 1972 with the opening of the first refuge by Chiswick Women's Aid. It was originally started by a group of feminists who wanted to do something about the position of women in society. They began with a march by 200 women and children and a cow in protest against the elimination of free school

169

milk, soon obtained a community women's meeting place and soon discovered that women were being battered and were in need of a place of refuge (Dobash and Dobash, 1979, p. 1; Rose, 1978a, 1978b and 1979; Sutton, 1978). Against the wishes of the local council, the community centre became a 24-hour refuge for battered women. With this seemingly inauspicious beginning a national and international movement had begun. In the USA, the BW movement began a few years later and its initial character, while to some extent informed by the British experience, was affected most specifically by the existing women's liberation movement and the anti-rape and anti-child abuse movements in America. The first American shelters specifically for battered women began in 1974 with the formation of Women's Advocates in Minnesota and in 1976 with the opening of Transition House in Boston (Schechter, 1982). Both these groups had their roots in the women's movement and were orientated to direct action. Transition House began in the apartment of two former battered women and Women's Advocates developed from a consciousness raising group that set itself the task of 'doing something' (Schechter, 1982; Leghorn, 1978).

In both countries, the new issue of wife abuse extended the recognition of women's oppression beyond the more personal concerns of consciousness-raising and public spheres of waged work, safety in public places and the like, and into the very heartland of private life, the family. More importantly, the movements sought explanations and solutions not only in forms of individual deviance, such as alcohol abuse, but also in the relations between the sexes from the most personal level to the wider social and cultural spheres. This included a consideration of the criminal justice system, the social services, medicine, religion, the economy and deeply-held and highly-revered beliefs in male domination and female subordination which underpinned and supported the use of violence (Dobash and Dobash 1977 and 1978; Massachusetts Coalition of Battered Women Service Groups, 1981; Warrior, 1982).

Soon after these early beginnings, although not always as a direct consequence of them, shelters began to open all over Britain, the continent and the USA. Throughout the 1970s, public attention was increasingly turned to exposing the existence of wife abuse. As awareness spread, women began to respond in increasing numbers either by forming new groups or by taking on the new issue as part of an existing consciousness-raising or women's liberation group. There was an explosion of activity, first in Britain and somewhat later in America.

Efforts to raise public awareness about the very existence of this abuse and its extent and severity required active involvement with the media and the public. Attempts to set up refuges, safe houses and telephone hotlines were often monumental tasks requiring hours of work, almost always without pay to raise funds, find accommodation, answer phones and deal with the details of opening and maintaining a shelter.[1] Most of all, the efforts and time were focused upon the women who had been beaten and were seeking some form of support and assistance.

Responses were developed through direct contact with the women who sought assistance, and formulated in terms of their particular problems and needs. As such, new issues arose constantly and innovative responses were quickly adopted, modified or rejected depending upon how useful or successful they were in practice. This innovative period was open, rather than rigid, and anything seemed possible including educating the public, pressing for changes in public agencies, and, for some groups, attempting to re-order the wider social conditions that underpinned the continued use of violence.

MAJOR ACHIEVEMENTS IN THE FIRST DECADE

During the first decade, major achievements were made by the BW movement at local and national levels. At the local level in both countries the problem was recognised and placed on the public and political agenda by activists. There were massive efforts to develop public awareness, gain support in the community and to obtain changes in the response of agencies of the state, particularly the criminal justice system.

Certainly the most important efforts at the local level were establishing refuges, safehouses and hotlines to serve the needs of women who had been battered and were seeking some form of assistance and/or escape from violence. By 1982 there were 719 shelters affiliated with the National Coalition Against Domestic Violence in America. On average, the American shelters each serve fifteen women and children who usually stay about two weeks (NCADV, 1982). This means that approximately 270 000 women and children were being sheltered annually by coalition shelters where once there was virtually no provision. A 1978 survey of refuges in England and Wales revealed that the average length of stay was five and a half months, and at any one time 900 women were residing in the

128 refuges with an average of six women and nine children per refuge (Binney *et al.*, 1981). None the less, it is sobering to realise that this number represents only a very small proportion of all the women who are battered each year and try to obtain shelter. In fact, a parliamentary select committee recommended that the initial target for refuges should be one family place per 10 000 of the population.[2]

In addition to the establishment of direct services to battered women through refuges and shelters, the grass-roots women's groups have expended considerable effort and demonstrated ingenuity in obtaining funding from a variety of private, corporate and government sources which they used in a number of diverse and innovative programmes. This is particularly true in America where the emphasis on large, comprehensive programmes is much greater than in Britain. The programmes include the development of educational materials, conferences and workshops, job training and advocacy for battered women, children's programmes, community outreach, race relations, provisions for counselling residents and staff, 'burn out' among staff, telephone networks, funding strategies and many others. The list is a tribute both to the energy and pragmatic innovation of the members of the movement, and to the inspiration they have given to others, including the men who began programmes for batterers, such as 'Emerge' in Boston and 'Raven' in St Louis.[3]

The efforts to obtain funding were much more intense in America than in Britain. They tended to concentrate on obtaining a relatively secure place in the allocations from block grants by establishing shelters as a priority and making battering one of the problems included in the allocation of federal funds, given to the states in the form of Aid to Dependent Children, housing, food stamps and the like. These provided a means by which some battered women, that is, those who are poor, might make claims in their own right. One of the most ingenious efforts to obtain funding has been the Marriage Tax. Since it is through entering marriage (legal or social) that a woman becomes the potential victim of the ancient practice of control of wives through chastisement, some states have taxed the marriage licence in order to help support refuges for victims of violence. Not only does the tax provide a stable source of funding for some shelters, it also makes a powerful political point about one of the causes of the violence.

NATIONAL ACHIEVEMENTS

The first developments at the national level began when the parliamentary select committee began public hearings in 1974 and, somewhat later, the US Civil Rights Commission held hearings on the issue of wife battering in January 1978. *Report from the Select Committee on Violence in Marriage* (vols 1 and 2, 1975) and *Battered Women: Issues of Public Policy* (US Commission on Civil Rights, 1978), are the British and American documentations of evidence taken from battered women, activists, researchers, lawyers and many others. The effect of the feminist analysis of the issue was such that in both countries the general orientation of the committees reflected quite strongly the notions that the violence was systematic and severe, that it was related at least partially to the status of women in society and that the state should respond quickly and positively both to the current victims of the violence and to the general problem itself. This perspective was much stronger in the American hearings than in the British. For example, in his opening comments, the chairperson of the US Civil Rights Commission hearings, stated:

> Many feel . . . that the focus should be on the wider cultural and societal influences which produce batterers. Such advocates note that prevalent cultural norms legitimize the use of physical force by a husband against his wife . . .   (US Commission on Civil Rights, 1978, p. 11)

Del Martin, a well-known American feminist and activist, was asked to give the opening address in which she clearly indicated the relationship between the violent abuse of wives and cohabitants and the subordinate social and economic position of women throughout society. She set the tone by focusing upon the institution of marriage, the supports for male domination and equal rights before the law and in employment. Those who followed during the two days of meetings gave similar analyses of the position of women in law, medicine and the criminal justice system.[4]

Although the general thrust of the evidence seemed to be that this was a distressing problem and one that would require considerable active support from government agencies if it was to be tackled, the general analysis of the problem focused on the inequality of women in the family and society. Some element of confusion and considerable disbelief was brought into the proceedings by Murray Straus, when he presented the research undertaken by himself and his colleagues,

Richard Gelles and Suzanne Steinmetz, and claimed that there were more battered husbands in America than there were battered wives. During the verbal altercation that ensued, two major points were made: the first was that all existing evidence from America and other countries revealed a consistent pattern in which the perpetrators of violence between marital partners is almost always the man, and secondly, the Steinmetz, Straus and Gelles research had very serious methodological shortcomings as the Conflict Tactic Scale used to measure violence resulted in misleading findings.[5] While even more scientific and political criticisms were yet to come, the negative impact of these findings was soon felt in some local shelters. For example, local officials withdrew funds from the shelter in Chicago with the caveat that if women are as violent as men, then why should women be provided with shelter when attacked. This episode foreshadowed future controversy between researchers and activists over the nature of the problem itself and who constituted legitimate spokespersons, or experts on the issue.

NATIONAL ORGANISATIONS

In America, discussions about forming a national organisation began in November 1977 at the International Women's year meeting in Texas. It was, however, at the 1978 Senate Hearings in Washington DC that those discussions began to be translated into action and The National Coalition Against Domestic Violence was born. Once formed, the NCADV established a steering committee with three directives: to set up an organisational structure, hold a national conference and lobby for national legislation (Schechter, 1982). The first national membership conference was held in 1980, in Washington DC. It was attended by 600 women from all forty-nine states (Brygger, 1982). Prior to this the steering committee had decided upon the goals for the fledgling national organisation:

1. To monitor and impact legislation relating to domestic violence and family policy.
2. To aid in the development of state and regional coalitions.
3. To develop a national network of shelters.
4. To educate the public to a non-acceptance of violence and to strive toward the complete elimination of violence in our society.
5. To support and initiate change in traditional sex-role expectations for women and men (NCADV, 1978, p. 15).

These five principles established the basic orientation to the issue of battering and task forces and committees formed the basic structure for conducting work and managing relations both within the Coalition and with outside agencies. The ideology was one of caring self-help and egalitarian organisations; the strategy was for direct action and lobbying for legislative change; the goals were social change for women in the family, society, the law and public policy.

By contrast, the earlier formation of the National Women's Aid Federation (NWAF), was not hindered to the same extent by geographic distance, although the time and expense of national gatherings was certainly not unproblematic. NWAF began in 1974, after the first meeting of the fledgling Women's Aid groups from England, Scotland and Wales. This was marked by the first major split in the movement between the vast majority who wished to form a democratic and egalitarian organisation (NWAF) and one group who wished to maintain central control and power (Chiswick Women's Aid) (Dobash and Dobash, 1979, p. 223; Rose, 1979; Sutton, 1978). As a consequence, the Federation was formed without the group which had so captured media attention that it was sometimes thought to be the only refuge in Britain.

The NWAF began with five basic principles:

1. To provide temporary refuge, on request, for women and their children who have suffered mental or physical harassment.
2. To encourage the women to determine their own futures and to help them achieve them, whether this involves returning home or starting a new life elsewhere.
3. To recognise and care for the emotional and educational needs of the children involved.
4. To offer support and advice and help to any woman who asks for it, whether or not she is a resident, and also to offer support and aftercare to any woman and child who has left the refuge.
5. To educate and inform the public, the media, the police, the courts, the social services and other authorities, with respect to the battering of women, mindful of the fact that this is a result of the general position of women in our society (NWAF, 1975 and 1978; Sutton, 1978).

A national organisation now exists for each country, England, Scotland, Wales, Northern Ireland and Ireland and almost every local Women's Aid group belongs to one of them.[6]

LEGISLATION

In Britain, legislative reform came relatively early in the history of the movement and is much more straightforward than the two-tiered system of national and state legislation that exists in America. Two major pieces of legislation were passed: the Domestic Violence and Matrimonial Proceedings Act, 1976 provided for injunctions, exclusion orders and arrest for violation of injunctions; the Housing and Homeless Persons Act, 1977 imposed duties on local authorities to house women who were made homeless through battering. While both represent advances in protection of victims neither has been without problems in enforcement, given the reluctance of police and housing authorities to comply with the laws (Binney *et al.*, 1985).

In the USA, legislative reform led to new laws in most states. Activity began with class actions brought on behalf of battered women against the police of New York City and Oakland, California, for their systematic failure to enforce the laws against assault. In theory, the new state laws have provided greater protection for victims, specified arrest procedures for offenders and heightened the enforcement of both. A few developed new procedures for victim support and alternative sanctions (Boylan and Taub, 1981; Hamos, 1980; Lerman, 1981). Each piece of legislation represents an enormous effort in educating, lobbying and building alliances with politicians. As always, the passage of legislation represents both change and compromise.

Finally, there has been an ongoing campaign for the passage of federal legislation to provide a source of stable and continuous financial support for the shelters. This began in 1978 with the introduction of the Domestic Violence Act (Bill) which failed with the election of Ronald Reagan (Schechter, 1982). The legislation to provide funding was reintroduced in a more modest form and has recently become law.[7]

DIFFERENCES BETWEEN AMERICAN AND BRITISH MOVEMENTS

Any summation of the achievements during the first decade of the British and American movements would be an understatement. While we have highlighted many of the similarities between them, particularly their initial orientations and achievements, there are also some fundamental differences. In the most general sense, the movements differ in ways that reflect the varied approaches to social problems taken in each country. There is a great orientation to the individual in America, while in Britain it is to the community. When translated into action, American attention is drawn to individual rights and personal problems. This leads to an emphasis on the law and the psycho-medico professions. Legislative reform is directed at providing individuals with the vehicle for obtaining personal rights in law, while a variety of therapeutic responses are developed to deal with techniques for coping and/or personal development. This involves a large number of lawyers and other professionals who often compete for predominance in funding, provision of services and as relevant experts. Sometimes these professionals are activists who view themselves as 'experts' working for battered women with a feminist perspective and stressing the necessity for wider social changes in addition to individual assistance. Although it is equally likely that experts may also come from outside the movement and offer competing anti-feminist solutions and perspectives.

In Britain, the orientation to community and state responses led to greater emphasis on the work of voluntary agencies, such as Women's Aid, and on changes in the support offered by state agencies such as housing and social work. Much less attention is paid to criminal justice and little to therapy. The approaches to funding are also very different. It is much more intensive in the USA, where there is no secure funding for shelters to provide accommodation at an affordable cost. Large mortgages must be paid and the commitment to very large, ever-expanding programmes with fairly well paid directors and professionals means that funding to a very high level is deemed to be crucial and often dominates programmes in a way that does not occur in Britain.

If the sheer volume of accomplishments is one of the most obvious characteristics of the battered women's movements, diversity is the other. This permeates everything from programme development to organisational structure and reflects both the energy and ingenuity of these movements. Ideology, tactics, short and long term goals for change continue to be worked out primarily through the processes of localised decision-making, programme developments, organisation building and resolution of conflicts.

These efforts have become increasingly difficult with the expanding conservatism of the governments in both countries and their widening attacks on social programmes. For example, NWAF has closed its office in London because of funding problems and refuges have had to close in both countries. As such the approach to the future will be one demanding continued efforts to maintain what has been gained and prevent erosion, because of cutbacks, while at the same time sustaining the sense of development that has characterised the brief history of the Battered Women's Movement.

REFERENCES

1. See, for example, the accounts in 'Learning from Women's Aid: A Paper from Northern Ireland Women's Aid', *Aegis* (September/October, 1978); Scottish Women's Aid Annual Report (1984); Welsh Women's Aid Annual Report (1984). Details are also given in Binney *et al.*, 1981; Evason, 1982; Pahl, 1978; Schechter, 1982; Warrior, 1976.
2. See the report from the Parliamentary Select Committee on Violence in Marriage, vol. 2, Session 1974–75 (London: HMSO, 1975) p. xxxi.
3. Some of the programmes for men who batter are described in 'Emerge: A Men's Counselling Service', *Aegis* (Winter/Spring, 1980); 'Men Against Violence Against Women', *Aegis* (Winter/Spring, 1980), 'Battering Men's Project', *Aegis* (Winter/ Spring, 1980).
4. See D. Martin, 'Overview: Scope of the Problem', USCCR *Battered Women: Issues of Public Policy* (1978) (Washington DC: US Government Printing Office), pp. 3–18; M. Fields, 'Wife Beating: Government Intervention Policies and Practices', USCCR, *Battered Women: Issues of Public Policy* (1978), (Washington DC: US Government Printing Office) pp. 228–87; A. Flitcraft, 'Shelters: Short Term Needs, A Response', USCCR, *Battered Women: Issues of Public Policy* (1978) (Washington DC: Government Printing Office), pp. 113–34.
5. See M. Straus, 'Wife Beating: Causes, Treatment and Research Needs', in USCCR, *Battered Women: Issues of Public Policy*, pp. 152–56 and 463–526, (Washington DC: US Government Printing Office); E. Hilberman, 'Response to Murray Straus', in USCCR, *Battered Women: Issues of Public Policy*, (1978), pp. 157–9, 527–31; E. Pleck, J. Pleck, M. Grossman and P. Bart, 'The Battered Data Syndrome: A Reply to Steinmetz', *Victimology: An International Journal*, vol. 2, no. 3–4 (1977), pp. 680–3; M. D. Pagelow, *Women-Battering: Victims and Their Experiences* (Beverly Hills, California: Saga Publications, 1981); R. E. Dobash and R. P. Dobash, 'Social Science and Social Action: The Case of Wife Beating', *Journal of Family Issues*, vol. 2, no. 4 (1981), p. 439–70; R. P. Dobash and R. E. Dobash, 'The Context Specific Approach to Studying Violence Against Women', pp. 261–76, D. Finkelhor *et al.* (eds), *The Dark Side of Families* (London: Sage, 1983).
6. Scottish Women's Aid, Ainslie House, 11 St Colme Street, Edinburgh, Scotland; Welsh Women's Aid, Incentive House, Adam Street, Cardiff, Wales; Irish Women's Aid, 143a University Street, Belfast, Northern

Ireland; Women's Aid Federation (England), 52/54 Featherstone Street, London EC1, (the latter no longer in existence).

7. For recommendations about state and federal legislation see *Attorney General's Task Force on Family Violence: Final Report* (Washington DC: US Department of Justice, 1984), pp. 96–107.

13 Masculinity and Violence
David H. J. Morgan

AUTHOR'S INTRODUCTION

Whether we are concerned with battles on the football terraces or the films of Clint Eastwood, the rational conduct of modern warfare or more individual and less controlled manifestations of aggression, the links between the terms 'masculinity' and 'violence' would seem to be straightforward and, for many people, almost 'natural'. Where women have engaged in, or been associated with, violent activities this involvement has usually been carefully circumscribed and indeed often stigmatised as unnatural or abnormal. As Virginia Woolf (1977) wrote:

> . . . to fight has always been the man's habit, not the woman's. Law and practice have developed that difference, whether innate or accidental. (p. 9)

The purpose of this chapter is not to deny that men have been implicated in all kinds of violence at all kinds of levels. If, as a sociologist, I am sceptical of the term 'innate' in this connection, I must recognise that Woolf's alternative, 'accidental', would appear to understate the issue. What I am attempting to do here is, firstly, to explore the everyday bracketing of the terms 'masculinity' and 'violence'. Rather than to assume some set of traits which are unambiguously linked to biological males, I seek to argue that what links these phenomena are *constructions* of masculinity, widely-held dominant and highly persuasive notions about what men are and, by implication, what women are. Such notions are rooted in, reinforce and are reinforced by the sexual division of labour, and behind this the deeper, more general, constructions of public and private, and of culture and nature. These notions are sufficiently variable and their links sufficiently complex to justify the adoption of a plural term, *masculinities*.

The other side of the equation, violence, is also equally various and diffuse. Here too I am not dealing with a single stranded and relatively identifiable phenomenon but rather a set of constructions and distinctions that are used and deployed within society. As with 'masculinities' I prefer to pluralise the term 'violences' (see Dobash and Dobash, 1979, p. 9). I am concerned with a set of complex processes within society, which include:

(a) Processes by which violence is recognised or identified as such. To a very large extent we are dealing with contested or competing definitions or understandings.

(b) Processes by which violence is legitimised (see Dobash and Dobash, 1979, p. 9). This is closely related to the first in that legitimised violence very often goes under some other name such as 'force' or 'restraint'.

(c) Processes by which violence is excused or condoned. Here violence may be recognised as such but may be excused or rendered as 'understandable in the circumstances', given the pressures, the provocations and so on.

(d) Processes by which violence is explained. This is closely related to (c) in that certain classes of explanations (for example, with reference to 'nature') might be said to 'count' as providing sufficient excuse.

Men and masculinity are implicated in all these processes to do with the construction of violence. Given the sexual division of labour and the particular position of men in relation to activities to do with the state and warfare, men may play a crucial role in defining the parameters within which violence is defined and understood. Striking examples of this would be judgements in the case of rape or domestic violence, including the murder or manslaughter of wives. A more detailed and rigorous investigation would, therefore, entail an examination of the relationships between men, masculinities and the processes by which violence is recognised, legitimised, excused and explained.

A second aim of this chapter is to begin to explore the possible links between different violences, between different 'levels' of violence. As has already been indicated, the term 'violence' is used to refer to an extremely wide range of situations, between, say, the immediate and direct interpersonal violence within the home and the much more remote violence that characterises modern technological warfare. Men are centrally involved at all 'levels' of violence but the links between these levels must be seen as something more complex (and often more contradictory) than the idea of some universal 'masculinity' being expressed in a wide range of contexts.

It should be noted at the outset that I am not primarily concerned in this chapter with sexual violence. The other chapters in this book are much more concerned with sexual violence and violences against women and I would not wish to deny the importance of these issues. Nor would I wish to deny that there are crucial and complex linkages to be made between the kinds of violence with which I am chiefly concerned and the concerns of many of the other chapters in this book. For example, as MacKinnon (1982) has argued, socially constructed definitions of masculinity and femininity (in terms of, for example, vulnerability, passivity, softness and their equivalent masculine contrasts) are strongly linked to dominant understandings of sexuality, especially heterosexual conduct. Moreover, the control that men exercise over the use and expression of violence, in almost all its forms, has among its consequences the control and intimidation of women and the maintenance of sexual divisions of labour and boundaries between public and private spheres. Nevertheless, this chapter is mainly concerned with the violence that men do to each other, in the pub, in the boxing ring or on the battlefield and only incidentally with the violence that men do to women.

SOME DISTINCTIONS

Rather than attempting to provide a definition of violence at the outset it would be preferable to recognise that it is a fluid, negotiated topic and that a sociological investigation is interested in its multiple and overlapping usages within a particular society. To that extent it is like any other term in wide use, with the possible qualification that its usage is more emotionally charged than many others. Illustrations of its contested nature abound, and constitute the source of considerable religious, political and moral debate. The pit-strike of 1984–5 provided many illustrations of the contested use of the term 'violence' as do debates about terrorism and corporal punishment.

In the multiplicity of usages that we are confronted with, one crucial distinction would seem to be between 'legitimated' and 'non-legitimated' violence. The term 'legitimated' rather than 'legitimate' is used to emphasise the point that processes rather than fixed structures or uncontested essences are being discussed. Indeed, in some cases it would seem that the legitimation process may be so effective that the violence almost disappears (corporal punishment in schools or at home, for example). As in the case of treason, where violence prospers none dare call it violence.

The legitimation of violence is closely linked to its position and practice in the sexual division of labour. Whether our focus be modern armies or military structures (see, for example, Enloe, 1983, pp. 127–30) or one which takes a much wider, cross cultural perspective (for example, Sanday, 1981a, p. 77) the dominance of men and the marginalisation of women in the business of warfare appears close to universal. We can see this as a part of a much broader nexus of relationships linking the exercise of power and the state, on the one hand, and the ideological maintenance of gender boundaries on the other. War is carried out in defence of 'our' women (Ehrenreich, 1983, p. 153), women are defined as 'the protected' (Stiehm, 1982, p. 367) even though, at the same time, they may be incorporated into men's wars in a variety of practical and ideological ways (Enloe, 1983; Arcana, 1983, p. 115).

The processes by which this legitimation is achieved are extremely various. Woolf, for example, noted the crucial importance of parades and national ceremonies and that military uniforms are often among the most splendid that regularly appear upon public display (Woolf, 1977, p. 25). Soldiers and uniforms are ever present at state and ceremonial occasions, times which celebrate (if not, perhaps, in quite the straightforwardly Durkheimian way argued by Shils and Young, 1953) themes of nation and solidarity and also, if more latently, themes of masculinity and the sexual division of labour. Legitimation of violence (which in effect often means the denial of the application of the signifier, 'violence') also occurs in mythologies and stories (Arcana, 1983, p. 135; Huston, 1982, p. 271). A key element here is the construction of the hero and the heroic. The hero is a man (Pearson and Pope, 1981) who overcomes odds and undergoes a series of trials (Propp, 1968; Wright, 1975) and more often than not displays the heroic qualities in combat with other men or on the battlefield. Combat may become a metaphor for other kinds of largely masculine activities such as living the Christian life in its 'muscular' version, engaging in business or commerce, climbing mountains or making scientific breakthroughs (for further illustrations see, for example, Dubbert, 1979).

One further way in which violence may be legitimised is through a process of normalisation. Whether we are considering the everyday play of small boys or the spectacular portrayal of battles in many of our art galleries, violence and its association with the masculine become part of the 'taken-for-granted'. One consequence of this is the denial of legitimacy for violence when it is carried out by women. Such violence may be seen as unladylike, unwomanly or as something demanding a special kind of explanation. In our own times, manifestations of violence on the part of women may be 'medicalised' that is, explained in terms which both define the behaviour as abnormal and link it with factors intimately connected with being a woman, such as pre-menstrual tension or post-natal depression (Edwards, 1984).

There are other distinctions that might be made. Legitimated violence, for example, would often seem to imply some notion of control or proportionality. However, a simple mapping of the uncontrolled/controlled distinction on to the non-legitimated/legitimated distinction is not possible. There is also a distinction, cutting across these, between 'understandable' and 'non-understandable' forms of violence. Some forms of violence are said to be 'beyond belief' and these forms are not necessarily those which seem to be the most uncontrolled. 'Calculated violence' may come under the heading of acts "beyond belief" while, "uncontrollable urges or passions" may be understandable or treated as such under certain circumstances' (Taylor, 1972). A further distinction, already implied in the discussion, is that between 'individual' and 'collective' forms of violence.

Such distinctions can, and no doubt should, be multiplied and refined. Let me for a moment emphasise the point, that I am dealing with a set of processes whereby violence is recognised, evaluated, classified and legitimated. These processes cannot be understood outside wider structures of power and control especially, in this context, in terms of the sexual division of labour and patriarchal institutions.

LINKS BETWEEN LEVELS

One abiding problem within sociology continues to be the question of the links and connections between different levels of analysis and how, indeed, these different levels are understood and conceptualised (Morgan, 1985). In very simplistic terms we may elaborate the distinction between the individual and the collective manifestations of violence within the latter distinguishing between 'group' violence (for example, street gangs) and more organised forms of warfare at a societal level. It may be possible to argue that the search for links is doomed from the start, that the levels or types of violences are different things altogether and should be treated as such. Such connections as are made, it may be argued, belong to polemic or rhetoric, rather than to analysis. One may have some sympathy with this view, although at this stage it would be unwise to close off this field of exploration prematurely. Nevertheless, such links that do exist must be considerably more complex than assuming that wars are manifestations of masculine violence (or aggression) writ large, just as it would be simplistic to assume that individual manifestations are enactments of ideological or cultural definitions of 'man as warrior'.

The analysis of violence in a group context would seem to be a vital part of this particular jigsaw puzzle. In this we would need to look at the ways in which group relations serve to legitimise, socialise and reproduce values and practices connected with violence. Here we would wish to explore the importance of peer group relations for those who are professionally involved in the practice and control of violence, especially the military and the police. We would also be interested in the way in which certain groups, sometimes called 'deviant groups', give recognition and legitimacy to violent behaviour and see the successful engagement in street violence as a mark of status or prestige. There are examples here in Whyte's (1943) 'corner boys' and Willis's (1977) 'lads'. We might also consider a whole range of institutionalised practices such as family feuds, playing the dozens or duelling which are given sanctions by the wider social networks and group relationships within which such activities take place.

Nevertheless, pervasive though these practices and manifestations are, and while the analysis of such forms of groups behaviour and sub-cultural expectations must be a valuable part of our exploration, there are pitfalls in this line of analysis. In the first place, one version of this line of analysis (the 'sub-culture of violence' theory) does seem to present all the difficulties associated with our sub-cultural theories, particularly the arguments around the 'culture of poverty' concept. In the extreme case, such arguments may be both racist and sexist. Thus, the implication of the 'mother-centred household' in these sub-cultural patterns of violence (or cultures of poverty) may be another version of blaming the victim, at least in so far as it removes these households from wider historical or structural considerations. In the second place, the argument that soldiers' behaviour and informal group relations represent some kind of carry-over from lower-class street or playground culture (Elkin, 1946a; Moskos, 1970) while persuasive, does suffer from an excessive concentration on the behaviour of subordinates. Platoons of soldiers may indeed carry over certain masculine tendencies from their street gangs or play groups and these may be emphasised in their patterns of speech, their emphasis on virility, on getting 'pissed', and so on (Elkin, 1946a and b, p. 1). However, might it not also be reasonable to suppose that the officers' mess carries over similar patterns of behaviour derived from elite educational institutions or sporting activities? In either case, the picture would need to be modified to examine the processes by which the relatively autonomous military structures use and shape and encourage patterns of group or sub-cultural behaviour experienced outside and prior to induction into the army.

In any event, the analysis of violence in group or sub-cultural contexts must examine the ways in which such groups *control*, and not simply encourage, violence. Groups of 'lads' or 'hearties' do not simply encourage indiscriminate violence, and prestige is most likely to go to someone who can handle himself when necessary (like Doc in *Street Corner Society*; see Whyte, 1943) rather than someone who lashes out in all directions. Calling the dozens, duelling and even bar-room brawling (Dyck, 1980) are forms of rule-governed behaviour.

However, the analysis need not be confined to the lower or subordinate echelons of military organisations. Some years ago, Frankenberg (1972) argued that the processes of top-level decision making, whether in wartime or peacetime, could be understood with the aid of insights derived from small-scale anthropological studies. Military decisions are taken by groups and the culture of top or elite groups is at least as deserving of close study (if often more difficult) than the relations among those who take the orders. This idea is interestingly developed by Janis (1971) in a paper called 'Groupthink Among Policy Makers' (in Sandford (ed.), pp. 71–89) and dealing specifically with some of the processes of decision-making at the time of the Vietnam War. Relative isolation and secrecy combine with similarities of background to produce a sub-culture in which hawkish qualities appear to be likely to have the ascendancy.

One obvious and 'taken-for-granted' uniformity of background which is not dealt with by Janis, or by most other analysts of top decision-makers, is the uniformity of gender. Yet masculinity, as Enloe (1983) argues, is one of the unheralded features of the 'military–industrial complex':

But virtually no analysts . . . of the military–industrial, complex have described the ways in which the network depends upon male bonding, male privilege and militarily derived notions of masculinity. (p. 193; see also Burstyn, 1983)

Thus, apart from the Senior Women Officers' Commission, the NATO elite is, she points out, an all-male club (*ibid.*, p. 131). It is interesting that a recent periodical presenting a super-masculine picture of war and weaponry is called *The Elite* (Dyer, 1985).

Group relations at all levels, therefore, represent one way in which the various levels of society and action might be related, between constructed masculine qualities and their individual manifestation and collective, and legitimised, forms of violence. It is important, to avoid reification and essentialism, to see this as a two-way process.

Another way in which these interactions can be seen to work is in terms of ideology. By ideology, I am referring to the processes by which certain assumed qualities are attached – anchored – to men and women and how these qualities are elaborated to explain or justify the differential distribution of men and women in the wider division of labour. Again, it must be emphasised that I am talking about an interaction; it is just as likely that the military and soldiering provide a set of metaphors for masculinity as the reverse. If war, as Virginia Woolf (1977) maintained, is a male institution, this should be seen as a matter of 'social and historical reality' rather than the outcome of any necessary connection with biological males. (Yudkin, 1982).

The ways in which ideology attaches masculine (and feminine) qualities to different tasks, statutes and practices is complex and various. For example, one particular pattern particularly associated with Mediterranean or Latin American cultures is concerned with notions of honour, reputation and its defence or protection (Peristiany, 1965; Pitt-Rivers, 1977; Horowitz and Schwartz, 1974). These cultures would seem to emphasise particularistic relationships, dense-knit networks, a rigid symbolic and spatial separation of spheres between men and women and an emphasis on honour as being particularly bound up with the reputation of those women – wife, daughters, sisters – attached to a man. In some cases this may lead to an understanding of the world as particularly threatening or hostile and a consequently limited extension of trust to those other men with whom one may come in contact (Weissman, 1981, p. 26). This particular nexus of honour and reputation would seem to be more properly related to notions of *machismo* than the more extended and metaphorical uses of that term in recent decades. In this context, then, masculinity is a personal quality, built up on a reputational basis in a context of dense networks and personalistic ties, something which is tried and tested by rules which are locally understood.

This contrasts, in an ideal typical fashion, with the kind of masculinity with which people in this country may be more familiar and which may be said to be associated with capitalism and the Protestant ethic. It is a more abstract construction of masculinity, a set of qualities or properties which may be said to be attached to men as a category rather than to particular men in particular situations. The reference, then, is to a more abstracted sense of men's *nature*. Increasingly over the last two centuries, the justification has been made in terms of science: men and women's natures come to be structured by scientific, perhaps psychologistic, understandings (Edwards, 1981). Thus, it is not a particular man defending the honour of a particular woman (and consequently his reputation) but generalised men excluding generalised women from particular statuses or roles on abstracted or scientific grounds:

> Western armed services . . . search for a difference which can justify women's continued exclusion from the military's ideological core – combat.   (Enloe, 1983, p. 138)

As physical strength decreases as a significant feature in the conduct of warfare (see, for example, McNeill, 1983), so the ideological site shifts to other qualities or properties, to do with, say, hormones or bodily cycles.

Little need be said, in this context, of the other major link between individual and societal levels, that of the socialisation process. This has been dealt with extensively in a variety of ways, social-psychological, psycho-analytical, sociological and historical. All that will be said here is to emphasise the complexity of the process and to underline a sense of the family-based household, within which such processes typically take place, as being a point of intersection for the public and the private, the individual and society, and for past and present to meet (Morgan, 1985). Some accounts of gender socialisation, in their textbook versions at least, focus upon the more active and obvious manifestations in terms of 'Action Man' for the boy and 'Barbie doll' for the girl. These accounts, and some, of course, have considerably more depth and subtlety than this, are accounts of the processes whereby gender differences and the inequalities are *reproduced* and maintained (Brittan and Maynard, 1984, pp. 71–112). Other accounts have a more active emphasis and consider the processes whereby masculinities and femininities are *generated*, focusing particularly on how women, in our culture, entrusted with the task of parenting as a full-time activity, produce boys and men with all the attributes commonly associated with that gender: self-sufficiency, strength, aggressiveness, and so on (Chodorow, 1978; Arcana, 1983).

SOME DIFFICULTIES

We may begin, therefore, to elaborate links between the different levels or kinds of violences in a variety of ways through the examination of group relationships, ideology and socialisation processes. But the movements and transitions between different violences are never straightforward; on the contrary, we encounter a host of paradoxes, puzzles and contradictions on the way. A few of these may be mentioned in the hope that their consideration may lead to a more sophisticated analysis. Most of these complications stem from the fact that in considering group or cultural contexts of violence we are as much concerned with the control of violence as with its encouragement:

1. The relationship between group or cultural norms and the expression of violence is considerably more complex than the phrase 'sub-culture of violence' might suggest. For example, 'scrapping' may be a common activity in some western Canadian bars (Dyck, 1980), yet men are not *obliged* to scrap in these contexts and are not thought of as 'unmasculine' if they define themselves as 'non-scrappers'. In contrast, certain types of scrappers known as 'chicken-shit bastards' (cowardly bullies) and 'rangatangs' (from orangutan) are feared and avoided rather than admired. Admiration may be accorded to the 'man who can take care of himself' but even that may not extend beyond the bar-room.

Certainly, the dynamics of interpersonal violence in group contexts, and its relationship to a sense of self and gender identity, are often complex indeed. Toch (1969), for example, in his often subtle analyses of violent encounters with the police shows a kind of game in which both sides, equally influenced by notions of masculinity, test each other to a point of no return (pp. 79–84). In attempting to show, by words or body posture, that one is capable of and willing to take care of oneself, a man may provoke that very outcome he is seeking to avoid.

In some cases, of course, a male group may exercise even stricter controls over the expression of violence, an example being provided by Weissman's (1981) elegant discussion of ritual brotherhood in Renaissance Florence. Here the immediate neighbourhood relationships are characterised by uncertainty, danger and a need to be ever on one's guard; Weissman uses the term 'angonistic' to describe relationships at the local level. Cutting across local-level relationships, however, there developed confraternities of *laudesi* (dedicated to the exaltation of God and the saints) and *disciplinati*, penitential flagellants. Here, 'true brotherhood' might be practised without fear or guilt or duplicity (Weissman, 1981, p. 79), and there was an emphasis on peaceable relationships.

2. Even where groups may encourage the expression of violence and qualities such as toughness, not backing down, being able to look after oneself, and so on, it is not necessarily the case that these qualities are ones which are required by a modern, bureaucratic and technocratic army (McNeill, 1983). Qualities which may be prized on the street may lead to the guardroom in the context of military disciplines.

3. Not only is it the case that modern rational military disciplines stand in sharp contrast to traditional heroic or manly skills but it would appear to be true that many modern societies have little place for their heroes once the conflicts that provided the occasion for heroism cease. Veterans, from World War I to the Falklands War, very quickly become a source of embarrassment or boredom. Perhaps the best heroes are dead heroes and the reputation in the cannon's mouth is a bubble that is easily broken.

4. Even where the modern army denies the opportunity to demonstrate traditional manly heroics, groups of buddies may find the opportunity to express masculinity in swearing, boozing, gambling and sexual adventures (Elkin, 1946a and b; Moskos, 1970; Dubbert, 1979, pp. 64–5 and 236–7). However, as organisational theorists have pointed out at some length, such solidarities may to some degree subvert traditional military values and be in opposition to their highly hierarchical structures. Thus an excess of zeal or militarism may be viewed negatively by the peer group and subject to a variety of punitive sanctions. Particularly in peacetime and among conscripts, getting by may be the central requirement and 'skiving' may be elevated to something of a fine art. The 'sad sack' may be an object of sympathy

rather than derision (Elkin, 1946b, p. 421) and Bilko may be as much a folk hero as John Wayne.

5. The divisions within the military are not, of course, simply divisions within the organisational hierarchy itself. There are also divisions which are continuations of divisions in the wider society, especially in terms of class and education. Enlisted culture, as Moskos (1970) describes it, is a typically male, working-class, young and unmarried culture (pp. 43 and 64). This constitutes a major line of distinction between the better-educated and more middle-class officer ranks (*ibid*. p. 42). Nevertheless, there may be more-educated enlisted men who may find themselves taking orders from less-educated NCOs. In short, class and educational differences are not suspended at the barracks door.

This too is well known; nevertheless it is worthwhile noting the differences within male organisations in these terms as a reminder that there are a variety of ways of being male or of 'doing masculinity', and that these may be shaped or influenced by particular class culture. Too often, it would seem, the paradigm of masculine behaviour is taken to be something derived from studies of working-class lads, the lower echelons of military or civilian organisations, football hooligans or street corner gangs. There may well be the danger of class stereotyping in all this and there is certainly a need to consider different models of masculinity which may be related to other divisions in society as well as having different kinds of relations to the practice of violence. The question of the relationships between masculinity and group decision-making has already been examined, but there are other relationships to be considered (see Tolson, 1977 and Ehrenriech, 1983, pp. 132–6 for some discussion of the relationships between class and masculinities). Perhaps class itself may be too crude a category. Thus, for example, we may talk of the 'public school ethos' and see this as being particularly related to the generation and reproduction of masculinity. Yet there are often subtle differences in the type of ideal man that different schools may be aiming at: the heartily all-rounder; the cultivated gentleman; the gentlemanly scholar; the healthy Christian, and so on. What we need to develop is an understanding of the range of masculinities that might be available, encouraged or permitted at any one time, the ways in which these masculinities relate, on the one hand, to the control and practice of violence and, on the other, to the system of social stratification.

CONCLUSION

This chapter has been deliberately exploratory and open-ended. The aim, firstly, has been to underline the need to pluralise the terms, to talk of 'violences' and 'masculinities'. It has attempted to argue that it is possible to trace links between different types or levels of violences, but that these links are often contradictory and nearly always complex. We can best understand these linkages by constantly reminding ourselves that we are dealing with constructions of masculinities and violences, constructions which are achieved, maintained and reproduced in a context of power inequality, whether that inequality be expressed in gender or class terms.

This chapter clearly would not have been possible without the continuing challenge presented to sociological practice by feminism and the consequent responses of some men to these challenges. However, there has been a tendency on the part of these men (for example Hoch, 1979; Fasteau, 1975; Reynaud, 1983) to present too uniform a model of male violence which, even where it is not designed to be biologistic or essentialist, may be read in these terms. This has the danger of understating the power of patriarchy; the benefits of which are enjoyed by gentle as well as by violent men. It may also stand in the way of understanding the complex patterns linking gender identities, ideologies and institutional settings, and hence in the way of attempts to control and change many of the violences within our society.

Acknowledgements
Special thanks to the editors, Jalna Hanmer and Mary Maynard, for detailed and most helpful suggestions. Also to Janet Finch, Kate Purcell and all who attended and commented upon my first reading of the paper at Hull, 1985.

My spell as a national serviceman in the Royal Air Force probably did me the world of good.

Bibliography

ADAMS, H. F. (1983) 'Work in the Interstices: Women in Academe', *Women's Studies International Forum*, vol. VI, no. 2, pp. 135–41.

ADLER, Z. (1982) 'Rape – The Intention of Parliament and the Practice of the Courts', *Modern Law Review* vol. 45 (November) pp. 664–75.

ADLER, Z. (1984) 'The CLRC's Report on Sexual Offences: Implications for Rape and Indecent Assault', *New Law Journal* (31 August), pp. 738–9.

AMIR, M. (1971) *Patterns in Forcible Rape* (Chicago: University of Chicago Press).

ARCANA, J. (1983) *Every Mother's Son: The Role of Mothers in the Making of Men* (London: Women's Press Ltd)

ARIEFF, A. J. *et al.* (1942) '100 Cases of Indecent Exposure', *Journal of Nervous Mental Disorders*, no. 96, p. 523.

ATKINS, S and HOGGETT, B. (1984) *Women and the Law* (Oxford: Basil Blackwell).

BACON, W. and LANSDOWNE, R. (1982) 'Women Who Kill Husbands. The Battered Wife on Trial' in C. O'Donnel and J. Craney (eds), *Family Violence in Australia* (Melbourne), pp. 67–93.

BALKIN, S. (1979) 'Victimisation Rate, Safety, and Fear of Crime', *Social Problems*, vol. 26, pp. 343–58.

BARRETT, M. (1980) *Women's Oppression Today* (London, Verso).

BARRETT, M. and McINTOSH, M. (1982) *The Anti-Social Family* (London, Verso).

BARRETT, M. and ROBERTS, H. (1976) 'Why do Women go to the Doctor?', Paper given to the BSA Annual Conference, Manchester.

BARRY, K. (1979) *Female Sexual Slavery* (Englewood Cliffs, N.J.: Prentice-Hall).

BARRY, K. (1982) '"Sado-Masochism": The New Backlash to Feminism' *Trivia*, no. 1, pp. 77–92.

BART, P. B. (1971) 'Sexism and Social Science: From the Gilded Cage to the Iron Cage, or the Perils of Pauline', *Journal of Marriage and the Family* vol. 33, no. 4, pp. 734–45.

BART, P. (1974) 'The Sociology of Depression' in Roman, P. and Trice, H. (eds), *Explorations in Psychiatric Sociology* (Philadelphia: F. A. Davis Co.) pp. 139–57.

BART, P. (1983) 'Women of the Right: Trading for Safety, Rules and Love. Review of A. Dworkin, *Right Wing Women*' in *The New Women's Times Feminist Review* (November/December) pp. 9–11.

BART, P. and O'BRIEN, P. (1984) 'Stopping Rape: Effective Avoidance Strategies', *Signs*, vol. 10, no. 1, pp. 82–101.

Bedfordshire Police Report on Acts of Domestic Violence Committed in the County between 1 February and 31 July 1976.

BEECHEY, V. (1979) 'On Patriarchy', *Feminist Review*, no. 3, pp. 66–82.

BELL, D. (1984) 'Police Dispositions of Domestic Violence', *Police Studies*, vol. 7, no. 3.

BELL, D. (1985) 'The Police Response to Domestic Violence: A Multiyear Study', *Police Studies*, vol. 8, no. 1, pp. 58–64.

BENEKE, T. (1982) *Men on Rape* (New York: St. Martin's Press).

BERNARD, J. (1973) 'My Four Revolutions: An Autobiographical History of the ASA', *American Journal of Sociology*, vol. 78, no. 4, pp. 773–91.

BINNEY, V., HARKELL, G. and NIXON, J. (1981) *Leaving Violent Men: A Study of Refuges and Housing for Battered Women* (London: Women's Aid Federation, England).

BINNEY, V., HARKELL, G. and NIXON, J. (1985) 'Refuges and Housing for Battered Women', in J. Pahl (ed.) *Private Violence and Public Policy* (London: Routledge and Kegan Paul).

BLAKELY, M. K. (1985) 'Is One Woman's Sexuality Another Woman's Pornography?', *Ms* (April) pp. 37–47.

BLAND, L. (1984) 'The Case of the Yorkshire Ripper: Mad, Bad, Beast or Male', in P. Scraton and P. Gordon (eds), *Causes for Concern* (Harmondsworth: Penguin) pp. 184–209.

BLAND, L., HARRISON, R., MORT, F. and WEEDON, C. (1978) 'Relations of Reproduction: Approaches through Anthropology', in CCCS Women's Studies Group *Women Take Issue* (London: Hutchinson).

BLEIER, R. (1984) *Science and Gender* (Oxford: Pergamon, Athene Series).

BOWKER, L. (1981) 'Women as Victims: An Examination of the Results of L.E.A.A.'s National Crime Survey Program', in L. Bowker (ed.) *Women and Crime in America* (New York: Macmillan).

BOYLAN, A. M. and TAUB, N. (1981) *Adult Domestic Violence: Constitutional Legislative and Equitable Issues* (Washington DC: Legal Services Corporations).

BRANDENBURG, J. (1982) 'Sexual Harassment in the University: Guidelines for Establishing a Grievance Procedure', *Signs*, vol. VIII, pp. 320–36.

BREGGIN, P. (1972) 'The Return of Lobotomy and Psychosurgery' in the *Congressional Record* (24 February 1972) pp. 5567–77 (Washington DC).

BREINES, W. and GORDON, L. (1983) 'The New Scholarship on Family Violence', *Signs* vol. 8, no. 3, pp. 490–531.

BRIDGES, P. (1981) quoted by O. Gillie, *Sunday Times*, 29 March 1981.

BRITTAN, A. and MAYNARD, M. (1984) *Sexism, Racism and Oppression* (Oxford: Basil Blackwell).

BROVERMAN, I. K., BROVERMAN, D., CLARKESON, F., ROSENKRANZ, P. and VOGELS, S. (1970) 'Sex Role Stereotypes and Clinical Judgements of Mental Health' in Howell, E. and Bayer, M. (eds), *Women and Mental Health* (New York: Basic Books Inc.) pp. 86–97.

BROWNMILLER, S. (1975) *Against Our Will: Men, Women and Rape* (New York: Simon and Schuster).

BRYGGER, M. P. (1982), 'National Coalition Against Domestic Violence' *Aegis* (Winter).

BUREAU OF JUSTICE STATISTICS (1983) *Report to the Nation on Crime and Justice* (Washington DC: US Government Printing Office).

BURGESS, A. and HOLMSTROM, L. (1974) 'Rape Trauma Syndrome', *American Journal of Psychiatry*, no. 131, pp. 981–5.

BURGOYNE, J. and CLARK, D. (1984) *Making A Go Of It* (London: Routledge and Kegan Paul).

BURSTYN, V. (1983) 'Masculine Dominance and the State', *Socialist Register*.

CAMERON, D, (1985) *Feminism and Linguistic Theory* (London: Macmillan).

CAMPBELL, B. (1980) 'A Feminist Sexual Politics: Now You See It, Now You Don't', *Feminist Review*, no. 5, pp. 1–18.

CARROLL, D. and O'CALLAGHAN, M. A. J. (1982) *Psychosurgery: A Scientific Analysis* (Lancaster: M. T. P. Press).

CHAMBERS, G. and MILLAR, A. (1983) *Investigating Sexual Assault* (Edinburgh: HMSO).

CHAMBERS, G. and TOMBS, J. (1984) *The British Crime Survey. Scotland* (Edinburgh: HMSO).

CHAPMAN, M. (1980) 'Operation Heartbreak', *Women's Own* (15 March 1980).

CHATTERTON, M. (1983) 'Police Work and Assault Charges' in Punch, M. (ed.), *Control in the Police Organisation* (Cambridge, Mass.: MIT Press) pp. 194–221.

CHESLER, P. (1974) *Women and Madness*, (London: Allen Lane).

CHODOROW, N. (1978) *The Reproduction of Mothering* (Berkley and Los Angeles, California: University of California Press).

CHOROVER, S. (1980) *From Genesis to Genocide* (Cambridge, Mass.: Massachusetts Institute of Technology).

CLARE, A. (1976) *Psychiatry in Dissent: Controversial Issues in Thought and Practice* (London: Tavistock).

CLARK, L. and LEWIS, D. (1977) *Rape: The Price of Coercive Sexuality*. (Toronto: The Women's Press).

CLARKE, J. (1981) 'Missing Dimensions in the Conventional Wisdom: the Market, the Family, Race and Contestation' in Tomlinson, A. (ed.) *Leisure and Social Control* (Brighton Polytechnic).

CLEMENTE, F. and KLEIMAN, M. (1977) 'Fear of Crime in the United States: A Multivariate Analysis', *Social Forces*, vol. 56, (December) pp. 519–31.

CLIFFORD, W. (1984) 'Official Policies to Help Victims of Crime in Europe', *Justice of the Peace*, no. 148 p. 43.

COLLIER, J. F. and ROSALDO, M. Z. (1981) 'Politics and Gender in Simple Societies', in S. B. Ortner and H. Whitehead (eds), *Sexual Meanings* (Cambridge: University of Cambridge Press) pp. 275–329.

CORRIGAN, P. (1977) *State Formation and Moral Regulation in Nineteenth-Century Britain: Sociological Investigations* (unpublished Ph.D thesis, University of Durham).

Criminal Injuries Compensation Board (1983) Nineteenth Report, Cmnd 9093 (London: HMSO).

Criminal Statistics 1982, Cmnd 9048.

Criminal Statistics 1983, Supplementary Tables.

DALY, M. (1978) *Gyn/Ecology* (Boston, USA: Beacon Press).

de BEAUVOIR, S. (1949–53) *The Second Sex* (London: Jonathan Cape).

DEEM, R. (1982) 'Women, Leisure and Inequality', *Leisure Studies*, vol. 1, no. 1.

DEEM, R. (1984) 'The Politics of Women's Leisure' (Paper presented at the Leisure Studies Association International Conference, University of Sussex).

DELAMONT, S. (1980) *The Sociology of Women* (London: George Allen & Unwin).

DELPHY, C. (1977) *The Main Enemy: A Materialist Analysis of Women's Oppression* (London: Women's Research and Resources Centre Publications).

DELPHY, C. (1981) 'Women in Stratification Studies' in H. Roberts (ed.), *Doing Feminist Research* (London: Routledge and Kegan Paul).

DELPHY, C. (1984) *Close to Home* (London: Hutchinson).

DENNIS, N., HENRIQUES, F. and SLAUGHTER, C. (1956) *Coal is Our Life*, London: Eyre and Spottiswode.

DIXEY, R. and TALBOT, M. (1982) *Women, Leisure and Bingo* (Leeds: Trinity and All Saints College).

DOBASH, R. E. and DOBASH, R. (1977) 'Love, Honour and Obey: Institutional Ideologies and the Struggle for Battered Women', *Contemporary Crises: Crime, Law and Social Policy*, no. 1.

DOBASH, R. E. and DOBASH, R. (1978) 'Wives: the "Appropriate" Victims of Marital Violence', *Victimology*, vol. 3–4.

DOBASH, R. E. and DOBASH, R. (1979) *Violence Against Wives: A Case Against the Patriarchy* (New York: Free Press).

Domestic Proceedings in Magistrates Courts (1984) (Statistics of Home Office Statistical Bulletin 14/84).

DUBBERT, J. L. (1979) *A Man's Place* (New Jersey: Prentice-Hall).

DuBOIS, E. and GORDON, L. (1983) 'Seeking Ecstacy on the Battlefield: Danger and Pleasure in Nineteenth-century Feminist Sexual Thought', *Feminist Review*, no. 13, pp. 42–54.

DUBOW, F. (1979) *Reactions to Crime: A Critical Review of the Literature* (Washington, DC: US Government Printing Office).

DUNNING, E. (ed.) (1971) *The Sociology of Sport* (London: Frank Carr).

DURHAM, A. (1984) 'Death of a Battered Mother', *New Statesman* (21 September).

DWORKIN, A. (1981) *Pornography: Men Possessing Women* (London: Women's Press).

DWORKIN, A. (1983) *Right-Wing Women* (London: The Women's Press).

DYCK, N. (1980) 'Booze, Bar-rooms and Scrapping: Masculinity and Violence in a Western Canadian Town', *Canadian Journal of Anthropology*, vol. 1, no. 2.

DYER, J. (1985) 'How Us Beat Them', *Guardian* (28 Feb 1985).

EDHOLM, F., HARRIS, O. and YOUNG, K. (1977) 'Conceptualising Women', *Critique of Anthropology* nos 9 and 10, pp. 101–30.

EDWARDS, S. (1981) *Female Sexuality and the Law* (Oxford: Martin Robertson).

EDWARDS, S. (1984), *Women on Trial*, (Manchester: Manchester University Press).

EDWARDS, S. (1985) 'Male Violence Against Women; Excusatory and

Explanatory Ideologies in Law and Society' in S. Edwards (ed.), *Gender, Sex and the Law* (London: Croom Helm) pp. 183–216.

EHRENREICH, B. (1983) *The Hearts of Men* (London, Pluto Press).

EHRENREICH, B. and ENGLISH, D. (1973) *Complaints and Disorders* (New York: The Feminist Press).

EICHLER, Margrit (1980) *The Double Standard: A Feminist Critique of Feminist Social Science* (London: Croom Helm).

ELKIN, H. (1946a) 'Aggressive and Erotic Tendencies in Army Life', *American Journal of Sociology*, vol. 51, pp. 403–13.

ELKIN, H. (1946b) 'The Soldiers Language', *American Journal of Sociology*, vol. 51, pp. 414–22.

ELLIS, H. (1933) *The Psychology of Sex* (London: Heinemann).

EL SAADAWI, N. (1980) 'Creative Women in Changing Societies: A Personal Reflection', *Race and Class*, vol. xxii, no. 2, pp. 159–74.

ENGELS, F. (1972) *The Origin of the Family Private Property and the State* (London: Pathfinder Press).

ENGLISH, D., HOLLIBAUGH, A. and RUBIN, G. (1982) 'Talking Sex: A Conversation on Sexuality and Feminism', *Feminist Review* no. 11, pp. 40–52.

ENLOE, C. (1983) *Does Khaki Become You?* (London: Pluto Press).

EVASON, E. (1982) *Hidden Violence: A Study of Battered Women in Northern Ireland* (Belfast: Farset Co-operative Press).

FABRIKANT, B. (1974) 'The Psychotherapist and the Female Patient: Perceptions, Misperceptions and Change' in V. Franks and V. Burtle (eds), *Women in Therapy* (New York: Bruner/Mazel).

FARLEY, L. (1978) *Sexual Shakedown* (New York: McGraw Hill).

FASTEAU, M. (1975) *The Male Machine* (New York: Dell).

Feminist Review (1982) vol. 11, Sexuality Issue.

FENICHEL, O. (1945) *The Psychoanalytic Theory of Neurosis* (New York: W. W. Norton and Company).

FINKELHOR, D. (1979) *Sexually Victimised Children* (New York: Free Press).

FIORA-GORMALLY, N. (1978) 'Battered Wives Who Kill', *Law and Human Behaviour*, vol. 2, no. 2, pp. 133–65.

FIRESTONE, S. (1971) *The Dialectic of Sex* (London: Paladin).

FITZGERALD, M., McLENNAN, G. and SIM, J. (1981) 'Law and Disorders: Histories of Crime and Justice', *Issues in Crime and Society*, Block 2, (D335) (Milton Keynes: Open University Press).

FLITCROFT, A. (1978) *Battered Women: An Emergency Room Epidemiology With A Description of a Clinical Syndrome and Critique of Present Therapeutics* (statement before the sub-committee on Domestic and International Scientific Planning, Analysis and Co-operation, Yale Medical School, 15 February 1978).

FLOR-HENRY, P. (1981) 'Psychosurgery Yesterday and Today: A Review', in Dongier, M. and Wittkower, E. D. (eds), *Divergent Views in Psychiatry* (Hagerstown, Maryland: Harper and Row Inc.) pp. 281–301.

FOREST, M. S. and HOKANSON, J. E. (1975) 'Depression and Automatic Arousal Reduction Accompanying Self-punitive Behaviour', *Journal of Abnormal Psychology*, no. 84, pp. 346–57.

FOUCAULT, M. (1979) *The History of Sexuality*, vol. 1 (Harmondsworth: Allen Lane, Penguin).

FRANKENBERG, R. (1972) 'Taking the Blame and Passing the Buck', in M. Gluckman (ed.) *The Allocation of Responsibility* (Manchester: Manchester University Press).

FREDEN, L. (1982) *Psychosocial Aspects of Depression* (Chichester: John Wiley and Sons).

FREEMAN, W. and WATTS, J. (1950) *Psychosurgery* (Springfield, Illinois: Charles C. Thomas).

FREUD, S. (1953) *Three Essays on Sexuality* (London: Hogarth Press).

GAMARNIKOW, E., MORGAN, D., PURVIS, J. and TAYLORSON, D. (eds), *The Public and the Private* (London: Heinemann).

GARDNER, H. (1984) *Frames of Mind* (London: Heinemann).

GEBHARD, P. H. *et al.* (1965) *Sexual Offenders: An Analysis of Types* (London: Heinemann).

General Household Survey (1973) (London: HMSO).

GIBSON, E. and KLEIN, S. (1961) *Murder*, Home Office Research Unit Report no. 4. Studies in the Causes of Delinquency and Treatment of Offenders (London: HMSO).

GILBERT, L. and WEBSTER, P. (1982) *Bound By Love* (Boston: Beacon Press).

GOLDBERG, D. and HUXLEY, P. (1980) *Mental Illness in the Community – The Pathway to Psychiatric Care* (London: Tavistock Publications).

GOLDSTEIN, P. (1984) 'Drugs and Violence Among Women' (paper presented to the American Society of Criminology annual meeting).

GOODE, W. J. (1971) 'Force and Violence in the Family', *Journal of Marriage and the Family*, vol. 33, no. 4, pp. 624–35.

GOODE, W. (1982) 'Why Men Resist', in B. Thorne with M. Yalom, *Rethinking the Family: Some Feminist Questions* (New York: Longman).

GORDON, M., RIGER, S., LeBAILLY, R. and HEALTH, L. (1980) 'Crime, Women, and the Quality of Urban Life', *Signs*, vol. 5 (Spring) pp. 144–60.

GOSTIN, L. O. and KNIGHT, L. (1980) 'Do the Doctors Know What They're Doing?', *Mind Out* (July/August).

GOTTFREDSON, M. (1984) *Victims of Crime: The Dimensions of Risk* (London: HMSO).

GOVE, W. R. and TUDOR, J. F. (1973) 'Adult Sex Roles and Mental Illness' in Freden, L., *Psychosocial Aspects of Depression* (Chichester: John Wiley & Sons, 1982).

GRAHAM, H. (1983) 'Do Her Answers Fit His Questions? Women and the Survey Method' in Garmarnikow, E. Morgan, D., Purvis, J. and Taylorson, D. (eds), *The Public and the Private* (London: Heinemann).

GRAY, J. and LEESON, J. (1978) *Women and Medicine* (London: Tavistock).

GRAYDON, J. (1983) 'But It's More Than a Game. It's an Institution', *Feminist Review* no. 13, pp. 5–16.

GREEN, E. and PARRY, J. (1982) 'Women, Part-time Work and the Hidden Costs of Caring' (paper presented to the BSA Annual Conference, University of Manchester).

GREENBLAT, C. S. (1983) 'A Hit is a Hit is a Hit . . . Or is It?', in D. Finkelhor, *et al.* (eds), *The Dark Side of Families* (London: Macmillan).

GRIFFIN, C., HOBSON, D., McINTOSH, S. and McCABE, T. (1982) 'Women and Leisure' in Hargreaves, J. (ed.) *Sport, Culture and Ideology* (London: Routledge and Kegan Paul).

GRIFFIN, S. (1971) 'Rape: The All-American Crime', *Ramparts*, (September) pp. 26–35.

GRIFFITHS, A. (1981) 'Some Battered Women in Wales: An Interactionist View of their Legal Problems', *Family Law*, vol. 11.

HAMOS, J. E. (1980) *State Domestic Violence Laws and How to Pass Them* (Washington DC: Office on Domestic Violence and National Coalition Against Domestic Violence).

HANMER, J. (1978) 'Violence and the Social Control of Women', in Littlejohn, G., Smart, B., Wakeford, J. and Yuval-Davis, N. (eds), *Power and the State* (London: Croom Helm, 1978).

HANMER, J. and SAUNDERS, S. (1983) 'Blowing the Cover of the Protective Male: A Community Study of Violence to Women' in E. Gamarnikow, *et al.* (eds), *The Public and the Private* (London: Heinemann).

HANMER, J. and SAUNDERS, S. (1984) *Well-Founded Fear* (London: Hutchinson).

HANMER, J. and STANKO, E. (1985) 'Stripping Away the Rhetoric of Protection: Violence to Women, Law and the State', *The International Journal of the Sociology of Law* vol. 13, p. 357–74.

HARE, E. H. (1974) 'The Changing Content of Psychiatric Illness', in Carroll, D. and O'Callaghan, M. A. J. (eds), *Psychosurgery: A Scientific Analysis* (Lancaster: M.T.P. Press Ltd).

HARTMANN, H. (1981) 'The Unhappy Marriage of Marxism and Feminism: Towards a More Progressive Union' in Sargent L. (ed.) *The Unhappy Marriage of Marxism and Feminism* (London: Pluto Press).

HARTSOCK, N. C. M. (1983) *Money, Sex and Power: Toward a Feminist Historical Materialism* (London: Longman).

HEATH, L. (1984) 'Impact of Newspaper Crime Reports on Fear of Crime: Multimethodological Investigation', *Journal of Personality and Social Psychology*, vol. 47, no. 2, pp. 263–76.

HERMAN, J. (1981) *Father–Daughter Incest* (Cambridge, Mass.: Harvard University Press).

HILBERMAN, E. and MUNSON, K. (1978) 'Sixty Battered Women', *Victimology*, vol. 2, pp. 460–471.

HINDELANG, M., GOTTFREDSON, M. and GAROFALO, J. (1978) *The Victims of Personal Crime* (Cambridge, Mass.: Ballinger).

HIRSCH, M. F., (1981) *Women and Violence* (New York: Van Nostrand).

HOBSON, D. (1978) 'Housewives: Isolation as Oppression', in CCCS Women's Studies Group, *Women Take Issue* (London: Hutchinson).

HOCH, P. (1979) *White Hero, Black Beast* (London: Pluto Press).

HORLEY, S. (1985) 'Fall-out in the Refuges', *New Society* (28 June).

HOROWITZ, R. and SCHWARTZ, G. (1974) 'Honour, Normative Ambiguity and Gang Violence', *American Sociological Review*, vol. 39, pp. 238–51.

HOUGH, M. and MAYHEW, P. (1983) *The British Crime Survey* (London: HMSO).

HOUGH, M. and MAYHEW, P. (1985) *Taking Account of Crime: Key Findings from the 1984 British Crime Survey*, (London: HMSO).

HOWELL, M. (1979) 'Can We Be Feminists and Professional?', *Women's Studies International Quarterly*, vol. II, no. 1, pp. 1–7.

HUDSON, D. (1981) 'Stepford Wives Syndrome', *Revolutionary and Radical Feminist Newsletter*, no. 7 (Women only publication, Summer 1981).

HUDSON, D. (1982) 'The Stepford Wives Syndrome – Psycho-surgery and Women' (paper presented to Feminist Social Work Conference, London, November).

HUDSON, D. (1984) 'The Psycho-control of Women: Lobotomy as a Method of Social Control', *CatCall*, issue 16 (Women only publication).

HUSTON, N. (1982) 'Tales of War and Tears of Women', in J. H. Stiehm (ed.) *Women and Men's Wars*, special issue of *Women's Studies International Forum*, (Oxford: Pergamon).

IMRAY, L. and MIDDLETON, A. (1983) 'Public and Private: Marking the Boundaries' in Gamarnikow, E., Morgan, D. Purvis, J. and Taylorson, D. (eds), *The Public and the Private* (London: Heinemann).

JACKSON, S. and RUSHTON, P. (1982) 'Victims and Villains: Images of Women in Accounts of Family Violence', *Women's Studies International Forum*, vol. 5, no. 1, pp. 17–28.

JAGGAR, A. M. (1983) *Feminist Politics and Human Nature* (New York: Rowman and Allanheld).

JANIS, I. L. (1971) 'Groupthink Among Policy Makers', in N. Sanford *et al.* (eds), *Sanctions For Evil* (San Francisco: Josey Bass).

JANOFF-BULMAN, R. (1979) 'Characterological versus Behavioural Self-blame: Inquiries into Depression and Rape', *Journal of Personality and Social Psychology*, vol. 37, no. 10, pp. 1798–1809.

JEFFREYS, S. (1985) 'Indecent Exposure', in d. rhodes and S. McNeill (eds) *Women Against Violence Against Women* (London: Only Women Press).

Judicial Statistics England and Wales 1983 and 1984, Cmnd 9370 and 9599.

KELLY, L. (1984a) 'How Women Define Experiences of Sexual Violence' (unpublished paper).

KELLY, L. (1984b) *Effects or Survival Strategies? The Long-term Consequences of Experiences of Sexual Violence* (paper at The Second International Conference for Family Violence Researchers, New Hampshire, USA, August).

KINSEY, A. C. *et al.* (1948) *Sexual Behaviour in the Human Male*, (Philadelphia: W. B. Saunders and Co.).

KITTAY, E. F. (1984) 'Pornography and the Erotics of Domination', in C. C. Gould (ed.) *Beyond Domination* (New Jersey: Rowman and Allanheld).

KLEIN, D. (1979) 'Can the Marriage be Saved? Battery and Sheltering', *Crime and Social Justice*, no. 12, pp. 9–23.

KLEIN, D. (1981) 'Violence against Women; Some Considerations Regarding its Causes and Elimination', *Crime and Delinquency*, vol. 27, no. 1, pp. 64–80.

KNIGHT, G. C. (1973) 'Additional Stereotactic Lesions in the Cingulum Following Failed Tractotomy in the Subcaudate Region' in L. V. Laitinem and K. E. Livingston (eds) *Surgical Approaches in Psychiatry* (Lancaster: Medical and Technical Publishing Co.).

KOSS, M. and OROS, C. (1982) 'Sexual Experiences Survey: A Research Instrument Investigating Sexual Aggression and Victimization', *Journal of Clinical and Consulting Psychology*, vol. 50, pp. 455–7.

LAND, H. (1978) 'Who Cares for the Family', *Journal of Social Policy*, vol. 7, no. 3.

LEDERER, L. (ed.) (1980) *Take Back the Night* (New York: William Morrow).

LEESON, J. and GRAY, J. (1978) *Women and Medicine* (London: Tavistock Publications).

LEGHORN, L. (1978) 'Grass Roots Services for Battered Women: A Model for Long-term Change', *Aegis* (July/August).

LEIDIG, M. (1981) 'Violence Against Women – A Feminist–Psychological Analysis', in S. Cox (ed.), *Female Psychology* (New York: St Martin's Press).

LEONARD BARKER, D. and ALLEN, S. (eds) (1976a) *Sexual Divisions and Society: Process and Change* (London: Tavistock).

LEONARD BARKER, D. and ALLEN S. (eds) (1976b) *Dependence and Exploitation in Work and Marriage* (London: Longman).

LERMAN, L. (1981) *Prosecution of Spouse Abuse: Innovations in Criminal Justice Response* (Washington, DC: Center for Women Policy Studies).

LEWIS, D. and MAXFIELD, M. (1980) 'Fear in the Neighbourhoods: An Investigation of the Impact of Crime', *Journal of Research in Crime and Delinquency*, vol. 17, pp. 160–189.

London Rape Crisis Centre (1984) *Sexual Violence* (London: The Women's Press).

LOSEKE, D. R. and CAHILL, S. E., (1984) 'The Social Construction of Deviance: Experts on Battered Women', *Social Problems*, vol. 31, no. 3, pp. 296–310.

LOWE, M. and BENSTON, M. L. (1984) 'The Uneasy Alliance of Feminism and Academia', *Women's Studies International Forum*, vol. VII, no. 3, pp. 177–83.

McCABE, T. and McROBBIE, A. (eds) (1981) *Feminism for Girls* (London: Routledge and Kegan Paul).

McCANN, K. (1985) 'Battered Women and the Law: The Limits of Legislation' in J. Brophy and C. Smart (eds), *Women in Law* (London: Routledge and Kegan Paul).

McCLINTOCK, F. (1963) *Crimes of Violence* (London: Macmillan).

MACDONALD, J. M. (1973) *Indecent Exposure* (Springfield, Ill.: Charles C. Thomas).

McFADDEN, M. (1984) 'Anatomy of Difference: Toward a Classification of Feminist Theory', *Women's Studies International Forum*, vol. 7, no. 6, pp. 495–504.

McINTOSH, S. (1981) 'Leisure Studies and Women' in Tomlinson, A. (ed.), *Leisure and Social Control* (Brighton Polytechnic).

MacKINNON, C. (1979) *Sexual Harassment of Working Women* (New Haven, Conn.: Yale University Press).

MacKINNON, C. (1982) 'Feminism, Marxism, Method and the State: An Agenda for Theory', *Signs*, vol. 7, no. 3, pp. 515–44.

MacKINNON, C. (1983) 'Feminism, Marxism, Method and the State: Toward Feminist Jurisprudence', *Signs*, vol. 8, no. 4, pp. 635–58.

McLEOD, E. (1982) *Working Women Prostitution Now* (London: Croom Helm).

McNEILL, W. M. (1983) *The Pursuit of Power* (Oxford: Basil Blackwell).

McROBBIE, A. (1978) 'Working Class Girls and the Culture of Femininity', in CCCS Women's Studies Group, *Women Take Issue* (London: Hutchinson).

MAROLLA, J. and SCULLY, D. (1979) 'Rape and Psychiatric Vocabularies of Motive', in E. Gomberg and V. Frank (eds), *Gender and Disordered Behaviour* (New York: Brunner/Mazel) pp. 301–18.

MARTIN, J. and ROBERTS, C. (1984) *Women and Employment: A Lifetime Perspective*, (the report of the 1980 Department of Employment/OPCS Women and Employment Survey, London: HMSO).

Massachusetts Coalition of Battered Women Service Groups (1981) *For Shelter and Beyond* (Boston: 120 Boyston Street).

MAXFIELD, M. (1984a) *Fear of Crime in England and Wales* (London: HMSO).

MAXFIELD, M. (1984b) 'The Limits of Vulnerability in Explaining Fear of Crime: A Comparative Neighbourhood Analysis', *Research in Crime and Delinquency*, vol. 21, no. 3. (August) pp. 233–50

MEDEA, A. and THOMPSON, K. (1974) *Against Rape* (New York: Farrar, Straus and Giroux).

Mental Health Act 1983 (London: HMSO).

MEREDITH, E. (1979) 'Some Possibilities in the Proceedings Used in Cases of Abuse in the Family' in Hanmer, J. (ed.) *Battered Women and Abused Children* (Occasional Paper no. 4. University of Bradford).

MILLET, K. (1972) *Sexual Politics* (London: Abacus).

MILLMAN, M. and MOSS KANTER, R. (eds) (1975) *Another Voice* (New York: Anchor Press/Doubleday).

MITCHELL, J. (1971) *Woman's Estate* (Harmondsworth: Penguin).

MITCHELL-HEGGS, N. A. and BARRACLOUGH, B. M. (1978) 'Use of Neurosurgery for Psychological Disorder in the British Isles during 1974–6', *British Medical Journal*, no. 2, pp. 1591–3.

MOGLEN, H. (1983) 'Power and Empowerment', *Women's Studies International Forum*, vol. VI, no. 2, pp. 131–4.

MOHR, J. W. *et al.* (1964) *Paedophilia and Exhibitionism* (Toronto: The University of Toronto Press).

MORGAN, D. H. J. (1985) *The Family, Politics and Social Theory* (London: Routledge and Kegan Paul).

MOSKOS, C. C. (1970) *The American Enlisted Man* (New York: Sage).

NAIRNE, K. and SMITH, G. (1984) *Dealing with Depression* (London: The Women's Press).

National Coalition Against Domestic Violence (1978) 'Ending Violence Against Women', *Aegis* (September/October).

National Coalition Against Domestic Violence (1982) *End Violence in the Lives of Women* (papers from the Second National Meeting of the National Coalition Against Domestic Violence, Milwaukee, WIS, NCADV, August).

National Women's Aid Federation (1975) *Battered Women Need Refuges: A Report from the National Women's Aid Federation* (London: Rye).

National Women's Aid Federation (1978) ' "He's Got to Show Her Who's Boss" – The National Women's Aid Federation Challenges a Man's Right to Batter', *Spare Rib*, no. 69, pp. 15–18.

Nebraska Feminist Collective, The (1983) 'A Feminist Ethic for Social Science Research', *Women's Studies International Forum*, vol. VI, no. 5, pp. 535–44.

NEULINGER, J. *et al.* (1970) 'Perceptions of the Optimally Integrated Person as a Function of the Therapists' Characteristics', *Perceptual and Motor Skills*, no. 30, pp. 375–84.

NEWBY, H. (1977) 'In the Field', in C. Bell and H. Newby (eds), *Doing Sociological Research* (London: George Allen and Unwin).

New York Radical Feminists, (1974) *Rape: The First Sourcebook for Women* (New York: Plume Books).

OAKLEY, A. (1974a) *Housewife* (London: Allen Lane).

OAKLEY, A. (1974b) *The Sociology of Housework* (London: Martin Robertson).

O'BRIEN, M. (1981) *The Politics of Reproduction* (London: Routledge and Kegan Paul).

OFFER, D. and SABSHIN, M. (1975) 'Normality' in A. M. Freedman, H. I. Kaplan and B. J. Sadock (eds), *Comprehensive Textbook of Psychiatry* (Baltimore: Williams and Wilkins).

PAGELOW, M. (1981) *Woman Battering* (California: Sage).

PAHL, J. (1978) *A Refuge for Battered Women, A Study of the Role of a Women's Centre* (London: HMSO).

PAHL, J. (1982) 'Police Response to Battered Women', in *Journal of Social Welfare Law*, pp. 337–43.

PAHL, J. (1984) 'The Control and Allocation of Money within the Family' (paper presented to the Second International Interdisciplinary Congress on Women, 'Gröningen, Holland).

PAHL, J. (ed.) (1985) *Private Violence and Public Policy* (London: RKP).

PARKER, S. (1971) *The Future of Work and Leisure* (London: MacGibbon and Kee).

Parliamentary Select Committee on Violence in Marriage (1975) *First Special Report from the Select Committee on Violence in Marriage Together with the Proceedings of the Committee* vols. 1 and 2 (London: HMSO).

PATTULLO, P. (1983) *Judging Women* (London: NCCL, Rights for Women Unit).

PEARSON, C. and POPE, K. (1981) *The Female Hero* (New York: Bowker).

PERISTIANY, J. G. (ed) (1965) *Honour and Shame* (London: Weidenfeld and Nicolson).

PERLOFF, L. (1983) 'Perceptions of Vulnerability to Victimization', *Journal of Social Issues* vol. 39, no. 2, pp. 41–61.

PINTHUS, E. (1982) 'Peace Education', *Quaker Peace and Service*, reprinted from *Friends Quarterly* (Winter) (Friends House, Euston, London NW1).

PITT-RIVERS, J. (1977) *The Fate of Shechem, or the Politics of Sex*, (Cambridge: Cambridge University Press).

PIZZEY, E. (1974) *Scream Quietly or the Neighbours Will Hear*, (Harmondsworth: Penguin).

POLLERT, A. (1981) *Girls, Wives, Factory Lives* (London: Macmillan).

PROPP, V. (1968) *Morphology of the Folktale* (Texas: University of Texas Press).

RABBITT, P. (1984) 'Investigating the Grey Areas', *Times Higher Education Supplement*, no. 14, 1 June.

RADFORD, J. (1982) 'Marriage Licence or Licence to Kill? Womanslaughter in the Criminal Law', in *Feminist Review* (Summer), pp. 88–96.

RADFORD, J. (1984) 'Womanslaughter: A Licence to Kill? The Killing of Jane Asher', in P. Scraton and P. Gordon (eds) *Causes for Concern* (Harmondsworth: Penguin) pp. 210–26.

RADZINOWICZ, L. (1957) *Sexual Offences* (London: Macmillan).

RAPOPORT, R. and RAPAPORT, R. (1975) *Leisure and The Family Life Cycle* (London: Routledge and Kegan Paul).

REYNAUD, E. (1983) *Holy Virility* (London: Pluto Press).

rhodes, d. and McNEILL, S. (eds) (1985) *Women Against Violence Against Women* (London: Only Women Press).

RICH, A. (1980) 'Compulsory Heterosexuality and Lesbian Existence', *Signs*, vol. 5, no. 4, pp. 631–60.

RICKLES, N. K. (1950) *Exhibitionism* (Philadelphia: J. B. Lippencote).

RIGER, S. and GORDON, M. (1981) 'The Fear of Rape: A Study in Social Control', *Journal of Social Issues*, vol. 37, no. 4 (Fall) pp. 71–92.

RIGER, S., GORDON, M., and LeBAILLY, R. (1978) 'Women's Fear of Crime: From Blaming to Restricting the Victim', *Victimology*, vol. 3, pp. 274–84.

RITTENMEYER, S. D. (1981) 'Of Battered Wives, Self Defence and Double Standards of Justice', *Journal of Criminal Justice*, vol. 9, pp. 389–95.

ROBERTS, B. (1972) 'The "Final Solution" to the Woman Problem', *The Second Wave II Magazine*, no. 1 (USA).

ROBERTS, B. (1984) 'The Death of Machothink: Feminist Research and the Transformation of Peace Studies', *Women's Studies International Forum*, vol. 7, no. 4, pp. 195–200.

ROOTH, F. G. (1971) 'Indecent Exposure and Exhibitionism', *British Journal of Hospital Medicine* (April).

ROSALDO, M. Z. (1980) 'The Use and Abuse of Anthropology: Reflections of Feminism and Cross-cultural Understanding', *Signs*, vol. 5, no. 3, pp. 389–417.

ROSALDO, M. Z. and LAMPHERE, L. (eds) (1974) *Women, Culture and Society* (Stanford: Stanford University Press).

ROSE, H. (1978a) 'In Practice Supported in Theory Denied: An Account of an Invisible Urban Movement', *International Journal of Urban and Regional Research*, vol. 2, no. 3.

ROSE, H. (1978b) 'The Development of Women's Aid' in *Up Against the Welfare State. Social Work*, *Community Work and Society*, unit 30 DE206 (Milton Keynes, Open University Press).

ROSE, H. (1979) 'Divided But Not Defeated! The Battered Women's Movement in Britain', *Aegis* (January/February).

ROSE, S., KAMIN, L. J. and LOWENTIN, R. C. (1984) *Not in Our Genes: Biology, Ideology and Human Nature* (Harmondsworth: Pelican Books).

ROWBOTHOM, S. (1973) *Woman's Consciousness, Man's World* (Harmondsworth: Penguin).

RUBENSTEIN, J. (1973) *City Police* (New York: Farar, Straus and Giroux).

RUBIN, G. (1975) 'The Traffic in Women: Notes on the Political Economy of Sex' in R. R. Reiter (ed.) *Towards an Anthropology of Women* (New York: Monthly Review Press) pp. 157–210.

RUDD, E. (1984) 'A Comparison Between the Results Achieved by Women and Men Studying for First Degrees in British Universities', *Studies in Higher Education*, vol. ix, pp. 57ff.

RUSSELL, D. (1973) *The Politics of Rape* (New York: Macmillan).

RUSSELL, D. (1975) *Rape: The Victim's Perspective* (New York: Stein and Day).

RUSSELL, D. (1982) *Rape in Marriage* (New York: Macmillan).

RUSSELL, D. (1984) *Sexual Exploitation* (Beverly Hills, California: Sage).

RUSSELL, D. and HOWELL, N. (1983) 'The Prevalence of Rape in the United States Revisited', *Signs*, vol. 8, no. 4, pp. 688–95.

SACHS, A. (1978) 'The Myth of Male Protectiveness and the Legal Subordination of Women: An Historical Analysis', in C. Smart and B. Smart (eds), *Women, Sexuality and Social Control* (London: Routledge and Kegan Paul).

SALAMAN, G. (1974) *Community and Occupation* (Cambridge: Cambridge University Press).

SANDAY, P. R. (1981a) *Female Power and Male Dominance* (Cambridge: Cambridge University Press).

SANDAY, P. R. (1981b) 'The Socio-cultural Context of Rape: A Cross-cultural Study', *Journal of Social Issues*, vol. 37, no. 4, pp. 5–27.

SARGANT, W. and SLATER, E. (1972) *Introduction to Physical Treatments in Psychiatry*, 5th edn (Edinburgh: Livingstone).

SARGENT, L. (ed.) (1981) *Women and Revolution* (Boston: South End Press).

SCHECHTER, S. (1982) *Women and Male Violence* (London: Pluto Press).

SCHEPPELE, K. and BART, P. (1983) 'Through Women's Eyes: Defining Danger in the Wake of Sexual Assault', *Journal of Social Issues* vol. 39, no. 2, pp. 63–81.

SCHNEIDER, E. M. (1980) 'Equal Rights to Trial for Women and Sex Bias in the Law of Self Defence', *Harvard Civil Rights – Civil Liberties Law Review*, vol. 15, no. 3, pp. 523–47.

SCUTT, J. (1981) 'Sexism in the Criminal Law' in J. Scutt and S. Mukherjee, (eds), *Women and Crime* (Australia: George Allen and Unwin) pp. 1–21.

SELIGMAN, M. (1975) *Helplessness* (San Francisco, California: Freeman).

SHARPE, S. (1976) *Just Like A Girl: How Girls Learn to be Women* (Harmondsworth: Penguin).

SHARPE, S. (1984) *Double Identity: The Lives of Working Mothers* (Harmondsworth: Pelican).

SHILS, E. and YOUNG, M. (1953) 'The Meaning of the Coronation', *Sociological Review*, vol. 1, no. 2, pp. 63–81.

SHULMAN, K. (1980) 'Sex and Power: Sexual Bases of Radical Feminism', *Signs*, vol. 5, no. 4, pp. 590–604.

SHUTTS, D. (1982) *Lobotomy: The Return to the Knife* (New York: Van Nostrand).

SILVERSTEIN, M. (1974) 'The History of a Short Unsuccessful Academic

Career', in J. Pleck and J. Sawyer, *Men and Masculinity* (Englewood Cliffs, N.J.: Prentice-Hall).

SIMPSON, G. E. and YINGER, J. M. (1965) *Racial and Cultural Minorities: An Analysis of Prejudice and Discrimination* (New York: Harper and Row).

SKOGAN, W. and MAXFIELD, M. (1981) *Coping with Crime* (Beverly Hills, California: Sage).

SMART, C. (1976) '*Women, Crime and Criminology* (London: Routledge Kegan Paul).

SMART, C. (1982) 'Regulating Families or Legitimating Patriarchy? Family Law in Britain', *International Journal of the Sociology of Law*, no. 10, pp. 129–47.

SMART, C. (1984) *The Ties That Bind: Law, Marriage and the Reproduction of Patriarchal Relations* (London: Routledge and Kegan Paul).

SMART, C. and SMART, B. (eds) (1978) *Women, Sexuality and Social Control* (London: Routledge and Kegan Paul).

SMITH, D. A. and KLEIN, J. R. (1984) 'Police Control of Interpersonal Disputes', *Social Problems*, vol. 31, no. 44, pp. 468–87.

SMITH, D. E. (1974) 'Women's Perspective as a Radical Critique of Sociology', *Sociological Inquiry*, vol. 44, no. 1, pp. 7–13.

SMITH, D. E. and DAVID S. J. (eds) (1976) *Women Look at Psychiatry* (Vancouver, BC: Press Gang Publishers)

SMITH, J. C., and HOGAN, B. (1978) *Criminal Law: Cases and Material* (London: Butterworths).

SPENCER, A. and McAULEY, J. (1985) 'Sticks and Stones May Break My Bones, but Names Will Never Hurt Me' unpublished paper presented to the 1985 Annual BSA Conference *War, Violence and Social Change*, held at the University of Hull, 1–4 April.

SPENDER, D. (1980) *Man Made Language* (London: Routledge and Kegan Paul).

SPENDER, D. (ed.) (1981) *Men's Studies Modified: The Impact of Feminism on the Academic Disciplines* (Oxford: Pergamon).

SPENDER, L. (1983) *Intruders on the Rights of Men: Women's Unpublished Heritage* (London: Pandora Press).

STACEY, M. and PRICE, M. (1981) *Women, Power and Politics*, (London: Tavistock).

STANLEY, L. (1980) 'The Problem of Women and Leisure: An Ideological Construct and a Radical Feminist Alternative' (paper produced for the Sports Council/Social Science Research Council Joint Panel on Sport and Leisure Research).

STANKO, E. (1985) *Intimate Intrusions: Women's Experience of Male Violence* (London: Routledge and Kegan Paul).

STARK, E., FLITCRAFT, A. and FRAZIER, W. (1979) 'Medicine and Patriarchal Violence: The Social Construction of a "Private" Event', *International Journal of Health Services*, vol. 9, no. 3, pp. 461–93.

STARKE, E. and FLITCRAFT, A. (1983) 'Social Knowledge, Social Policy, and the Abuse of Women: The Case Against Patriarchal Benevolence', in D. Finkelhor, *et al.* (eds), *The Dark Side of Families* (Beverly Hills, California: Sage).

STEIMETZ, S. K. and STRAUS M. A. (eds) (1974) *Violence in the Family* (New York: Dodd, Mead and Co.).

STEWARD, S., and GARRATT, S. (1984) *Signed Sealed and Delivered – True Life Stories of Women in Pop* (London: Pluto Press).

STIASNY, M. (1983) *Gender Relations in Education* (a dissertation in part fulfilment of the requirements of the MA Degree in Sociology of Education, University of London, Goldsmith's College).

STIEHM, J. H. (1982) *Women and Men's Wars* Special issues of *Women's Studies International Forum* (Oxford: Pergamon).

STOLLER, R. S. (1976) *Perversion; The Erotic Form of Hatred* (London: Harvester Press).

STORR, A. (1977) *Sexual Deviation* (Harmondsworth: Penguin).

STRAUS, M. A. (1977) 'Sexual Inequality, Cultural Norms and Wife Beating', in J. R. Chapman and M. Gates (eds), *Women into Wives* (Beverly Hills, California: Sage).

STRAUS, M. A., GELLES, R. J. and STEINMETZ, S. K. (1980) *Behind Closed Doors: Violence in the American Family* (Garden City, New York: Anchor Press/Doubleday).

STRAUS, M. A. and HOTALING, G. T. (eds) (1980) *The Social Causes of Husband-Wife Violence* (Minneapolis: University of Minnesota Press).

SUTTON, J. (1978) 'The Growth of the British Movement for Battered Women', *Victimology: An International Journal*, vol. 2, pp. 3–4.

TALBOT, M. (1979) *Women and Leisure* (London: Social Science Research Council/Sports Council).

TAYLOR, L. (1972) 'The Significance and Interpretation of Replies to Motivational Questions: The Case of Sex Offenders', *Sociology*, vol. 6, no. 1.

TOCH, H. (1969) *Violent Men* (Chicago: Aldine).

TOLSON, A. (1977) *The Limits of Masculinity* (London: Tavistock).

TOMLINSON, A. (ed.) (1981) *Leisure and Social Control* (Brighton: Brighton Polytechnic).

TOMLINSON, A. (1983) 'The New Hope for Leisure: Some Comments on Labour's Manifesto' in G. Jarvie (ed.), *The Politics of Leisure* (Leisure Studies Association newsletter supplement).

TONG, R. (1984) *Women, Sex and the Law* (New Jersey: Rowman and Allanheld).

TOOTH, G. C. and NEWTON, Mary P. (1961) *Leucotomy in England and Wales 1942–1954* (Ministry of Health, Reports on Public Health and Medical Subjects, no. 104, London: HMSO).

TWEEDIE, J. (1975) 'Womanslaughter', *Guardian* 20 January.

TYLER, T. (1980) 'Impact of Directly and Indirectly Experienced Events: The Origin of Crime-Related Judgments and Behaviors', *Journal of Personality and Social Psychology*, vol. 39, no. 1, pp. 3–28.

US Attorney General's Task Force on Family Violence (1984) *Final Report* (Washington DC: US Government Printing Office).

US Commission on Civil Rights (1978) *Battered Women: Issues of Public Policy* (Washington DC: US Government Printing Office).

VALENSTEIN, E. S. (1977) 'The Practice of Psychosurgery: A Survey of the

Literature (1971–6)' in *National Commission for the Protection of Human Subjects of Biomedical and Behavioural Research*, appendix (Washington DC: US Department of Health, Education and Welfare).

VALENSTEIN, E. S. (ed.) (1980) *The Psychosurgery Debate* (San Francisco: W. H. Freeman).

VOGELMAN, Sue, S. *et al.* (1979) 'Sex Differences in Feelings Attributed to a Woman in Situations Involving Coercion and Sexual Advances', *Journal of Personality*, vol. 47, no. 3, pp. 420–31.

Von HENTIG, H. (1948) *The Criminal and His Victim* (New Haven, Connecticut: Yale University Press).

WALKER, L. (1978) 'Battered Women and Learned Helplessness', *Victimology*, vol. 2, pp. 525–34.

WARD, D., JACKSON, M. and WARD, R. (1969) 'Crimes of Violence by Women', in D. Mulvihill *et al.* (eds), *Crimes of Violence* (Washington DC: US Government Printing Office).

WARD, E. (1984) *Father–Daughter Rape* (London: The Women's Press).

WARDELL, L., GILLESPIE, D. L. and LEFFLER, A. (1983) 'Science and Violence against Wives', in D. Finkelhor *et al.* (eds) *The Dark Side of Families* (Beverly Hills, California: Sage Publications) pp. 69–84.

WARRIOR, B. (1976) *Working on Wife Abuse* (Cambridge, Massachusetts: Transition House, Women's Centre, 46 Pleasant Street).

WARRIOR, B. (1982) *Battered Women's Directory*, 8th edn, (Cambridge, Massachussetts: Transition House, Women's Centre, 46 Pleasant Street).

WASIK, M. (1982) 'Cumulative Provocation and Domestic Killing', *Criminal Law Review*, pp. 29–37.

WASOFF, F. (1982) 'Legal Protection from Wifebeating: The Processing of Domestic Assaults by Scottish Prosecutors and Criminal Courts', *International Journal of the Sociology of Law*, vol. 10, pp. 187–204.

WATSON, J. (1968) *The Double Helix: A Personal Account of the Discovery of DNA* (London: Weidenfeld and Nicolson).

WEIS, K. and BORGES, S. S. (1973) 'Victimology and Rape: The Case of the Legitimate Victim', *Issues in Criminology*, vol. 8, no. 2, pp. 71–115.

WEISSMAN, R. F. E. (1981) *Ritual Brotherhood in Renaissance Florence*, (New York: Academic Press).

WEST, D. J. (1976) *Understanding Sexual Attacks* (London: Heinemann).

WESTWOOD, S. (1984) *All Day, Every Day* (London: Pluto Press).

WHATLEY, W. (1617) *The Bride Bush or Wedding Surmon* (1975 reprint, English Experience Series).

WHITEHEAD, A. (1976) 'Sexual Antagonism in Herefordshire' in D. Leonard Barker and S. Allen, (eds), *Dependence and Exploitation in Work and Marriage* (London: Longman).

WHITEHORN, K. (1984) 'Relax – We're Only Working Women', *Observer*, 18 November, p. 11.

WHYTE, W. F. (1943) *Street Corner Society* (Chicago: University of Chicago Press).

WIDOM, C. and MAXFIELD, M. (1984) 'Sex Roles and the Victimization of Women: Evidence from the British Crime Survey' (paper presented at the annual meeting of the American Society of Criminology).

WILLBANKS, W. (1983) 'The Female Homicide Offender in Dade County, Florida', *Criminal Justice Review*, vol. 8, no. 2, pp. 9–14.

WILLIAMS, J. and HOLMES, K. (1981) *The Second Assault: Rape and Public Attitudes* (Westport: Greenwood Press).

WILLIS, P. (1977) *Learning to Labour* (Farnborough: Saxon House).

WILSON, E. (1983a) *What is To Be Done About Violence Against Women?* (Harmondsworth: Penguin).

WILSON, E. (1983b) 'The Context of Between "Pleasure and Danger"': The Barnard Conference on Sexuality', *Feminist Review*, no. 13, pp. 35–41.

WILSON, P. (1978) *The Other Side of Rape* (St Lucia: University of Queensland Press).

WIMBUSH, E. (1985) *Women, Leisure and Well-Being: An Interim Report* (Centre for Leisure Research, Dunfermline College of Physical Recreation).

WINKLER, R. (1977) 'Current Psychosurgery in Australia: Local Concerns' in J. S. Smith and L. G. Kilohe (eds), *Psychosurgery and Society* (Oxford: Pergamon Press).

WINTER, A. (1972) 'Depression and Intractable Pain Treated by Modified Prefrontal Lobotomy', *Journal of the Medical Society*, vol. 69, pp. 757–9.

WOLFGANG, M. E. (1958) *Patterns in Criminal Homicide* (New York: Wiley).

Women's Studies Group (1978) *Women Take Issue* (London: Hutchinson and Centre for Contemporary Cultural Studies, University of Birmingham).

WOOLF, V. (1977) *Three Guineas* (Harmondsworth: Penguin) 1st pub. 1938.

WRIGHT, W. (1975) *Sixguns and Society* (California: University of California Press).

YOUNG, G. (1980) in *Hansard*, *Written Answers* (6 July 1981) p. 32.

YOUNG, K. and HARRIS, O. (1978) 'The Subordination of Women in Cross-cultural Perspective', in *Papers on Patriarchy* (Conference, London 1976) (Brighton: Women's Publishing Collective).

YOUNG, M. and WILLMOTT, P. (1973) *The Symmetrical Family: A Study of Work and Leisure in the London Region* (London: Routledge and Kegan Paul).

YUDKIN, M. (1982) 'Reflections on Woolf's *Three Guineas*' in J. H. Stiehm (ed.), *Women and Men's Wars*, special issues of *Women's Studies International Forum* (Oxford: Pergamon).

Index